BIG CATS

BIG CATS

FACING BRITAIN'S WILD PREDATORS

RICK MINTER

Whittles Publishing

Published by
Whittles Publishing Ltd.,
Dunbeath,
Caithness, KW6 6EG,
Scotland, UK

www.whittlespublishing.com

Forest image on cover courtesy of
bluecinderella – http://www.flickr.com/photos/bluecinderellee/2423017040/

ISBN 978-184995-042-8

Printed and bound by
Severn, Gloucester

CONTENTS

ACKNOWLEDGEMENTS

The mystery cats of Britain present us with a morass of a subject – the deeper you probe, the more complex it becomes. Scrutiny and debate are crucial to make any progress and I have learnt much through my local and national networks. Beyond the benefit of mutual learning, though, there's another reason I work in groups: the subject can be bruising. Mainstream views are changing as awareness of the cats dawns, but a rump of people are still harsh about those who study big cats. In this atmosphere, moral support from your peers can help you stay sane.

In presenting a book, there are many people to thank: first and foremost my stalwart publisher Keith Whittles and his staff. Getting ideas published and circulated is part of the learning process we need in this area. Like many writers with a day job I have stretched deadlines and had family distractions. Whittles have stuck by me and I hope they find it worthwhile.

Below is a list of people who've helped me on this journey. It includes those who have inspired, informed and reassured me, and some who have challenged me. It is not a complete register, and many eyewitnesses as well as friends, colleagues and contacts have encouraged me, from my hairdressers (who even pass on sightings) to my neighbours who scan the papers for me. Sometimes they may be being polite, but I hope they are as intrigued as they appear to be. The list below includes names from my main national grapevine, Big Cats in Britain. The book owes much to them and their co-ordinator Mark Fraser, and I recommend their website as a reference source.

Steve Archibold	Danny Nineham
Nigel Brierly	Jules Pretty
Ian Bond	Ian Rotherham
Daniel Elliot	Chris Sandys
David Hetherington	Jake Scott
Cheryl Hudson	Bool Smuts
Linda Long	Rik Snook
Coryn Memory	Nigel Spencer
Chris Moiser	Shaun Stevens

A close circle of advisers has shaped this book more than they might realise. They include Mark Fletcher, Chris Johnston, Jonathan McGowan and Peter Taylor. Their approach is one of continual exploration and enquiry and I gain much from the sounding board they offer. Between them they checked many of my drafts, giving important tips and honest feedback. What appears in the text is my responsibility alone.

Amongst the cast I have to highlight one other person, somebody you will soon meet in the book: the irrepressible Frank Tunbridge. Frank, local to me in Gloucester, is an inspiration, both for his probing mind and his fierce independence. He has taught my family more on wildlife than anyone has. He is a reminder that the real outdoors is far more fun and scary than computers and game consoles, and that rediscovered books with dusty covers can offer many rich pickings. Google hasn't yet conquered Frank.

Finally, to the essential support team of my whole family. They have confronted me on this topic more than anyone, and suffered more as a result of its grip. They respect the subject but dislike the baggage that goes with it, often for good reason. I will remain bad at taking their advice but I hope it keeps coming.

Carol Cowley took this photo at 6.20 am on a February morning in 2011. She was approaching a wood on the South Downs in West Sussex, when her Jack Russell dog became nervous. Carol watched in surprise and fright as a large black panther emerged from the wood and came to within 30 yards of them. Carol keeps a camera with her and took one photo as the cat came broadside. She said the cat looked up when it heard the camera click, but ignored her and the dog and walked on. Carol watched the panther for just 30 seconds in total. Due to its stocky form Carol thinks the cat may have been pregnant. The photo has been brightened due to the low light in which it was taken.
Photo: © Carol Cowley

PREFACE

I have a confession. I've not read all the books and pamphlets on UK big cats, yet they are within reach on my shelves as I write. I've consulted them and enjoyed chunks of many but, sadly, I find the core bits dull. And although I do suggest one website, I loathe the internet image of British big cats. The sites display a world of chattering anoraks indulging in the shock of out-of-place animals. I'm being harsh, I know, but the subject is portrayed as if it were little more than solving a puzzle or cracking a code, as if one day it will all be over. Detective work matters, but we need to consider the wider connections of our vagrant cats and the effects of big predators in nature and on our psyche.

Some of the big cat books are in part tedious for one main reason: they churn out people's reports with no context. Sighting after sighting is listed as if each is a revelation. Eyewitness reports of cats of different shapes and sizes are vital so, yes, sightings and witness accounts are the foundation of the topic and should inform and guide us. And every encounter with a possible big cat is indeed noteworthy to the people and for the area concerned. But an emphasis on sightings can be overdone. Without analysis, they can dilute the essence. I may be guilty of this in what follows, but I have tried to strike a balance.

The other obsession, understandably, is pictures. There is a desperation for something visible, a need to reveal the secret animal. For me, photographs are desirable but not essential. They can be forever nit-picked, as we will see later, and yet they are seen as the end game, as vital and definitive proof. I do not agree. They are a distraction from other good evidence and are just part of the set of clues and information we need. And to think there is a finale, to consider that the subject somehow ceases, insults the process – this is wild nature, dynamic and interactive, something we might find stirring. It is an infinite game, not a set-piece session of Cluedo.

The subject of our mystery cats is burdened with opinion and everyone feels qualified to hold forth. I am frequently told that 'so and so', a bigwig in some organisation or a professor somewhere, doesn't believe in big cats being here, as if this is news that should bring our work to a halt.

But it does not matter. I'd expect people to be guarded on this topic, especially if they've not seen and heard what I have seen and heard. There is no rush to become aware of big cats in our countryside. This book is not designed to convert anyone. There are questions for us to tackle, when we are ready, about how we study and relate to these cats. If this book helps our readiness, it will have done its job.

There may be natural scientists who regard the book as shallow, full of cut corners and weak postulations. I accept the risk of such a response, but I would stress the spirit in which this work is offered: it's aiming to offer pointers, provoke debate and awaken a gentle realisation that something is afoot. My roots in social science feel the need for rigour too. Trends in human observation and emotion need justifying if they are to count and be recognised, while the cats themselves leave a range of signs and are sometimes captured on film. I hope enough snippets of evidence are offered and claims supported while the book holds its audience and engages minds.

To the strict scientists who think I am hasty in my assessment of the big cats here, I say this: when would you start this debate? How and on whose terms, given that it is so far-reaching? A predator's landscape of many dimensions is before us to survey and to study. A mystery animal is becoming real. The great challenge is to make evident what is invisible. The cats always have the upper hand so their lives will stay mostly hidden, but why not discover what we can?

Meanwhile there are farmers – some fascinated, some anxious – who appreciate a friendly contact with whom to swap notes. There are people who can lead the way to the predator now, but there are rules of trust to learn and new partnerships to forge.

Parts of the text may seem earnest, but I hope compensation comes with the reality and drama described elsewhere. And I make no apology for the more profound thoughts. We all have a responsibility to stay measured as we consider this new wildlife before us. The cats force us to think about their world, our self and ourselves.

The deer in our woods are alive to the large carnivores which now stalk them. Some people's dogs and horses have sensed large cats and, by their reactions, alerted their owners. Nature knows and shows us that new and extraordinary animals have melted into the landscape. The emergence of Britain's big cats invites us to think afresh as we experience our own outdoors.

Rick Minter

COMING TO YOUR SENSES

'Some people have quietly concluded that there are a few big cats living undercover in Britain. It sounds like a tall story to me. But knowing what I do about leopards, anything is possible...'

(Jonathan Scott, narration for 'The Secret Leopard',
Natural World, BBC2, 2010)

We view leopards and pumas as majestic and enigmatic. They are large wild felines, unknown to us. Sometimes graceful, sometimes fierce, they dwell in the depths of far-off lands. Watching footage of a leopard killing and consuming an antelope is a stunning and humbling experience. I've just watched on YouTube an African leopard clamping its prey at the throat. The ambushed impala kicks and shudders limply as the asphyxiating clasp takes effect. The instant the deed is done, the leopard moves swiftly to the rump of the prey and immediately shears into the flesh, lest any lurking scavengers arrive. The night scene is floodlit by safari vehicles. Tourists whisper in excitement at what they are seeing, cameras flash relentlessly and guides brief their clients. The situation is both dramatic and serene, a perfect demonstration of a large carnivore at work, dispatching and consuming prey. The impala's swollen body suggests it was pregnant. This is nature's harsh code, not ours.

Watching the leopard at work on its own patch, its hard-defended territory in Africa, may be a powerful moment, but it is also highly packaged. The spectacle is played out before a gallery of camera-snapping tourists. The event is far removed from our own ordered existence, in which our lives rarely encounter the frisson of risk or the discomfort of the deep outdoors. The visitors, the adventurers behind the camera lens, have got their prize. Their global travel, their holiday money and their hopes have all been rewarded. The action over, they have a striking moment to hold on to until the reality check: the retreat to the world of pavements, central heating, packaged food, Wi-Fi and Twitter feeds.

After much consideration, I want to suggest there is an alternative reality just around the corner, in the comforting charm of the British countryside. A cut-price safari is available here. Large cats which we regard as symbols of wilderness – the likes of the leopard, the mountain lion, our once-native lynx and maybe some we don't yet know of – have established their own homes here. They can occupy spaces from deep Exmoor valleys to the conifer-cloaked Scottish hills, and from rugged Welsh pastures to the arable lands of East Anglia and Humberside. As I finish this book, in May 2011, reports of panthers have come from locations as diverse as a Cornish estuary in southwest England and the coast of Sutherland in northeast Scotland. And feral cats are not just living in remote places: they are reported in the open farmland of middle England and in derelict spaces on the edge of towns. They can inhabit the same places we do, living in our shadows. According to reports, they cross carriageways at night, they use underpasses, traverse old railway lines and shelter in quarries, old tunnels, derelict buildings, and mines. Our nature reserves, commons and golf courses are part of their larder. We have no impala and dik-dik for them to trail, but we have an abundance of deer, including roe, fallow, muntjac and sika. Becoming alert to theses secret cats, and sensing some of their signs, is part of the cut-price safari.

TOWARDS ENLIGHTENMENT

It may seem audacious to propose big cat territory throughout Britain, but I am not alone. There are many closet followers of these mystery mammals and yes, we do keep pinching ourselves. But if I am ever worried about being labelled a crank, I can defer to my local police force. They are matter-of-fact about the presence of big cats, breeding big cats, in the area. The nation's top broadcasters are on the case too: the topic has cropped up on mainstream TV from a cast including Bill Oddie and Ray Mears, as we shall see later.

If large carnivores are sometimes around the corner in our countryside, how do we feel about that? Is it cause for concern, a reason to rejoice, something to study or all of these things? The issues need to be thought through and talked through. This book is designed to help us reflect calmly on the situation, to help us consider getting used to some new animals in the countryside. Animals which are all about extremes, the most elusive on the planet but sometimes dramatic and conspicuous when in action, animals which go unnoticed but which can also leave tangible signs. And, like big predators the world over, creatures which can be revered and feared, loved and loathed.

I hope this book can help us grapple with what might be termed the discovery stage of our big cats – to help people feel that they are allowed to raise the prospect of large wild cats living in the countryside.

A black leopard keeps to cover in its large enclosure in Africa.
Photo: Mark Fletcher

In the environment and nature sectors with which I am most closely linked, some people deny the subject, others shuffle with unease at the very words 'big cats', while others again are eager to explore the issue, sensing something fresh and relevant, a new ecology which asks questions of what we think we know. Acclimatising to the presence of big cats and all that they represent is not easy, but we should perhaps begin by being more open.

With awareness may come ambivalence as we think about new types of carnivores in our land. This may be all the more reason to embark upon a research stage, to distinguish facts from assumptions where we can. Research will inform us in various ways. It may help us learn more and consider any responses we make, for we should be considered rather than hasty in our actions. I have not compartmentalised this book according to the stages listed below, for they are not always sequential and not always distinct. Perhaps, however, they represent the scope of how we should prepare our minds and think further.

UK Big Cats - stages of awareness

The sequence of becoming aware of and attuned to big cats in our landscape might be as follows:

Discovery and awareness

Research, survey and understanding

Response, possibly including education, information, and advice

My point is that we should learn what we can about these animals before we make any response, especially of a formal type. Our personal views might vary and may change over time or as we find out more. I hope, though, that we would all agree that the research stage is important if we wish to understand these animals better, and appreciate their lifestyles and the effect they may have on our environment.

TABOO QUESTIONS

Reports of big cats across Britain are unremitting, but there is more to the subject than these moment-in-time observations. Our wildlife and our landscapes may be changing, gradually and subtly, because of the presence of these new big predators. Does this matter? Will it affect many of us as we go about our daily lives? Will it have an influence on other wildlife and will it alter the ways in which people use and experience the outdoors? And should anyone or any organisation be bothered enough to do something to understand the nature of what could be happening?

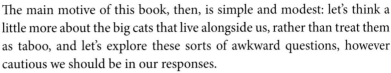

The main motive of this book, then, is simple and modest: let's think a little more about the big cats that live alongside us, rather than treat them as taboo, and let's explore these sorts of awkward questions, however cautious we should be in our responses.

I appreciate that my tone on big cats here in Britain may smack of political correctness. I do not believe, however, that the cats should rule people's lives, affect their livelihoods and be accepted at any price. There is a balance to be struck and some rules to be aware of and, so far, the clandestine cats seem to be on the right side of this balance and these rules. But what about the human side of this balance? I find that people act responsibly in handling a big cat situation. From worried parents to dog owners, to farmers, to surprised car drivers and ramblers and, on the occasions when they are consulted, official bodies, the reaction is measured. There are, of course, different views depending on the context. 'I like the idea of them living quietly here, eating rabbits. There is plenty of space in Herefordshire for us to live alongside them,' said one eyewitness a while back. Many would agree, while the cats keep to natural prey. But when livestock becomes a target, the mood can change. 'My tolerance ends when my stock are killed,' said a pedigree sheep breeder to me in Herefordshire this May, after a large lamb, a ewe and a prize ram had been dispatched one at a time in cat-like attacks over a period of six weeks. She sensed a new alien presence. An intruder had upset the natural order on her land. Such situations seem sporadic, and livestock attacks seem contained or intermittent. They rarely linger as an ongoing curse. But experienced help and advice needs to be offered to landowners and anyone feeling under pressure from big cats. Avoiding the subject means that this doesn't happen, so people improvise, devising their own solutions. They get tips from others who have had a big cat visit and they find their way to informal help. This system works up to a point and I am part of it, but I know its limits. I see the families unsettled by a visiting cat. It is commendable that people want to find a responsible way forward, and we avoid pitchforks heading for the hills.

WORLDS APART?

Some people feel that a big cat passing through the neighbourhood from time to time becomes savvy – in its own best interest, it gets to know some rules. We will look at this again later, but one example comes from Frank Tunbridge, a colleague here in Gloucestershire. I recall it well, as Frank and I were sitting in my kitchen having our monthly catch-up about big cats as the incident was phoned through. I could half-hear the phone conversation unfold and realised it was notable. It came from a corner of the county where sightings are common, where we have come to expect routine reports. Some of them may be of the same animal,

The puma or mountain lion at home in Montana, US. The photo was taken in a large habitat enclosure. Photo: Patty and Jerry Corbin

apart from when there are colour distinctions. The informant was a lady who rented a field for her horse and foal. She had had two sightings of a black, panther-type cat in the field. She was not fazed by the events and felt the cat gave her a wide berth as it passed through. On the occasion of her second sighting her foal had bounded up to the cat when it saw it. The lady normally had a black lurcher with her, although she had left it behind that day, and the foal and the dog would enjoy a play together, the foal racing to greet the dog. She felt the foal's action was simple to explain – it had assumed that the big black cat was the dog. She watched in trepidation as the foal raced to the cat at the top of the field. The cat sat still, disdainful. It let out a threatening snarl and the foal beat its retreat, quickly returning to its mother. Foals, especially at a small stage, may be a target for a big cat, and this is a worry Frank and I sometimes hear raised by horse owners. This lady, though, was unperturbed and felt no need to protect her horse or foal. She felt she understood the cat, and was totally comfortable with its occasional presence. She said she sensed that the cat was female and Frank agreed that this might be a good hunch. His reasoning for agreeing with her was the regularity of the cat's appearance, for he had been on its case, glimpsing it once at dusk and meeting locals who had too. It seemed to have a small territory, making it more likely to be female. It was also slight in build rather than of big, swaggering form.

The lady had one more observation to make, which endeared the cat to her. 'It shows me what it can do,' she said. 'It leaves carcasses, including one of an eaten-out fox, in the middle of the field, right where I can see.' This was the animal's message, the lady thought, of co-existence. 'It's telling me, "This is how I live. You've no need to worry, or to bother me."'

NATURE THAT EXCITES

As I write this, in the spring of 2011, a campaign group is challenging the proposed trapping and removal of beavers from the River Tay in an action proposed by the agency Scottish Natural Heritage. This, despite the fact that an official trial of released beavers, monitored and carrying implanted ID chips, is being carried out at Knapdale and will inform any further releases of beavers if it's decided to bring them back more widely in Scotland. The beavers on the Tay were seen as far back as 2001. It is generally accepted that the five that founded this population escaped from a wildlife park. The reaction to the Tay beavers tells us something about people's connections with free, unmanaged wildlife. When people first noticed beavers on the Tay they didn't run to the authorities and they didn't blab to the press. They kept quiet. People who were in the know seemed content for nature to take its course. They may have felt the beavers were best left to do their thing before public policy caught up with them.

I think the example in Tayside holds some clues, for I've seen this very reaction applied to big cats too. Although some eyewitnesses avoid reporting big cats for fear of ridicule, there are other motives too. Some people would rather not face up to big cats being around. They feel it's something we should keep to ourselves, rather than broadcast, and not something on which we should venture an opinion. I understand that view entirely. If a topic is surrounded by so much speculation, why pronounce on it with confidence? And, as in the case of the Tay beavers, some people don't wish to disclose something they feel is special when the consequences are unknown or even feared.

After one of my talks on big cats, a Cotswolds farmer who'd seen a panther in nearby woods wanted to challenge me. 'Isn't it like knowing a good beach – shouldn't you keep it to yourself?' he asked, forcing a rather agonised reply from me. I was, I said, simply reporting what I felt needed to be known. If people walk, play or camp, for instance, in areas where the cats are sometimes seen, then some of them might like to be aware of the fact. That was all. I wasn't suggesting he carry a gun with him, I wasn't suggesting staying at home and I wasn't inviting him to be over-protective of his kids. I was just saying that a big cat may be present, sometimes, although mainly active at night, and by knowing that and by being a bit vigilant, he'd notice much more around him anyway. Remaining on alert would reveal all manner of tracks and signs of common wildlife and he would hear more birdsong in its many variations. All these parts of the natural world would come into much clearer focus. 'Enjoy it!' I said.

I finished my response to the farmer and the Cirencester audience by saying that I would prefer them to get a reasoned message from me rather than dubious information from people with a different agenda. I got a receptive hearing that day – although perhaps the gathering was self-selecting – and people were curious, polite and largely sympathetic. Since that talk in Cirencester I have done many more, often alongside Frank Tunbridge. I have briefed a great variety of bodies, from the Mammal Society to the Exmoor Society, from farmers' groups to Women's Institutes, Natural History Societies and civic societies. I've facilitated several workshops and spoken at two national wildlife conferences. All told, I have held discussions, mainly in the form of a collective gathering, with well over a thousand people on the topic. At many of these events I have deliberately sampled people's views and the responses are remarkably consistent. I am confident that research and survey is a well-supported option to take as a response to our big cats.

NATURE THAT ASKS QUESTIONS

The UK wildlife depicted in our textbooks is not always the complete picture. Real nature is out there, regardless, more contaminated than we imagine and doing its own thing. Our wildlife has become globalised: a cocktail of species are evolving on these shores, with origins that are a blend of native, exotic, traded, escaped, licensed and unlicensed. Britain is now a land of cosmopolitan species, from the jungle-like Japanese knotweed, which first spread from Victorian gardens and estates, to the raucous ring-necked parakeets screeching away in London parks. Our tainted and mixed-up nature has different effects on the landscape depending on where it appears. Japanese knotweed is seen as damaging to ecosystems and can cost huge sums to clear, but how about the spreading Himalayan balsam, the new blaze of popping purple we can see on summer walks? Some defend it as a late-season host for insects and an aid to pollination, while others see it as a rampant and worrying change, taking a stranglehold on our river banks. The signal crayfish in our rivers and lakes is clearly invasive and damaging, ousting our native crayfish and disturbing the freshwater ecology, but not all aliens are bad news. Some naturalised arrivals can soon feel like long-lost friends. Witness the little owl, 'the Frenchman', which we now commonly hear at dusk. It arrived through the 1800s and had spread country-wide by the 1930s. It filled a vacant niche and is today our most noticed owl. So where do we draw the lines? What are the cut-off points in acceptance, and what are our criteria for impacts and effects? The way we regard our changing nature is as much cultural as scientific. We should be honest in our motives for separating the bits of nature we like from those which we want to control.

ENERGISING THE ECOSYSTEM

I once escorted a New Zealand ecologist on his first trip into the British countryside. As we surveyed the pastoral scene from the ridge of the Malvern Hills on the Herefordshire-Worcestershire border, he marvelled at the shaggy, wildlife-rich common land which had escaped the cleans-

A Eurasian lynx demonstrates its camouflage in a
habitat enclosure in a Bavarian Forest.
Photo: Miha Krofel

9

ing of modern farming. He remarked on the soft but regimented character of orchard plots, he picked out the roughly-grazed horse paddocks and he noted where the pastoral estate-land bounded the more intensive agricultural fields. He was fascinated by these first glimpses of an unfamiliar land, but there was a limit to his diplomacy: 'Your landscapes lack energy!' he declared.

Here, was the brutal verdict of an outsider from someone who has clout in his own country. In one clipped sentence he wrote off our countryside as dormant, bland and missing something. Our countryside may be pretty. It may be scenically striking across large swathes, and it may have all manner of artefacts which make it a cultural delight. But if you see the land, its vegetation and its wildlife as a living, dynamic entity, then much could be regarded as rather sterile.

FEELING THE DRAMA, SENSING THE WILD

Many people, especially from the world of ecology and wildlife conservation, are expressing this view these days. There is a vigorous debate about how to add that missing spark to the landscapes of Britain and 're-wild' them. A step on the way to this is widely referred to as 'landscape-scale conservation'. These are the tags for the latest thinking in how we should improve the lot of the UK's wildlife. Landscape-scale conservation and re-wilding mean moving beyond wildlife gardening or tinkering with small nature reserves, to create bigger spaces for nature, where it can do its own thing, to ebb and flow as a whole ecosystem. The people pushing this agenda suggest bigger units of land for nature reserves, a less prescribed and deliberate management of the land, and the introduction of grazing animals to pressurise the vegetation, creating more micro-habitats within it. This involves creatures like Exmoor ponies and Highland cattle, or even bigger, wilder herbivores to graze and browse, to create the disturbance and the niches for other wildlife, from insects to butterflies, to adapt to. The ultimate expression of this system might be beavers creating glades where woods meet river corridors and wild boar rooting around, their snouts ploughing the woodland floor, dispersing seeds and leaving fresh mounds of soil for fungi and insects to get to work on.

The desire for this new-style conservation is not just based on the richer ecology it will bring, but on a recognition that it has a vital human dimension too. It is exciting, both visually and emotionally. It can bring lyrical power to the land. It is the perfect response to the lack of energy noted by my New Zealand friend.

And this 'new nature', this new thinking about 're-wilding', is not a pipe dream – some of it is happening already, such as the Great Fen project, north of Cambridge, where fenland systems are being re-wetted and joined up. Another renowned example is the restoration and expansion of native Caledonian forest in community projects like Trees for Life in the stunning terrain of Scotland's Glen Affric, and in the official beaver trials noted above in Argyll. But alongside visionary projects, a return to the wild is coming about because of some people's dubious behaviour. While an official reintroduction of wild boar might never have been sanctioned, the animal has 'accidentally' returned to British habitats in which it once flourished, having jumped the fences of farms where it was supplying prized low-fat meat.

In most 'complete' ecosystems, the agricultural and the wild herbivores (the grazing animals) and the deer are influenced by large predators. The grazing animals' movement through the year and by night and by day is affected by a wariness of what stalks them. The predator, whether canine or feline, is a key agent in the ecosystem process. Remove the predator and the deer will often need more intervention by man, especially to curb the numbers, and to keep the herbivores from concentrating on sensitive habitat where tree seedlings can be munched away like salad.

So beaver and boar are coming back, in different ways, as missing links in our ecology. But another creature, the master of concealment, has sneaked unnoticed into the landscape too. A big feline predator is here, in various guises. The most radical part of the re-wilding agenda is underway. The return of this predator is a cause of satisfaction amongst many people from all shades of opinion, yet I would suggest that celebration is premature. The big cats do largely go unnoticed and rarely create concern, but when they do, we need to support those who feel anxious, be it the sheep farmer under pressure or the worried dog walker who meets a curious panther. The arrival of the alpha cat needs to be acknowledged, but until we learn how and when to troubleshoot – though maybe not literally – co-existence cannot be complete. That is the challenge.

THE LORE OF THE CATS

The Mystery Moggy

A panther who roamed Severn Vale
Fooled trackers who always would fail
He gave them the slip
With their bait of catnip
Folks said it was just a tall tale

(Seen at a Gloucestershire village fete, 2010)

MARGINAL CREATURES

All societies and cultures pay homage to the notable creatures which live alongside them. Real and fantasy animals can be represented in art, literature, storytelling, verse, and in humour and hoaxes. Predators, with their power, their fierce image and their grace and guile, usually get particular attention in this folklore. Unknown beasts and mystery animals were often depicted in symbols and sketches at the edges of maps, becoming more familiar and more fully represented if they lived on in people's minds because they became real or were celebrated so much in myth. The fringe of the map was the stuff of 'Here be dragons!'

As we come to recognise our own assortment of panthers and pumas, they are creeping into our folklore. Their flirty and tantalising image – 'Are they here or not?' – has guaranteed the attention of local media. They are a gift for the headline writers, a modern-day beast lurking in the landscape, one we cannot pin down. But we are entering a stage when our big cats are changing their place in our perception. Increasingly, they are moving in from the margins of our mind or the edge of our consciousness. Attention on prime time TV and regular newspaper reports, along with gossip at professional conferences as well as in the pub, is putting them on the map. And for some people, at least, in Britain, they are in full view.

REAL DRAMA?

The BBC Radio 4 play by Simon Bovey, *Red in Tooth and Claw*, broadcast twice in recent years, is uncannily real. It depicts a farming family piecing together clues, realising they have a big cat visiting their land, sometimes taking sheep. They and neighbouring folk wrestle with the situation. As the sheep-killing continues, reactions differ – people relate to the animal in different ways and there are rifts. A big cat has cast its spell over a landscape and over a community. The question of what to do is more tormenting than the animal itself. Then, at the end, comes a harsh, agonising lesson. 'The only beast in the woods is the one we take with us,' is the lasting message. The play was inspired by Simon Bovey's own sighting of a big cat in a Surrey woodland. It demonstrates the worth of quality drama, for it is played out for real, without the final impact, across many parishes to which I'm invited to share the thinking on how to handle a big cat's spell.

I'm told that a play once staged in Exmoor focused on the high-profile local legend, the Beast of Exmoor. Flashes of the creature sprang up through the performance, as key characters in the play confronted their own representation of the beast. Suspense was maintained throughout the production until a final scene revealed the actual beast, showing it as a hydra-like entity, a composite creature representing all the various bogeymen plaguing people's minds.

And, on a more whimsical level, big cats have even made it into modern comic strips. In the *Beano*'s 2010 summer special, Roger the Dodger takes up the challenge of the Beanotown Gazette to photograph a big cat. He dabs spots on his own moggy and nearly fools the newspaper editor, until the dubious scale is noticed and Roger is found out. Roger, his mission a failure, declares that only an idiot would think there really was a big cat on the loose. As he utters these scornful words, a leopard eyes him up from an overhanging branch…

BRANDING 'THE BEAST'

Rumours can be invented, spread, twisted, and scoffed at over pints in the pub. And when it comes to the product placement of big cats, nothing much seems to beat local beers and ales. A fierce and rugged image, a modern-day mystery and, not least, the tag of 'the beast' is close to perfect for a brand. To their credit, two traditional breweries have used their local panther stories to represent leading beers amongst their stock. The Grainstore Brewery from Leicestershire and Rutland produces Panther Bitter, while Exmoor Ales in Somerset supplies Beast Ale from 'The Dark Side of the Moor'. It would be bad form to endorse specific beers, of course, but local trackers, not surprisingly, testify to the powers of these products.

Whether you think they are real or imagined, the Beast of Exmoor and the Beast of Bodmin have become iconic labels. These are mighty legends which live on, sustained by ongoing local rumours, some of

which my sources suggest are well-founded. The Beast of Bodmin has even become a hot chicken curry option in one of the town's fast food takeaways. In the Exmoor National Park visitors' magazine, the kids' puzzle section includes a spotter's guide, with points awarded for different features of the area. Toughest of the lot, and very much in the frame, is The Beast – a black panther, perhaps glimpsed in the wild or noticed on a beer label, or seen in the flesh at the local Exmoor Zoo. If you come across this element of Exmoor's identity, you earn 100 points, easily trumping all other features and landmarks. Other areas seem as beset with big cats as are Exmoor and Bodmin – more so, even. Yet reputations stick. When documentaries are made, from home or abroad, the script writers have Bodmin, Exmoor and the Surrey Puma fixed firmly in their minds. Brands like these cannot be contrived. Branding has to be earned, by a combination of local and national attention.

Places which have considered exploiting their 'big cat country' image include the Kintyre Way, a long-distance path in southwest Scotland. The 88-mile route winds from Tarbert to Southend in Kintyre. When new funds for maintaining and promoting the path were announced in 2009, big cat sightings were part of the image sold to people. Some of the funds were earmarked for wildlife initiatives, including the Kintyre Way Big Cat survey, to which users of the route can report any sightings. Remote trail cameras were proposed for any hotspots. Here, then, is a big cat initiative taking its place alongside other measures to market a recreational feature of the countryside. Rather than shrug off the big cat rumours, the site's managers want to use them as an asset. It's all a matter of attitude and the sensitivity with which you raise the topic.

There may be a market for guided walks, field trips or even safari-like big cat vigils, but nothing has yet been devised, as far as I know. I suspect anyone spending a day tracking in the Gloucestershire country-side with my friend Frank Tunbridge, or elsewhere with Frank's counterparts, learning about the different signs the cats leave and hearing of people's encounters in the area, would feel transported and enlivened by their introduction to wild predators and how to sense them. I've often planned the brochures in my mind. And maybe it's not far-fetched, for in April 2009, the local press in Worcestershire announced that visitors were coming to the county in search of its secret panthers. Hotel and bed-and-breakfast managers told Destination Worcestershire, the county's tourist board, that people, following up big cat reports, were visiting the county specifically on the trail of the beast. The tourism staff there were considering developing trails and a website for people wanting to investigate the beast's existence.

So at least two specific areas are poised to harness the visitor potential of their big cat fame. With imagination and flair, they may well pull it off. Will we one day see rivalry between the tourist slogans, boasting 'the best big cat experiences'? Maybe there is scope for yet more legends.

A BEAST OR A BLUFF?

Being alert to a possible doctored photo or contrived story adds a complication to studying out-of-place big cats. The topic is tricky enough already, but hoaxes go with the territory, and one may as well accept and enjoy the challenge. There are good trick photos and rubbish ones. The more obvious and perfect a big cat's outline in a photo purporting to come from the UK countryside, the more suspicious we should be. These days, with Photoshop and similar computer aids, it's a doddle to come up with something passable to circulate on the web. The deliberately naff attempts, of one's own moggy in the garden labelled as the local predator, are actually more fun and have more impact in raising a smile on YouTube and the like.

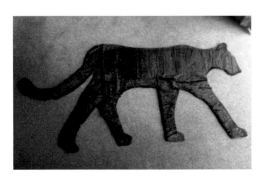

The cut-out image used for the Staines Advertiser's *2011 April Fool's picture.*
Photo: Staines Advertiser

The best hoaxes show imperfect images, with an animal, or what might be an animal, partially in view, slightly obscured, at an annoying angle, or looking something like a dog but slightly more like a cat. These are the tricky ones that could be for real, and they are guaranteed to get attention. The *Staines Advertiser* got it right for April Fool's Day 2011. If they had resisted quoting local expert 'Christian Lyons' in the accompanying article, the picture might by now have been prominent on the web, paraded by some as conclusive evidence. The story was plausible. The angle and the distance from the camera of the animal allegedly seen through the woods by a cyclist was just as it happens, and was similar to many accounts from across middle England. The supposed panther may have been a scale cut-out figure, but it wasn't as two dimensional as the expert cat twitchers are used to. It seemed to have texture and shadow. The crafty journalists had stuck on fur – a trick to remember!

Another way to make pranks plausible is to use a location with some big cat history where there is already a rumour to build on. In this respect, too, the *Staines Advertiser* got it right, but unwittingly – they didn't know they'd chosen the very place where readers claimed to have spotted mystery cats, but posts on the newspaper's blog soon pointed this out.

The prize for the most effective hoax so far goes to a clever silhouette of a panther in a pasture next to Charlbury station in Oxfordshire. The cut-out profile has good scale and proportions and was placed in position following local big cat reports in the past. Year after year it results in carefully described accounts of a panther on the loose, sent to local and national big cat groups by well-meaning train passengers. Local big cat researcher Steve Archibald explains why this hoax is particularly successful: 'It looks like it is moving because there are trees between the track and the cut-out. When the train is in motion it gives the impression that it is the cat which is moving instead.' Steve himself receives around three reports of the Charlbury panther a month, either direct or via Thames Valley Police.

WHAT SHOULD WE CALL THEM?

Technically, big cats are the species that can roar and make up the *Panthera* genus: lion, tiger, leopard, jaguar and snow leopard (although the snow leopard cannot roar). The cheetah is a genus of its own, and the two species of clouded leopard are a distinct subfamily. The other 29 species of cats are in the *Felis* genus, and cannot roar, so the puma (also known as cougar and mountain lion), despite being the same size as a leopard, is not officially a 'big cat'. All cats have a bony link between the throat and the voice box, called the hyoid. In *Panthera* cats it vibrates to create the roar, as it has a ligament attached. In *Felis* cats there is no ligament

The Charlbury Panther – Britain's most commonly reported big cat.
'You can't miss it, really, when you're gazing out of the train window. It is
really convincing – people won't have it when you tell them it's a cut-out,' says
Oxfordshire big cat researcher Steve Archibald.
Photo: Steve Archibald, bigcatsightings.com

attached to the hyoid bone, so no vibration and no roar. The sounds the cats make is important in working out what they might be, and whether they belong to *Felis* or *Panthera*, but the official 'big cat' name is rather academic to most people's general interests. Another classification point is the overall status of cats as the family *Felidae*, or felids.

As imprecise as it is, I mostly use the term 'big cats' throughout this book to label the range of misfit panther-, puma- and lynx-sized cats to which I refer. There is no other useful and widely understood alternative with which I am comfortable. The clunky terms 'Alien Big Cats' or 'Anomalous Big Cats' are sometimes used elsewhere, often crunched to the rather anaemic shorthand of 'ABCs'. The cats here may well be regarded as alien or anomalous, but the same cannot be said of the formerly-native lynx, which may be naturalising anyway. They may well be regarded as exotic but again, the lynx is an exception, and if we examined some with a lineage of several generations, it might soon justify classification as its own evolving subspecies. Thinking, then, about the status and labels of these cats is more than folklore: it might be important science in terms of genetics and evolutionary paths. These are our cats, in our land. Are they contaminating our landscape and habitats or might they become regarded as honorary natives? How about the Scottish mountain lion, *Puma celtica*, the Britannia panther, the Leopard of the Shires? One day our guidebooks may be rewritten – I can already imagine the Cotswold Way Spotters' Guide to Big Cats. Some people would be chuffed and others horrified.

I also use the term 'feral' for the cats but peri-feral may have been a better choice. Newly-recognised creatures deserve new terms, surely? Fresh words could reflect that we barely know these animals, even on the outside, and that in their transition from peri-domestic to peri-feral, they occupy in-between spaces in nature and in our minds. 'Wild' or 'truly wild' are also useful ways of considering them. It is not for me, though, to suggest titles for this unrecognised wildlife. The lore of the cats will evolve and has still to develop. Just as the puma has multiple labels across the Americas, from cougar in the west to panther in the east, from the ghost cat to the horse pirate via catamount and painter, they will carry on being the Beast, the Panther and the Big Cat, according to our media and our own moods. As the cats force us to think about parts of our community and ourselves that are rarely examined, their names will emerge as we forge relationships with them.

THE BIG CAT LIBRARY

Beasts, predators and panthers make good fodder for stories and literature and some of the main published titles are summarised below. The list indicates that big cats are starting to be used to inspire and excite modern fiction.

A surprising amount of reference material has already been written about the evidence and reporting of big cats, going back well over a decade. Meeting most of the authors, hearing them speak and watching them defend their work, I'm aware just how clued-up these people are – some intelligent minds and some intrepid people have applied themselves to the theme. Many of the same types of incidents, evidence, reactions and rumours which crop up today, and are being reported in current trends, were being noted and discussed in literature many years ago. Some of the books and references below are written to convey a particular agenda and a favoured theory but, overall, the body of writing on the UK's big cats contains consistent messages at its core. Maybe that in itself tells us something.

CARTOONS, CHILDREN'S STORIES AND NOVELS

Bod - the Beast of Bodmin Moor
Endymion Beer. 2006. Halsgrove

A clever cartoon story book following the trail of Bod the black panther as he ventures across Bodmin Moor and further afield in the landscapes of southwest England. He meets a female feline Min, who adds to the fun and frolic.

A scene from Bod the cartoon cat from Bodmin. Courtesy: Endymion Beer

Hox
Annemarie Allan. 2007.
Floris Books

It is heartening to see the lynx enter children's fiction in Britain. This story follows a young boy's relationship with two lynx in Scotland as they embark upon a journey away from potential perils at an animal research centre.

Safe for Life
Katherine Reynolds. 2009.
Ideas4Writers

A sequel to the award-winning children's adventure novel *Born to Dance*. Dylan de Polka, the tap-dancing star of the Happy Days Circus, and his canny feline friend, Red Tabby, take on the ruthless Jago Reaver and his villainous sidekick, Frankie. They are intent on stealing the circus animals' much-loved home, Great Park. Katherine Reynolds' books are superbly written and are great adventure stories for children up to a reading age of around 12. Patrick the Panther appears in this second story.

Black Cat
Martyn Bedford. 2001. Penguin Books

This is a story for adults which brings the beast legend centre stage. A couple realise much about their own deeper personalities and their fringe existence as they track a possible black panther on the moors. As the plot unfolds, the author introduces many of the thorny issues associated with investigating big cats. He has clearly done his homework.

REFERENCES ON UK BIG CATS

Merlin. The Story of a West Country leopard
Trevor Beer. 2008. Ryelands

Merlin follows the fate of a black leopard after he is released and adapts to a feral life in southwest England, stalking prey and keeping away from human activity. This is a clever concept of a book and one of the most helpful texts for thinking about how a leopard would behave in the depths of the British countryside.

The Path of the Panther
Ian Bond. 2011. Big Cats in Britain, britishbigcats.blogspot.com

Mammal specialist Ian Bond has kept a diary of big cat reports across northeast England for over ten years. He plots the sightings and discusses them with some of his fellow ecologists in the region. This book brings together the reports and the author's thinking on trends in what might be happening. This is a valuable account from a region less well known than others for mystery cats. The author's measured and scientific approach adds to the stature of the book.

Big Cats in Britain Yearbook
Mark Fraser (ed.). Annual publication from Big Cats in Britain
britishbigcats.blogspot.com

Mark Fraser heads the investigative group Big Cats in Britain. Each year he collates sightings and reports and commissions essays and comments from amongst the amateur researchers who follow the subject. The Yearbook presents the ideas postulated by this community. Mark Fraser stresses that the different components of the Yearbook carry no endorsement but are conveyed as they are – people's own reports and thoughts and occasional snaps of what they've encountered.

Big Cat Mysteries of Somerset

Chris Moiser. 2005. Bossiney Books

Zoologist Chris Moiser has produced three short books on UK big cats, each documenting reports and possible evidence from specific counties. They are a neat introduction to the subject and some of the most straightforward and readable texts available on the big cat mystery, focused on southwest England but with lessons for the whole UK. Bossiney Books have published the Somerset version, plus a separate volume on Devon and Cornwall, while the booklet on Dorset is produced by Inspiring Places Publishing.

Mystery Big Cats

Merrily Harpur. 2006. Heart of Albion Press

After casting aside all the main theories for the origin of big cats in the UK, Merrily Harpur promotes daimons as a key explanation for people's encounters. This book suggests that the cats are not real furry animals. Understanding the concept of daimons turns out to be a puzzle in itself, but other aspects of the book are rewarding for those who are deeply hooked. She has since produced a shorter book, *Roaring Dorset*, which provides a helpful summary of trends in big cat reports across Dorset.

Big Cats Loose in Britain

Marcus Matthews. 2007. CFZ Publishing

A book for those who want to appreciate the breadth and volume of sightings in earlier decades of the big cat phenomenon, especially across southwest England.

Cat Country. The Quest for the British Big Cat

Di Francis. 1983. David and Charles

Presents the controversial hide-out theory, which suggests that the bulk of the UK's big cat reports relate to an indigenous cat undiscovered by science which has lived and evolved undercover. This may seem radical, but whatever your conclusions, Di Francis' well-argued work is certainly thought-provoking.

The Beast of Exmoor

Di Francis. 1993. Jonathan Cape

A riveting account of the commotion on Exmoor through the 1980s, as farmers lived with livestock losses and people reported mystery animals which may or may not have been responsible for them. The area came under siege from the media, and trophy hunters and the military moved in to target the rogue animal(s). Di Francis went behind the lines too, and documented events as the immortal story took shape.

The Beast of Exmoor – fact or legend?
Trevor Beer. 1984. Countryside Productions, Barnstable

Another fine piece of detective work on the mystery cats of Exmoor, describing the author's follow up to witness reports, his tracking, sometimes alongside Nigel Brierly (see *They Stalk By Night*, below) and setting out his own thoughts on why both dogs and large exotic cats could be responsible for the sightings and the sheep kills, a point that is perhaps still very relevant today. He finishes the booklet with admiration for the beast(s): 'Whatever else, it has made our lives that much more interesting.'

Illustration by Trevor Beer of the big cat he watched on Exmoor in 1984.

Mystery Cats of the World
Karl Shuker. 1989. Robert Hale

I know little about the realm of cryptozoology but for those who do, Shuker is a guru with a reputation for rigour and thorough treatment of the subject in hand. This book is now tricky to acquire but is recognised as an important reference. The first sections, up to page 97, grapple with some of the fundamental evidence and science behind the UK's experience with exotic cats. Later in the book, the section on the long-limbed onza found in Mexico, which has seemingly evolved for more open grassland conditions, may have parallel lessons for some of the UK sightings.

The Surrey Puma: the Natural and Unnatural History of Britain's First Alien Big Cat

Roman Golicz. 2005. Don Namor Press

A helpful chronology of the Surrey Puma reports through the 1960s and 1970s, supplemented with some well-researched analysis. Unfortunately, the dense text of this booklet makes it a challenge to read, but it acts as a definitive guide to the saga of the Surrey Puma.

They Stalk by Night: the big cats of Exmoor and the Southwest

Nigel Brierly. 1989. Yeo Valley Productions, Bishops Nympton

Nigel Brierly devoted much time to investigating evidence and speaking to locals on Exmoor through the 1980s. This booklet presents his findings in a systematic and engaging way. He has advised many people who study big cats and this booklet has become an influential one which these investigators keep to hand. It is also important for having introduced the possibility of darker or black pumas, a subject which remains controversial but which some encounters suggested at the time.

ECOS: a Review of Conservation

www.banc.org.uk

Neil Bennett

If you want to consider the UK's big cats in context and study the links with other nature conservation topics, including the management of alien species and approaches to re-wilding Britain's landscapes, *ECOS* is the main place to look. It is a non-academic journal, published three times a year. I am thoroughly biased because I help edit it, but you will not find these matters discussed regularly elsewhere.

SEEING AND SENSING –
THE GREY EVIDENCE

The Will-o'-the-Wisp is out on the marsh,
And all alone he goes;
There's not a sight of his glimmering light
From break of day to close;
But all night long, from dusk till dawn,
He drifts where the night wind blows.

(Annie Campbell Huestis, 1900)

KNOWING THE JIZZ

At least once a month, someone will contact me out of the blue to tell me, in a stunned voice, that they've seen or encountered a big cat. Mostly they are emphatic, conveying their report with great conviction and confidence: 'It couldn't have been anything else!' 'It was definitely a big cat!' Sometimes they noticed it because their dog suddenly got nervous or made a noise they'd never heard from it before, or because their horse quivered in a way they'd never known, or because they saw an animal being mobbed by crows. Scale is crucial to a sighting and many people try to find a yardstick in the landscape, either at the time or afterwards. High shoulder blades, powerful back legs and haunches and a long, often sweeping tail are other hallmarks. The words 'slim', 'sleek', 'fit', 'powerful' and 'muscular' are often used, all marking out the condition of a predator in the wild.

Often it is the movement, fluid and deliberate, which alerts people and helps them register something distinct. It is not in their normal visual reference and is unlike a dog, even if at first they thought it was. It's happened to me, for 40 seconds in Cumbria, as a sleek black animal, low to the ground, moved nonchalantly along a hedgerow. It was 80 metres ahead of me, oblivious to me or, more likely, ignoring my presence. The first ten seconds were spent puzzling over an odd-looking isolated Labrador, the next ten involved the rapid realisation that it might be a panther and a check of the animal against all the options I knew. Next, spinning together in my head, came shock, unease, awe and amazement.

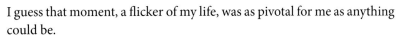

I guess that moment, a flicker of my life, was as pivotal for me as anything could be.

But my best big cat sighting of sorts was a dog – yes, a dog – because of what it taught me about instant reaction. I was with a carload of ecologist friends, enjoying a tour of marshes on the Isle of Sheppey in Kent. As we looked up from watching greenshank, away in the flat and shaggy landscape we saw a black, mastiff-type dog. The weather was clear and the dog stood out, a moving mammal in the landscape, 50-odd metres away. Before I blurted out what I could see, I thought I'd wait for other views. Sure enough, my three companions quickly announced their surprise at seeing a dog lost in the marsh. Here was the kind of situation where many witnesses have reported unexpectedly seeing a cat, in the middle distance and with no human around. The dog looked bemused and forlorn, its movement was erratic and it lacked confidence for the location in which it found itself. It was the mass of the average panther but it lacked the jizz of a cat, and we all knew at once what it was. I know the word 'jizz' has evolved to have other connotations these days, but it remains an important concept in the recognition of wildlife – the instant impression and characteristic of an animal or bird. The jizz is a crucial element in many sightings, as it is form, poise and movement that can clearly distinguish feline from canine.

DARING TO CONFESS

People who make reports of a cat are mostly tentative. As they introduce themselves on the phone they are feeling for a sense of whether I'm both trustworthy and sane. Their report often comes with the strict condition that the location remain a secret, and there will often be concerns about the animal being pursued or shot. 'They won't be culled, will they? To be honest, I find it all rather exciting!' said one macho chap who'd spotted a panther one morning while dog-walking near Dursley in Gloucester-shire. I was once offered money to help protect a regularly-seen cat. I explained I doubted anyone could manage that, money or no money. The incidents are often laced with emotion – some people are worried, others elated. Some people are desperate to see the animal again and it stays in their mind as a powerful force. The words, 'I felt privileged' are used sur-prisingly often. Others want rid of it and never to see it in their mind or on their property again. Some of the informants want advice, especially if they own land or animals, and want to check what practical measures to take if the feline visitor returns. Listening to people's queries can feel like offering counselling, whatever their emotions.

Once, in Somerset, a lady I'd never met rushed to embrace me in front of customers in the pub where she worked, such was her relief in hav-ing 'the big cat man' turn up to hear her story. A black panther frequently

Andrew Dempsey describing one of his two big black cat sightings on the Cotswold edge, east of Cheltenham. He found a fresh deer kill at this location too.

Andrew Dempsey found this fresh roe deer carcass at the location of a big cat sighting in Gloucestershire. The deer's body was still warm. A large amount of fresh consumption had occurred, and the stomach displaced and left. See carcass descriptions in Chapter 5. Photo: Andrew Dempsey

walked through the fields in view of the pub, and she watched it regularly. Once, over 30 customers shared the experience, and a man phoned his relatives back home in New Zealand, knowing they would be asleep but eager to tell them he was watching a panther in the distant English fields. The lady thought the cat must be male, for it was large, powerful and muscular. She once noticed him at close quarters, lying on a boundary wall as she cycled to work. This was a closer meeting, the only time he had seen her. Now, after getting used to views of this showcase creature from the window, he'd gone unseen for several weeks and his absence was troubling her. We discussed areas close by which he might like: the adjacent deer park, the steep hidden valleys along the local hills, and even the more tucked-away bits of the coast. She agreed she'd been lucky to see the panther so many times – well over 20, she thought – but it was all too special to let go. She yearned to see that majestic animal again.

Witnesses and informants are ordinary citizens in all walks of life: people driving, especially at night, dog walkers, horse riders, farmers, teachers, engineers, milkmen and even off-duty policeman – three in the last two years, in fact. As my other half once said to me: 'It must be all true – these people are so normal.' I am reluctant to distinguish between class or creed, age, levels of education or whether people have experience in observing wildlife and mammals. A local paper in Scotland once sought an ecologist's verdict on an eyewitness report, but the witness was a receptionist at a veterinary practice. It seemed perverse that the evidence of a person who saw different-sized dogs and ordinary housecats all day, every day, should need a second opinion. I work with nature conservation specialists and count many as good friends. Some won't trust the ordinary citizen's reports of wildlife. I think that's too sweeping. I'll give a lorry driver as much of a hearing as a lizard expert if they are both rational and robust in what they describe. For those who do prefer the view of a professional outdoorsman, though, a person dealing with the natural world every day, try the following report from the Scottish Highlands, west of Inverness (page 28).

While I get told of a big cat once or twice a month, Frank Tunbridge is notified weekly. Frank puts himself about. He will frequently crop up in the local papers, on radio and regional TV, and you'll find him first on a web search. Big cats in this part of Gloucestershire lead you to him. He runs car boot sales, especially around Stroud, meaning hundreds of people nod a hello to him every week, every season. If there's word on the street about a mega-cat somewhere, it will get to Frank. The phone calls, the reports, the emails and referrals from press and radio between us don't stop. If it goes quiet after two or three weeks, something seems up, but then there can be two on the same day. A half-eaten deer carcass on a back road one Sunday resulted in three separate reports that morning

22 October 2007, approx. 7.20 a.m.

Minor road from Achilty to Little Scatwell, about 200 metres SE of Luichart Power Station; north bank of River Conon. Approximately NH 396 568

Morning was clear with intense sunrise to southeast which caused me to stop and admire as the whole sky seemed to be blood red. As I moved the vehicle forward an animal bounded across the road approximately 20 metres in front of me. It moved northerly across the road and was very dark. It was the colour that alerted me. The animal was long and black with a long tail. It disappeared into an area of rising birch woodland on the north side of the road. I scanned to see if it would reappear and it did. I watched the animal walk steadily uphill through the birches. It was then that I could gauge its size. It was obviously a cat from the way it moved and the tail was long and curved. The animal was bulky-headed with small ears and a broad face. At one point it stopped and looked back down the hill from a distance of about 100–150 metres. Bigger than a Labrador and with muscular shoulders. The only thing that I could think of was a panther. It then moved more swiftly up hill and was lost from view. The entire sighting lasted approximately five minutes.

I have travelled through southern Africa and have seen (at close quarters) leopard in the wild. The only difference between a leopard and the animal that I saw was the colour. The same heavy-headed appearance, the slouch of the shoulders, the sweeping, curved tail were all the same. This is a situation that I never saw myself experiencing! And it is strangely difficult to admit to oneself that that is the animal that one saw, let alone report it.

(Duncan Macdonald, Highland Council Countryside Ranger)

– one to me, two to Frank. On his inspection Frank didn't even conclude that the deer was a big cat victim, but it shows that people are primed on the issue, and false alarms or unproven cases are part of the deal. As I check this chapter at the end of May 2011, Frank has had 27 reports in his logbook since January. In December 2010 he had ten reports just in the one month. Several other reports have gone straight to the press. The winter months always yield more sightings, not least because of less cover in the landscape, so the trend of reporting itself is consistent. The good people of Gloucestershire are telling us something.

Frank and I may have some kind of handle on the situation but, in truth, we have no idea what is really going on. Some people, maybe most,

Plenty of action on trail of Big Cats

Frank Tunbridge

The Stroud News and Journal maps out some of the area's recent big cat sightings. This reporting often prompts other people to come forward with their sightings in the locality.
Photo: Stroud News & Journal

PROFESSIONAL killers like the SAS do not announce their intentions, or broadcast their presence, otherwise they ~~would very soon become~~ ... ple, a deer kill/paw prints on trees or posts, or unusual droppings/paw prints – please feel free to call me, Frank Tunbridge – in confi- ~~dence, to report the above or~~ ...

don't tell anyone of their cat encounter, even within the family. It can be hard to admit that you've seen a non-existent mammal which is meant to be in Africa, Asia, the Rocky Mountains or the zoo. So while some people feel compelled to talk, others tell no-one. People stay silent for various reasons: they might fear ridicule, or want to protect the animal or not want to cause a commotion in the area. For some, though, the powerful moment, whether it was special, frightening, awkward or a mixture of all three, is just too hard to put into words. In my own locality, and at the talks I give, I find people who have never previously mentioned their experience but who are prepared to recount it then, given a willing audience who will not mock them.

Estimates of national levels of sightings have ranged from 1,200 to well over 2,000 a year, and the guess is that about one in ten sightings is actually filed somewhere. There are no central records and no co-ordinated stats, even across police forces. Apart from to the police, reports get sent to local papers and radio, websites, or to national bodies such as Big Cats in Britain, while some even make it to Defra (Department for Environment, Food and Rural Affairs), as we will see later. Gauging the scale of sightings when they are dispersed in so many directions is therefore fraught with problems. We can still only speculate at the overall pattern.

Sceptics would say that the sightings and reports are suggestive, building on each other as people get in on the act. There may be a hint of that, but a very different psychology is usually at work, meaning that people feel more confident to report their experience once they hear of activity from the same place. For others, though, the big cat moment remains under wraps and they remain steadfastly quiet. I agree that we do need to factor mis-sightings into the equation, but it is under-reporting rather than invention and exaggeration which characterises the statistics.

PARISH-WIDE, COUNTY-WIDE OR NATIONWIDE?

The media love big cat reports – they are a gift for them. Any story, whether plausible or flakey, is bound to get attention and provoke heated views. Most reports are immersed in the detail of their own local mystery, following up a sighting, examining a mystery footprint or hearing of a farmer's concern. Local people's views are heard and often an 'expert' in the area, from a zoo or wildlife body, or a big cat researcher, is sought for comment. There is, though, an angle which these accounts usually miss as they focus on their particular corner of the world: that they are not alone. The same thing is happening next door, in the next county and even nationwide. In an online poll in August 2009 (far, admittedly, from rigorous science, as the sample size is unknown and the respondents self-selecting) the *Scottish Daily Record* newspaper asked: 'Do you believe there are 'big cats' roaming wild in Scotland?' The response after several days stood at 87% saying 'yes'.

The national scope and the extent of the media coverage can be appreciated by viewing the press reports compiled by Mark Fraser on the Big Cats in Britain website. The list rattles on month after month, year after year. It speaks for itself, it has UK dimensions. The topic doesn't go away. Page 32 shows a list of big cat headlines from a month in 2008, and again in 2010.

Some newspaper reports gain momentum, as readers pipe up about sightings following others nearby. And views are polarized. I've seen readers complain, fed up with what they take to be too much hype on big cats in the Gloucestershire press: 'It was a dog or the witness was high,' said one dismissive commentator on a thread last year. Note that the lists of headlines on page 32 are just from England. Wales and Scotland would provide more. For the media, both national and local, our mystery big cats remain a potboiler, courting controversy and giving scope for shocking headlines.

THE RUMPUS ON THE WEB

There are researchers and diehards who debate big cats daily through such groups as Big Cats in Britain, but around the web, in specialist groups and in local newspapers, a rash of comment can break out when, following a sighting or query, someone mentions a panther or puma. Groups involved with farming, wildlife, game, bushcraft, the paranormal and dogs – even car-driving groups – have all swapped notes, argued and shared sightings on their web forums. The sceptics in each camp have weighed in, not buying what the witnesses assure them is true. Some people keep an open mind and remain curious, politely asking questions of their peers. But beyond these reasoned views, all shades of opinion can be found, with views expressed both mildly or with the force of a bludgeon. These debates in cyberspace are nothing if not feisty but, alas, they are rarely well-informed.

I saw a big cat on milk round!

Big cats in the Forest? You bet

Big cats on the prowl – and that's official

Huge prints mean a puma not a pet

'I narrowly escaped big cat smash'

Panthers really are out there in the UK

Workers spot big black cat in field

'Our eyes just fixed on each other... It was without question the big cat'

'I was up this tree when I saw beast'

Big freeze brings big cats

A selection of newspaper headlines announcing big cat encounters in Gloucestershire.

Local newspaper headlines from June 2008

Paw Prints Awaken Rumours of Big Cats *The Shropshire Star*: 25 June
Is this Paw Print a Panther? *Rutland & Stamford Mercury*: 24 June
Was This Paw Print Left by a Tiger? *Asbourne News and Telegraph*: 18 June
Huge Black Cat Spotted in Woods *Northants Evening Telegraph*: 16 June
What is Killing the Moorland Lambs? *Huddersfield Daily Examiner*: 14 June
Mystery Big Cat Spotted in Woods *Northampton Chronicle*: 14 June
On the Hunt for the Beast of Bevendean *Brighton Argus*: 13 June
'I Saw the Beast of Bevendean' *The Argus*: 13 June
More Sightings Reported of Mysterious Big Cat *This is Somerset*: 12 June
They Want You to Spot the Big Cats Too *Metro*: 9 June
Beast Attacks Lambs on the Mendips *This is Somerset*: 6 June
Have You Seen a Big Cat on the Prowl? *Peterborough Evening Telegraph*: 5 June
1995 Sighting Adds to Panther Mystery *Stafford Post*: 5 June
Big Black Cat is Still Out There Somewhere *Loughborough Echo*: 5 June
Predator on the Prowl *This is Somerset*: 5 June
Big Cat Spotted Soaking up the Sun *Sheerness Times Guardian*: 5 June
Further Sighting of a Big Cat *Tavistock Times Gazette*: 4 June
Southwark 'Puma' Spotted *Southwark News*: 2 June

Local newspaper headlines from March 2010

Large Cat Spotted near Yeovil? *Yeovil Express*: 22 March 2010
Expert: Paw prints in Yorkshire Dales 'definitely' from a wild big cat *The Westmoreland Gazette*: 18 March 2010
Savaged Sheep -was it a puma? *West Somerset Free Press*: 19 March 2010
Colne Walker Finds Puma Paw Print in Snow *Lancashire Telegraph*: 18 March 2010
Big Cat Spotted in Sedgemoor *Bridgewater Mercury*: 17 March 2010
Cat Sightings a Real Mystery *Hartlepool Mail*: 9 March 2010
Report Reveals Suffolk Big Cat Sightings *Evening Star*: 8 March 2010
Is Claws on the Prowl Again? *Evening Star*: 6 March 2010
Beast Sightings investigated near Runcorn *Runcorn and Widnes Weekly News*: 4 March 2010
Mystery of Cat Sightings Deepens *This is Somerset*: 2 March 2010
Wildlife Expert Ian Bond Says Big Cats Prevalent Across North *The Journal (Sunderland)*: 2 March 2010

THE CATALOGUE OF MISTAKES

Some people spot a panther, upright and poised. Its reactions, though, are suspect. It doesn't respond to nearby birds. It flutters in the breeze.

It is, after all, a black bin bag. Other people dismiss a bin bag they see cast near a hedge – until it gets up, shows its long tail and slinks off. Researcher Nigel Brierly, in his book *They Stalk by Night*, tells of a lady near Yeovil who, in 1981 nearly stumbled upon two cats mating, one on top of the other, as she mistook them for a log as she walked out of a local wood. The cats separated and took off as she passed near. They were bigger than her golden Labrador dog.

There are a range of candidates to be confused with a cat, including logs that really are logs, deer and foxes moving stealthily in low light and otters, which although way below panther scale, have a fluid rolling movement which can be taken for feline. Dogs are less often a cause for confusion. Lurchers, especially those discarded by poachers, can lead to misidentification but dogs have, by and large, a very different jizz.

It is large domestic cats, outsize ferals and designer cats which can be the key candidates for muddle. Frank Tunbridge was once invited to check a 'lynx' that had arrived at a lady's remote mobile home, enjoying the food being offered at the back door. She insisted it was a lynx – it matched a photo she'd seen in the newspaper. Frank reluctantly made a 90-minute drive just in case but, sure enough, he arrived to meet a cat with a normal-length tail and no tufted ears. A Bengal cat was lying in the lady's arms. From Maine Coons to Bengals – and a new one coming our way, the savannah cat – some people have no experience of designer cats and are easily misled.

Some sceptics suggest that people dredge a creature from their subconscious, projecting an animal buried in their minds. A variant of this is 'believing leads to seeing', when people expect to see panthers in their midst. Perhaps both can happen, but is this going on week in, week out across Britain? I think not. People also describe animals they don't know. Puma kits are quite distinctive, with brown blotchy spots in the early months. Witnesses do not know that, and they have no idea of the hallmarks of an adult puma – a creamy muzzle and a rope-like tail – yet some describe them with great precision.

The proportion of reports subject to mistakes, mis-sightings and pure invention is hard to call, but I suggest it is low. A reliability weighting for a sighting is suggested in the checklist on page 42. Suspect and airy ones are filtered out early by any seasoned investigator and many informants are honest about their level of confidence, as we'll see below. We do need to be tough on the evidence and yes, we do need to spot the mistakes – it goes with the territory. Any good researcher watches for the pitfalls, from people's false expectations over footprints to misjudged black housecats. Constructive challenges are welcome and crucial, but much of the nit-picking from sceptics is nothing but knee-jerk fuss. The response from these sceptics is in some ways self-fulfilling, for it serves to suppress some of the reports and potentially vital clues. But let me turn the tables. Let me pose a question to some who squirm at the sightings and suggest that there is a deeper reason for the sceptics' discomfort: aren't some of them simply in denial?

THE EXMOOR ZOO EXPERIMENT – SILHOUETTE SPOTTING

The rigour of people's sightings is always argued over, especially in relation to people's judgement of scale. So hats off to Exmoor Zoo which, in a programme on UK big cats for the History Channel, conducted a simple but effective low-tech experiment on people's grasp of it. Masterminded by naturalist Trevor Beer, the zoo laid out a series of scale cut-outs of different cats. The size and shape ranged from domestic cat to jungle cat, then to lynx, puma and panther. The colour differences were there too, to see if light and dark shades made any difference. A sample of over 100 visitors to the zoo in the space of a day were taken aside and asked to turn around for a five-second view of some of the shapes. The tests were done for distances of 50, 100 and 150 feet. The results were a surprising and overwhelming success. Just about all the participants (96%) were able to judge size and colour accurately: people registered the size of each cat for exactly what it was. I think these results should carry weight and give us more confidence in people's impressions of an animal's size. The conditions were admittedly fairly clear and the land pretty flat, while it's rarely like that in the 'real' outdoors, where slopes, lighting and dodgy weather can all play a part. But the public passed their test at Exmoor Zoo and showed that, by and large, they can gauge the category of scale of an object in a spontaneous situation.

REACTIONS – FROM PAINTING TO PUTTING DOWN THE GUN

A number of witnesses go to great lengths to mark their big cat event. There are all manner of reinforcing signals suggesting that something exceptional has occurred. I've known people buy expensive night-vision equipment, hoping to get a better view of a mystery feline on their land. A husband and wife cancelled their wildlife charity membership when they were scoffed at by the receptionist when reporting a four-minute panther sighting on a nature reserve. Two cool teenage lads were keen to brief me on the black coloration in leopards and jaguars, having been spurred on to learn more after seeing a black panther in the fields overlooked by their house, and a butterfly recorder spent an hour on the phone with me, bowled over by the wildness he had sensed when watching a big cat. Immersed in nature all his life, this was new territory, a new feeling for him.

People want proprietorial rights on the cat they've seen: 'Nobody is to shoot that cat, and if anyone does it will be me,' said one deer stalker. Elsewhere, I've known of an alarmed father seeing a panther in fields near his garden, worried it might eye up his children over the fence. Assuming he'd need to take on the intruding cat with a gun, he contacted tracker and researcher Chris Johnston for advice. Chris briefed him on the cats and their lifestyles and, sure enough, this helped the father relax. He kept wary, but wiped away any notion of the cat pacing out his property. In time, the turnaround was complete: he became an advocate for the cats and keen to learn more.

Frank has twice been contacted by individuals with a terminal illness, with little time left to live and keen that he should know of their secret sighting of an exotic cat. One of these was a woman who'd marvelled at a giant cat visiting her remote woodland garden. She described how Frank's newspaper reports of pursuing big cats were a highlight for her. She held the animals in her mind and they lit up her life.

THE SURROGATE CAMERA

Another way people react is to illustrate what came their way. They may not have captured it on camera, but they have been inspired to depict what they observed. Various illustrations by eyewitnesses appear throughout this book. Shown here is the scale cut-out cat produced by artist Peter Drewett, from Montcoffer near Banff, following his sighting in January 2009. He told the *Banff Journal* that he was so thrilled by the sighting that he got up in the middle of the night to make a life-sized

Peter Drewett's replica of the large black cat which visited his property.
Photo: Banff Journal

cardboard replica. He described the cat as being around a metre in length and completely black, with no other markings:

> I had a very good sighting of the cat, which was about 65 feet away from me. At first I thought it was a large black fox, but that thought only lasted about a nanosecond. I am used to painting wildlife, and this was definitely a cat. It was about three feet long, and I would say it was about six or seven times the size of the domestic cat I used to have. It had such distinctive movement, lithe and supple as it slunk away through the grass. It slipped through a fence and bounded across the field till it was out of sight. It was beautiful, just incredible. I only wish I'd had a longer sighting and had my camera handy.

IN THE WORDS OF THE WITNESS…

Reports of big cats are not just a visual thing. 'Sightings' can be smells, sounds, a glimpse of yellow-green eyes in the night, experiences shared with other people and one's pets or horses. The encounters can range from the briefest of glimpses to full-on confrontation, when people want to get away from the cat and might have reason to be scared.

One way of considering the various reports is to break them into types, and consider what they mean. A crude structure might be as follows:

Types of big cat encounter

Glimpse – some witnesses less confident

Longer sighting – movement and behaviour noted

Multiple sighting – people have a chance to discuss the object seen

Regular sighting – animal seen on several occasions in similar location by same people

Consistent location – the same place gives rise to reports from different people, independently, with no knowledge of the others

Close up encounter – very close to the animal

Incident – livestock attacked, dog threatened

Smells – cat scent detected at a possible territorial feature or leaf/soil litter scrape

Sounds – calls heard which equate to vocalisation of large *Panthera* or *Felis* cats

Night eyes – yellow/green eyes seen in spotlights or headlamps. Large and widely-spaced

Animals react – dogs react (freeze in an anxious state or wish to pursue the animal, depending on dog breed); horses spooked and nervous

I won't offer immediate examples of all these categories of sighting because most will crop up through the book. But let's begin here with three 'glimpses', cases where people have a striking few seconds when they register an animal which is completely unexpected.

THE GLIMPSE FROM THE CAR

Only one of these three witnesses is categorical in his view that he saw a big cat, and he even draws a conclusion as to the species. Together the three accounts pick up different characteristics which influence what they might have seen.

Hertfordshire, March 2010, Sam Nightingale

I work in Harpenden. On my way to work this morning I was driving down the A10 just north of Hertford and on the cattle bridge that goes across the road, I saw what looked like a big cat. It was about the size of a Labrador dog and it caught my eye. It was about 20 feet away and I saw it for about five seconds. I am no cat expert but the way it walked, with its shoulders moving and the prominent shoulder bone – it was prowling slowly across the bridge – it looked like what you see on the nature shows, it was all black and against the white sky of the morning it stuck out like a sore thumb. The tail was almost as long again as the body but not quite. It was like a shallow half-moon.

Forest of Dean, Gloucestershire, July 2003, John Beart

I was traveling on a narrow back road through the woods when a big cat emerged from the bracken and crossed the road about 50 metres in front of the car. It was July, late afternoon, very bright, excellent visibility, with no other car in sight and I was going up a long incline so it was about level with the windscreen giving me a perfect view. As I passed the place it had crossed, I saw it from behind climbing up a bank into the trees. It had jet black, gleaming fur, the head and body shape of a cat and the unmistakable long looping tail, and it moved like a cat. It unmistakably was a member of the leopard family, with absolutely no possibility of mistake. I cannot describe my shock. I was thunderstruck, astonished and bewildered, as I had absolutely no idea there could be anything like it moving around in Gloucestershire.

Forest of Dean, Gloucestershire, January 2008, Jane Spray

Driving from Cinderford towards Brierley, at dusk at about 4.55 p.m. today, at the beginning of the straight, downhill part of the

A4136 which leads to Brierley, I had a very brief sighting of what looked to me very much like a big black cat. It was already at the right hand edge of the roadway when I first saw it, a dark, black shadow against the dark grey of the tarmac, and it quickly crossed the road, slipping invisibly into the undergrowth. It was about the size of a not-too-large deer, but a completely different shape, and with different movement, much more horizontal, longer, low-slung, with a fast, fluid, almost streaking, purposeful movement.

The head was not large or prominent: it seemed like a small extension of the body in the same overall horizontal plane, and I didn't get much impression of the tail, except that it wasn't held high or fluffy like a dog or I think I'd have noticed it more. The shape and the movement were cat-like and very fast. I'm used to seeing deer, foxes and badgers etc. crossing Forest roads, and have seen the wild boar, but this was not like any of these.

MULTIPLE WITNESSES

One of the most notable cases of a multiple sighting in recent years was at Balcombe School in Sussex in October 2008. The cat was seen for around 30 seconds, sitting by a woodland close to a school playground. According to the *Mid Sussex Times*, classroom assistant Rosemary Robertson saw the animal while in the fenced playground with a class of four-year-old children, 12 of whom watched the cat. One of them stated in a media interview that it was 'exciting but also a little bit scary'. Mrs Robertson said: 'It was like a ginger tom but three times the size... I have looked up on websites since and it was definitely the sound a puma makes.' In his letter to parents, headteacher Terry Harris said: 'Since the sighting we have informed the police, who are currently investigating the location of the sighting, secured the perimeter of the school and informed Balcombe Estate.'

THE CONSISTENT LOCATION – FROM HAMPSHIRE TO CENTRAL SCOTLAND

Just about half of Gloucestershire seems to be a consistent location for big cats. Several iconic woodlands have provided reports over the years, and the Cotswold Way could have its own sightings directory. Frank and I often feel the county could be branded Big Cat Country. But let's look elsewhere for another location where sightings come in clusters. We could consider Shotts and Wishaw in the Central Belt of Scotland, south-east of Glasgow, where the local paper, the *Wishaw Press*, has totted up 13 reports over recent years and has begun a Panther Watch. One witness in March 2011 claims the following remarkable sighting along the path from walking his dog: 'It was a panther, just as nice as you like, reversing down a tree with a magpie in its mouth – I could see it clearly. There is no doubt in my mind. I'm not talking about a big, black domestic cat – this thing was seriously big. You're looking at least 40 cm high and about a metre long. That's without its tail. It also had quite a long tail, at least a foot to 30 cm. Me and the dog just froze at the sight. I was stunned by the size of it. It then just turned, walked over the wee hillock and was gone.'

Another I know of, in the middle of the chalk landscape of Hampshire, is the Alresford bypass. The road traverses open arable land and has splendid wide verges, providing a green corridor of scrub and grassland. I've seen deer along the side and I suspect the stretch acts as a refuge for wildlife across the open farmland. In July 2010, Lisa Trigg reported a 30-second sighting of a two-and-a-half foot long black cat from her car, a few hundred metres from the end of the bypass. She said: 'I was driving towards it, the cat was trotting down the road and crossed right in front of my car and disappeared through a hedgerow to my car window side. It had pointed ears and a long straight tail, probably the length of the cat's body.' The coat was 'black and very shiny'. She described the animal as seeming young in appearance and it did not appear to be adult size. The animal was totally unconcerned by her presence and she viewed it from just a few feet away. She also found a report of a sighting in the same area by a delivery driver the previous January. In the local paper he described a big black cat emerging from the side of a house before leaping over a ditch and into a hedge just 30 yards in front of him. He described the animal as very muscular, two feet tall at the shoulders, with dark fur and having a metre-long tail. 'It was definitely a big cat and a powerful-looking animal. It was the way it leapt over the ditch, I have never seen anything like it.'

As well as these two accounts I know of three other reports of large black cats around this area over as many years. There is nothing rigorous in my observation of the Alresford bypass: I've simply noted it as a cluster amongst the steady stream of reports. But what, if anything, does this particular density of sightings mean? Is it significant? Is it part of a route taken by one or more cats? Is it a coincidental set of sightings or mis-sightings? Is it no different from neighbouring bits of Hampshire, or is something going on? Unless and until we do our homework on the cats, and study and survey a sample or areas, we'll be left to guess.

THE CLOSE-UP ENCOUNTER

The close-up encounter is sometimes from the car, sometimes in front of the cat and right in the open. In this situation the reaction of the person is important to avoid aggravating the cat. These encounters are chances for the Holy Grail photo, but one can appreciate that the witness has other things on their mind: such as trying to stay calm, keeping the cat at length and maybe enjoy the moment if they can. Emily Shiers, as below, believes she found herself close to a cat in 2010. Her report is of interest for two reasons: firstly, because she had a young child with her and watched the cat's reaction to it, and secondly, because she can testify to the prejudiced reaction one can get when reporting a big cat sighting.

Stroud, October 2010, Emily Shiers

The cat was slowly walking up a field on the edge of Stroud in which my two-year-old nephew Nathanial and I were standing. We were killing time before picking up Nathanial's older brother from school. Nathanial saw it first and started to say, 'Oh, puss!' – making me look around. It was a medium sandy-brown colour with darker spots and it was tall and lean, although not skinny. Its fur had a coarse appearance. The overall look was 'all legs'. Its tail was long and slim, held parallel to its body. It had a similar-shaped head to a Siamese cat, which was slightly out of proportion to its body, seeming too small. In relation to a dog's scale it was the size of a fully-grown German shepherd. I wonder if it was a hybrid due to the difficulty of exactly identifying it against photos of the standard species I've seen on the web.

Although it wasn't threatening (it seemed curious) it was obviously Nathanial's presence that made me slightly concerned and

'I know what I saw and it was a big cat'

Emily Shiers and her nephew Nathanial at the location where they encountered a big cat at Stroud.

Photo: Gloucestershire Media

By Jo Barber
citizen.news@glosmedia.co.uk

NURSING assistant Emily Shiers was stunned when she came face-to-face with a 'big cat' as she walked to pick up her little nephew from school.

Emily, 33, from Stonehouse stumbled across the large beast in a field near Callowell School at Farmhil, Stroud.

"I was amazed and awe-struck at the same time," said Emily, of Little Australia.

"It was just minding its own business.

"If people want to laugh at me they can, but I know what I saw.

"To tell the truth I didn't really clock it at first, for a split-second, until I realised what it was."

Her big cat sighting happened last Thursday afternoon at about 2.30pm.

Emily said the animal was about two feet high to its shoulder and roughly five feet long, including its tail.

It was around 10 feet away from her.

Emily's younger nephew Nathaniel, two, noticed it first.

ready to flee. After a few seconds I considered reaching into my bag for my phone camera, but was more concerned about keeping hold of Nathanial. I felt awestruck at this beautiful yet somewhat out-of-place creature. As we were around the corner from the school, I immediately went to the main gate to tell parents what I'd seen, and suggest they be alert to a possible big cat being around.

People's reactions to my sighting have varied from the curious and fascinated to the almost abusive – some of the negative comments made on newspaper websites have been quite unpleasant. The strangest reaction was somebody meowing at me on a bus! As I keep saying to people who don't believe me: I know cats and I know what I saw! The experience has left a strong impression, as I still often visit the place where I saw what I now consider 'my' cat, with a camera and the hope of seeing it again.

SIGHTINGS CRITERIA – TOWARDS SOME RIGOUR

My own method of logging reports has nothing to recommend it. While Frank notes them chronologically and carefully in his logbook, I keep notes in a file and tabulate them when I make time, often hurriedly before a talk. Ian Bond in the northeast of England uses mammal recording software to plot the sightings on a map, and Big Cats in Britain has a volunteer who pinpoints reports on a Google maps system. Anyone on the case should do something similar if they are watching for trends, clusters and possibly even territories. We should also make a thorough checklist of points from each sighting, both to gather the information on offer and to judge the report's plausibility. It is here we come to one of my grumbles. We need to tighten the way we monitor big cats. It is a homespun effort. Among the few brave souls who research and investigate, we make progress but, in truth, we are playing at it. The full tools for the job are still needed, wherever they might come from and whoever decides to help out.

ARE WE CAMERA-READY?

Even with a camera to hand and a cat in sight, it would take 10–20 seconds at least to grab the device, flick the right button and get it whirring into action – digital equipment is not actually that instant. Would the cat still be there in that time, and would the witness think to act in such a quick-witted way? Would many people be sufficiently composed, and would they even think to take a picture rather than experience the moment? Assuming that we should be swamped with good photos shows ignorance of the cats and their propensity to flee when being watched at close quarters, and the capabilities of humans and their cameras.

Big cat sightings – checklist

- Location:
- Date:
- Time:
- Weather:
- Daylight/crepuscular/darkness:
- Number of witnesses:
- Description of situation and what was seen:
- Distance of animal(s) from witness:
- Number of animals:
- Any smells:
- Any sounds/vocalisation:
- Any other field evidence: e.g. footprint, dropping, carcass of prey
- Scale of whole animal:
- Objects used to help gauge scale:
- Key features of animal:
- Head:
- Body:
- Tail:
- Ears:
- Overall height:
- Length (nose to rump):
- Tail length:
- Description of movement:
- Reaction of other animals (e.g. dog, horses, nearby birds):
- Other field evidence:
- Duration of sighting or encounter:
- Situation of sighting (walking, driving, horse riding etc.):
- Animal's activity during sighting e.g. chasing deer, rabbit in mouth, tail visible?
- Witness experience with wildlife, animals:
- Witness reaction and emotions:

Overall weighting

Reliable

Probable

Possible

Uncertain

Definitely not

One person who did have a camera with them when encountering a big cat, and a cat he was half-ready for, was researcher Chris Johnston. Here's his feedback on the reality of such a situation:

My most memorable moment in investigating big cats was after 13 years of research, when I finally got to see my first big cat in the British countryside. I was following up a sighting in Lancashire and had arranged to meet the person there, but I arrived early so went for a walk where the cat had been seen. While looking into a wood through my binoculars I could not believe it – there was a big black cat lying on the edge of the wood. It turned its head to the right, then to the left, and then just looked right at me with those amazing eyes. Although I had been actively looking for big cats, when I saw one it was hard even for me to believe in what I was seeing. I had a video camera with me but I was totally captivated by the moment and never even thought of using it, I could not take my eyes off this beautiful creature and just stood there, admiring it. It was an unforgettable experience, and I have no regrets about missing any photos – the memory of the sighting was a reward in itself.

Chris Johnston's illustration of the large black cat with a white blaze that he witnessed in Cumbria.

An eyewitness who did have a camera phone to hand, but who failed to record what he was watching, was Daniel Elliott, an experienced observer of wildlife who spends his life in the outdoors, managing fisheries. He has no regrets about missing recording the animal and is under no illusions about the tough task of filming a big cat in the wild, given all the factors which come into play at the time, as he recalls below:

My second big cat sighting was near Rendcomb in Gloucestershire in August 2008, and I did have a camera phone to hand. It lasted for the best part of three minutes – a big black panther was there before me. This should be ample time to snap some footage and gather something solid – in theory. However, time taken standing in awe of what's before you, moving to a better vantage point and then fumbling around with a camera phone is soon sapped away before the animal retreats. All I had was a shaky image and audio of me huffing and puffing as I tried to scurry up a hill in pursuit of a shot. While lacking evidence, I had the experience of something that will stay with me forever. That'll do fine.

Even when a camera phone is used, the results are likely to be frustrating. This was the case with the Kirchin family who noticed a big cat along a track as they drove through the back roads of Holden Hill area in Devon in July 2009. The dark blob on their camera phone and the small resolution means that the image does not print well, but can be seen on this book's blogsite. Andrew recalls the incident:

My wife, daughter and I were driving along a winding lane be-tween Holden Hill and Dawlish when I decided to try a new route and got lost. As we came around a sharp right-hand bend there was an un-gated track going off to the left giving vision along it of about 150 yards. As I looked along the track I could clearly see a large black animal walking away from us about two-thirds of the way along the track. I stopped the car and pointed it out to my wife and daughter, who immediately stated what I was thinking: 'Oh my God, it's a puma!' I pulled the car onto the track entrance and turned off the engine. The cat turned and was clearly aware of our presence – I would say it was about 100 yards away.

Despite the concern of my wife I got out of the car and approached it, getting to about 50 feet away before it sensed me and confidently stood up, turned and walked off. I got close enough to estimate that its shoulder would have been higher than my knee. It had an incredibly long tail and very pronounced ears. The three of us saw it clearly and it was very plain that this could not be a domestic cat – it was more the size of a Labrador. In total we watched the cat for about three minutes.

My daughter took the attached picture on her phone. I know it is inconclusive but it was taken from a good distance and you can see clearly its size in relation to the long grass in the centre of the track.

BEING PATIENT OR BEING LUCKY

British TV enterprises have flirted with ideas for seeking out our big cats but have never invested realistic levels of time and money to probe the subject properly, as they would do overseas in Asian or African leopard country, for example, or in puma territory in the States.

In 2007 Channel 5 was actively planning a TV series to investigate the UK's mystery cats. They considered possible presenters, including Nick Baker, and two researchers spent several months considering how it all might work. One idea was to have a Big Cat Response Unit at the ready, so film crew and reporter could immediately descend on a location, interview eyewitnesses, look for evidence and, hopefully, film the real thing soon after the animal was spotted. A 'Response Unit' on big cats sounds pretty swashbuckling for TV – attention grabbing and high profile. But, alas, it would be doomed to failure. The chances of filming a cat one or two days after a sighting are remote – the cat could be literally miles away or, if at close quarters, lying low while the camera crew clattered through its territory. Unless they were unbelievably lucky, all that such a programme could achieve is yet more vivid accounts of people's sightings – lots of quotes from witnesses stunned by what they'd seen, but no pictures of exotic felines.

The Channel 5 website announced the prospective programme through much of 2007, and their researchers were deluged with sightings reports – there seemed an abundant choice of where to go. But reality dawned, the proposal was dropped, and a risky investment halted. Britain's big cats had failed their TV audition.

So what would it take? What would deliver the prize of a panther smiling to camera, deep in our own wildwoods? To serve up the footage required would require key locations to be flooded with remote cameras. This would take time and effort, and film-makers are worried that they might get no reward. The cameras would be needed at strategic locations on a cat's suspected perambulation, the logjams or crossover points on its trails and tracks. But these are often places where people pass through as well, day and night: bridges, tunnels, cycleway crossovers and links across converted railway lines. Inevitably, the cameras are at risk from theft or tampering – positioning the equipment in the British landscape is a whole lot different from selecting a trail in the Rocky Mountains or a Sri Lankan forest.

Mark Fletcher is an award-winning wildlife film-maker who works with the BBC's Natural History Unit. With an interest in the UK's big cats, he and narrator Jonathan Scott sneaked an enticing comment into the finale of their 2010 documentary on leopards for the BBC's Natural World series. Near the end of the programme, the scene switched from Africa to Britain… 'As sightings have increased,' Jonathan Scott read, 'some people have quietly concluded that there are a few big cats living undercover. It sounds like a tall story to me! But knowing what I do about leopards, anything is possible.' This cryptic ending is one of the best indications yet that some of the wildlife buffs who make our nature programmes have an interest in big cats here, and may know more than they let on.

Other TV concessions to the taboo topic have included Bill Oddie's clever 2010 documentary on alien species, which included panthers and pumas on the list. 'An animal which on the one hand may be here, and on the other hand may not be here…' he teased. Even the BBC's flagship *Springwatch* and *Autumnwatch* broadcasts have indulged in big cats during their 'Unsprung' episodes, as they chat on a sofa about the quirks of wildlife. They have listened to accounts of viewers' sightings and discussed a deerkill photograph with open minds. Chris Packham has mentioned tracking a lynx in his local woods and has explained that some big cats are out there 'in low numbers' and that you might come across the signs they leave behind. *Autumnwatch* also hosted an email comment board on big cats. During Autumn 2010 it was one of the busiest threads on the programme's website, attracting many detailed big cat sightings, lots of queries from people intrigued about the cats and plenty of scorn from sceptics. It quickly became the usual bun fight between the enthusiasts with plenty to tell and the scoffing individuals who will only be satisfied with a verified dead body or DNA-ed droppings delivered to their desk.

FILMING BIG CATS IN THE WILD – LESSONS FROM JAGUAR COUNTRY

Getting more and better footage of big cats in the wild in Britain is one of the greatest challenges in the quest for greater acceptance. Like it or not, photographs and film will be more influential than pictures of paw prints, poo and half-eaten deer. Film-maker Mark Fletcher explained the complexities of filming cats in the wild specifically for this book:

> It is not just time, but how much money you risk throwing at a filming exercise that may not be successful. Millions of pounds have been spent trying to film jaguars and leopards in the wild. For example, I was one of the first documentary makers to film a wild jaguar sequence, despite decades of filming in places where jaguars live. It was only possible because turtle researchers had written of jaguars taking green turtles on a turtle nesting bed in Costa Rica. The scientists had noticed drag marks and discovered turtle bodies, half-eaten, in the jungle behind the beach. I budgeted the filming at about £20,000, including infrared camera traps and a cameraman and me on location for two weeks. The risk was that the jaguars would not return to the turtle to eat a second night, particularly if the area had been disturbed. The beach was about ten miles long, and a kill could happen at any place along the shore.
>
> Each morning before dawn, a turtle researcher patrolled the beach looking for a turtle kill for us. We were very lucky. On about the

tenth day we found one, and carried all the equipment on foot five miles to the site. I set up a remote system, and, almost unbelievably, we got a shot of the jaguar returning to the kill that night. We were very lucky, and it was easy compared to most attempts to film jaguars and leopards.

Leopards have only been filmed extensively in the wild in the Masai Mara, in small private reserves in South Africa, in Sri Lanka, in the reserve there, and a few other places. These leopards are well habituated, their habits known to the trackers, and adapted to and familiar with tourists. Anywhere else is much harder, and most of the footage used in films is from these few places. Cats are much more easily filmed in large enclosures, using a habituated or captive animal. My guess is that the number of wild leopards that have been found habituated enough to follow and film is quite small.

In Oman, the scientists have been tracking leopards for a long time, and can trap them and put on radio collars, but very rarely see them free in the wild. The leopards simply stay over the horizon. That is the norm. Snow leopards have only ever been filmed properly once, and that required a massive operation. The team knew of a leopard that in winter lived near to a village and was occasionally taking small goats and sheep. They filmed for two winters and by sheer luck found the leopard was denning within sight of a road.

The snow leopard and her cubs were only filmed around the den, the river valley and the road, and as soon as it moved away, it disappeared into the mountains. Filming the hunt for *Planet Earth* was a fantastic achievement. The cat left the den in summer, and moved up into the mountains, and despite trying to track it for months, it was never seen. It returned to the same den in the autumn, and was trapped and radio collared. It disappeared again in the spring and hasn't been seen since, despite the collar. My guess is the total cost of the effort would buy a small house in England, but the huge effort resulted in some fantastic footage.

I don't think it is at all easy to film leopard or jaguar unless you know a place where they kill regularly, returning to the kill, or a den. Leopards move dens every few days, and almost always move if anyone finds them. Leopards have never been filmed successfully with dead bait, or call-back techniques. However it is relatively common for leopards to be trapped in large cages by researchers who know what they are doing. It requires specialist equipment and expertise. Even then, it can take months, even in areas of quite high leopard density. The leopards are usually then radio collared – the only way they can be tracked with any degree of certainty. Catching a wild leopard on film is not easy anywhere in the world, even with well-studied leopards.

I have enjoyed many long chats with Mark Fletcher during the writing of this book, and it has benefited from his wisdom. I rather suspect that in the coming months and years, Mark will have a key influence on our further discovery of Britain's undercover cats.

THE YOUTUBE GALLERY

YouTube is a handy source of some people's filming of alleged large cats. Interesting cases – including ones from Shropshire, Herefordshire and Hertfordshire – fall into the 'definitely possible' category. Others – a cat ambling across a field in Derbyshire, for example – might be more in the oversized feral category, seemingly long in the body and tail and pretty muscular. Although clearly much bigger than the average mog, it in no way resembles a dark leopard or anything similar. Any cat of that size (say two feet, head to rump) could be a large feral or maybe a young 'something else', although perhaps it is unwise to make these assumptions, as pictures such as these need precise scaling to better indicate what we are watching. Sometimes the picture includes a convenient yardstick for scale, but often there is nothing, and all we can do is swap opinions on what may be a panther, a standard housecat or even a fox.

As this book is being completed, YouTube is carrying a new snippet, now doing the rounds amongst big cat enthusiasts. Yet again it demonstrates the problems of filming from a distance unless you have top-notch equipment at the ready. The footage is labelled 'Big black cat hunting crows to the west of Westonzoyland'. A farmer and two friends are looking over an extensive open field, holding the camera in a battering wind – crucially, the camera has no zoom. They suddenly notice a panther-like black dot on the far side. It is clearly a large animal and does not appear to be a deer or a dog. It suddenly surges through the expanse of field, then stops near the hedgerow and walks, perhaps in stalking mode. The three observers instantly remark on its speed, behaviour and movement, which they all liken to a cat rather than a dog. They quickly conclude they are watching 'a jaguar or panther'. They try to scale the animal in comparison to the five-foot high hedgerow. Like many other sightings, it is the form of the animal, including the very long tail, but especially its movement, which gives the greatest clue that they are watching a large cat. They also discuss going closer but wonder if that is safe and wise. It is a classic clip to watch, conveying the spontaneous reaction of eyewitnesses.

Elsewhere on YouTube there are plenty of dubious offerings, as with any fringe topic. However, I'd single out Jet Black, an interview with a no-nonsense farming family from Shropshire, hearing how they came to terms with a visiting panther in 2004. 'He decided to stop with us for about a week,' and 'Looked in a very fit condition' are amongst the family's remarks. They even managed some footage of the animal, whatever its scale, away in the distance. Their account, and their calm realisation that they'd need to be on guard, reminds me of many long chats I've had in farm kitchens.

TIDDLES - THE MYSTERY HIGHLAND CAT

As I finished off this book in April–May, photographs of a cat, taken by Lisa Sydenham at Embo in Scotland, provided a splendid 'stop press' moment. They demonstrated the range of reactions which distant photographs can generate; they illustrated the importance of repeat measurement of photos; and, with wonderful timing, they served up a story close to the book's publisher Whittles, just south of its base in Dunbeath in Caithness.

Lisa Sydenham and her sister Alana were travelling back to Dornoch on 27 April 2011, passing through the small settlement of Embo. They spotted what they first thought was a black Labrador moving at the far edge of a sown field, a distance later measured at 180 metres. As they watched, though, they felt the animal was much more cat-like. Stopping the car, Lisa grabbed her camera and captured seven photographs showing the cat move at different positions. The photos are dated and clearly taken from the same spot, showing the cat's progression along the field edge.

Describing the events, Lisa said: 'It spotted me and crouched down in the grass before walking off. We must have watched it for about five minutes in all.' The animal's movement was 'different from a dog – graceful'. It was 'an amazing experience', she remarked. She noted the high shoulder blades as distinctively cat-like, and two pheasants flew up close to the cat during its stalking posture. The sighting, along with two of the photographs, was taken up by national newspapers and by the *Ross-shire Journal*: here was a possible panther, backed up with photos. Some people emailed the newspapers to dismiss the pictures as a housecat, but everyone who has heard from Lisa regarded her as a plausible witness and, contrary to claims from the doubters, she did not go to the press wanting money; she simply felt people should know about the presence of what she and Alana thought might be a feral big cat.

I noted one big cat enthusiast dismissing the pictures as 'Tiddles' on a blog, and some other big cat investigators were equally unimpressed, despite the lack of graspable scale in the photos. They were too quick to judge, I felt, and must know that, whatever the spread of opinion, repeating the photos with a scale measure is the key rule. Meanwhile, the *Scottish Sun*, before it ran the story, consulted Frank Tunbridge for a view. Frank said that the pictures were interesting, that he didn't think the cat was necessarily a domestic size or form, but that he felt the case remained open due to lack of clear scale. But his open-minded views were not printed. The *Scottish Sun* hyped up the incident, preferring its own dramatic account of a beast in search of dinner.

The story was supplemented by reports of a local deer kill and sheep kills, with landowners suspicious of a big cat. Dornoch has had its share of big cat sightings in the past. Northern Constabulary Chief Inspector Paul Eddington, an experienced police wildlife crime specialist, said there had been several very credible sightings of big cats in the area in previous years.

After the kerfuffle in the press, Lisa and Alana decided to do scale comparison pictures of the photographed cat, knowing that the results would be helpful whatever the outcome. They prepared an outline cat figure and a marked measuring pole, as shown in the photographs here. Alana walked with the props along the main margins of the field where the cat was seen, while Lisa took photographs from the exact previous location, with the same camera and zoom extension. The new photos were sent with the originals to film-maker Mark Fletcher to align. As the two sets of pictures were overlain on Mark's software, the tree canopies merged perfectly, indicating a precise match. This meant a reliable gauge and proof of the Embo cat's scale. The cat was not a 'Tiddles' at all, but neither was it a panther. It registered at close-on 60 cm from nose to rump. The largest of my own two black adult moggies is 41cm in the body, but such domestics can occasionally reach 60 cm. The Embo cat could be a range of things, perhaps most likely a large feral or, more intriguingly, a cat, young or mature, of more exotic or mixed origin. From its behaviour, as watched by Lisa and Alana, it appeared more wild than domestic in its character. Knowing it was being watched, it stayed confident and kept to itself, unwavering in intent.

Lisa and Alana did feel the measurement would be greater, and were surprised at the result. But key questions remain. What triggered Lisa and Alana to notice this cat at well over 100 metres as they drove past the field, and to mark it out as something different? And why did it hold their attention, making them feel that it could be adult panther size? Do one's emotions help build and confirm expectations? Does something acting and behaving as a feral animal rather than a domestic pet hold one's attention more, because it is unfamiliar? Something about the jizz of this cat stood out for these particular witnesses on this day.

Whatever the Embo cat is or is not, it is a lesson for us all. The temptation to swap opinion in such cases is strong, but we do best to hold back, check and measure. Lisa and Alana have demonstrated how to do this. Meanwhile, 'Tiddles' may have company. Following the *Ross-shire Journal*'s coverage of the incident, Alana learnt of another sighting two weeks later. At around one o'clock one morning, a man spotted a large cat a couple of miles northwest of Embo. Reporting it to the police, he said

Above: Two of the original photographs taken by Lisa Sydenham in Embo in April 2011. A cat of unknown size moves along a field edge and up a bank, 180 metres away from the camera location.
Photos: Lisa Sydenham

Left: Alana Sydenham with props for comparison photos to judge the size of the cat photographed at Embo. The cat silhouette measures 70 cm head and body, 50 cm tail and 40 cm to shoulder. Once an adult cat is at or beyond this scale it may be an interesting specimen.
Photo: Lisa Sydenham

it was 'the size of a big dog, black shiny coat and big eyes'. The watch for the Highland panther continues…

WHAT IF WALLABY SIGHTINGS WERE SO PREVALENT?

Let's for a moment imagine that all these reports were not of feral big cats, but of another out-of-place animal: wallabies. Small populations of red-necked wallabies have in the past established themselves for several generations both in Sussex and in the Peak District, so they can escape and breed and be viable for some time, although harsh winters are not to their liking. They were monitored by Derek Yalden of Manchester University, one of Britain's foremost mammal experts. The Peak District population was known because its origins were traced to a 1940s release from a menagerie when the owner went off to fight in World War Two. Early records included road casualties taken to the police station in Buxton. While quite shy, the animals are not secretive like a big cat, leave distinctive footprints and droppings and can be observed relatively easily in daytime.

Parma wallabies as well as red-necked wallabies are present on the Isle of Man, perhaps having escaped from a wildlife park. Isolated cases of wallabies have been recorded in Scotland and in Bedfordshire. If the big cat sightings were instead glimpses of wallabies, would we give them more weight? Would widespread and regular reports, as we have of big cats, mean more attention from wildlife bodies and a greater inclination to study and understand what was happening? I suspect that in a couple of universities at least there would be wallaby research projects charting the populations, and wildlife bodies would be trying to understand the ecological ripple from these animals. But big cats are a different proposition. They are awkward to study on a practical level, concealing themselves and remaining on the move, and they are mentally awkward too, living beyond our comfort zone. So we shy away and they remain unknown.

SO MANY SIGHTINGS, BUT SO WHAT?

As a social scientist, it intrigues me that here in Britain, the weekly build-up of sightings pretty much counts for nothing. I fully understand the calls for hard evidence, the best and most clinching, and we'll look at that later. 'Science needs a body,' I keep hearing. Well, yes, to a point, but if we're not on the case, we'll miss any evidence which might be lying right before us, such is the transient nature of the cats' signs. Bodies, after all, may get scooped away, as we'll also consider later. Sightings and encounters are integral to the process and we can learn a lot from them. Read any overseas literature in which big cats are surveyed and studied and you'll see the worth of the ordinary person's report, backing up and helping to interpret what's found in the field.

Commenting to the *Observer* in 2003, Professor Alayne Street-Perrot, from the geography department of the University of Swansea, said: 'Either massive numbers of country people are experiencing social psychosis or there is something out there that is worth investigating.' This observation seems just as relevant today …

This March 1998 edition of the Sussex Express *contained still pictures taken from footage of an apparently panther sized cat foraging in a field for four minutes. The cat was filmed by local resident David Ward-Streeter from his house overlooking the field. Courtesy:* Sussex Express

CAT PEOPLE – THE SLEUTHS AND TRACKERS

'You know my methods – apply them. How often have I said to you that when you have eliminated the impossible, whatever remains, however improbable, must be the truth?'

(Sherlock Holmes in Arthur Conan Doyle's
The Sign of the Four)

There are many people with only a passing interest in the UK's big cat puzzle who are quick to pass judgement, mostly doubting that there could possibly be any giant felines roaming these shores. If there were, then wouldn't they be the first to know? You can meet their like in many blogs and email threads across the web. But whatever these armchair critics think, should the view from their computer screen count? I prefer to listen to those who venture out into the landscape, the wind in their face, scouting for traces of cats. It is these authentic minds which are advancing our knowledge. The press calls them experts, re-searchers, enthusiasts or investigators. They are also labelled – by some people – cranks, nutters and worse. It goes with the territory. Whatever we choose to call them, they are the real leaders, the pioneers who are putting their reputations on the line. There are several across the UK, from all kinds of backgrounds, some from within groups like Big Cats in Britain, and some striving away as loners in their own local patch.

What does their task entail? For most, it involves time listening to witnesses, advising people after a panther encounter and building a relationship with their local media. They also log reports, contribute to websites, check tracks, suss out locations for camera traps and even try to fathom out territories. In this chapter we'll hear direct from a sample of these people, chosen because of their experience and their influence, and ranked among the doyens of the tracking community. Their views on the cats vary, as is to be expected, as we are all learning. They share, though, one common trait: they are all tough on the evidence. They are often more doubting than the sceptics, for they have seen it all: many false dawns, many promised pictures, and many visits to see excited people who have not, after all, got meaningful evidence in their hands or on their land – they might have done, but they weren't equipped, or ready in time. Here are the trackers' own stories. Here is a reality check on life on the front line, in the quest for Britain's big cats.

Nigel Brierly
Area: Exmoor

Nigel is now in his 90s and is widely regarded as one of the founding fathers of the UK's big cat research community. He still makes time to proffer advice, reach for hidden gems in his library and offer insights on evidence and sightings. For him, the mystery is still unravelling, but we are making progress, with new minds at work on the subject and new people to carry the baton. Here, Nigel offers thoughts and lessons from the 1980s Exmoor saga which played out before his eyes, and gives a few pointers for the future.

THE INVASION OF EXMOOR

Spring 1983 is a time I will never forget… I live with my wife Doreen in an isolated house on the edge of Exmoor and surrounded by sheep farms. Drewstone, a farm close to us, was finding carcasses of a full-grown ewe freshly killed almost every night. Young lambs were also disappearing. The farmers were at a loss as to what sort of animal was killing their sheep. They knew all about dog kills and could speedily deal with them, but this was different, 'something that ought not to be there,' as one farmer put it. Dogs invariably kill in the daytime whereas the sheep were being picked off singly at night with no disturbance to the rest of the flock.

A cage trap large enough for an adult puma-type cat used by Nigel Brierly without success in the 1980s. Nigel points out that cage traps need to be watched regularly to avoid dogs and other animals entering. The trap door needs to be designed to avoid potential injury to animals and people. Photo: Nigel Brierly/ Fortean Picture Library

The farmers, armed with rifles, together with hounds from the hunt, searched all the local woods without success. At Drewstone, a man who was a crack shot and formerly a big game hunter manned a mobile chicken house which was moved at night from field to field but the killer always killed in an adjoining field.

Then it was the turn of the marines. A detachment was billeted in one of the sheep sheds at Drewstone. They took a few shots at shadowy targets, with no result. By the time the local police and the NFU arrived, the police were alarmed by the number of rifles about. The NFU went from farm to farm warning farmers to search their haylofts in case the animal was using one as a lay-up spot.

With growing press publicity a motley collection of 'beast hunters' arrived. There was an expert dog catcher from Plymouth whose method was to trail a joint of meat through the woods, confident that he would catch the beast within a week! But I met on a nearby farm Sgt Eddie McGee, head of a tracking school in Scotland at the time and noted for tracking a multiple murderer in the North of England a few years earlier. He had just brought into the farm a dead lamb with large claw marks on its shoulders and the skin of a rabbit. He was quite convinced that he was not following a dog – unlike the view of the marines and the police at the time. He left abruptly after two days. (He has, of course, gone on to have a celebrated career in tracking and survival skills.)

Finally, Di Francis arrived. She had been studying big cats throughout the country for a number of years and had just finished her book, *Cat Country*, which was a real eye opener. It was the first time the big cats were taken seriously. The Beast of Exmoor was born! From this time on I caught the big cat bug. All my interest in natural history took second place to this so-called beast. It was surprising to find how many people had seen big cats of various colours, ranging through black, black-and-white, white, grey, and brown. Most people I spoke to about the cats were farmers and country people and quite capable of seeing the difference between a dog and a cat.

Eventually I decided to write a small book, *They Stalk by Night*. The main motive for writing it was to show there was plenty of evidence for pumas in the wild here but, at the time, very little for panthers which were generally favoured by the press.

THE SOURCE OF THE CATS AND THE FUTURE

I believe there has been a small population of big cats in Britain ever since the First World War and that the numbers have steadily increased up to the 1960s. From the 1960s up to the early 1980s the numbers increased rapidly due to releases and escapes from the

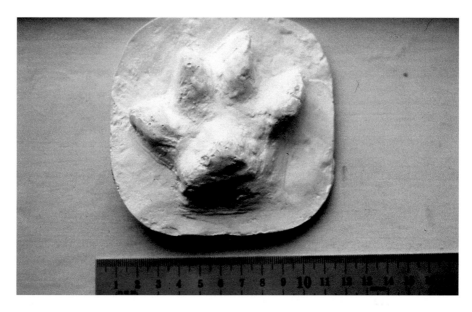

Plaster cast of footprint from the 1980s in Devon thought to be that of a puma. Nigel Brierly made this cast at the edge of a pond where a cat was thought to drink.
Photo: Lars Thomas/Fortean Picture Library

spread of wildlife parks and private collections, peaking in 1976 with the passing of the Dangerous Wild Animals Act.

There has been evidence of big cats breeding in the wild up to the present day. I also believe some hybridisation has occurred between lynx and puma and one cannot dismiss the possibility of human intervention, such as artificial insemination. Big cats with collars have been seen in Cornwall, Wales and Somerset. By 2020 I would expect the population of big cats to be lower than today but that will depend on factors such as the size of the deer and rabbit populations at the time. I would be happy if there was a lower population since I believe in the conservation of our native species such as brown hare, a favoured prey of the lynx and the puma, which is already scarce in some areas where it was once plentiful.

Mark Fraser
Area: UK
Website: www.bigcatsinbritain.org.uk

Mark Fraser is one of Britain's leading investigators on big cats. He has chaired and co-ordinated the research group, Big Cats in Britain, for 11 years and has tracked cats and followed up sightings across the UK for

Mark Fraser takes a break while advising on a big cat documentary.

over 20 years. He is at the hub of sightings reports, media requests, queries and information which arrive thick and fast on a daily basis. One of his main challenges is filtering all the material – he has the relentless task of considering what may be robust enough to relay to fellow researchers and what appears more dubious, needing to be passed on with a health warning.

Mark's contribution below is an edited version of an input to the *Farmers Weekly* email blog on big cats in 2009. Several of us were in a heated exchange with an unreasonable sceptic, which is a common hazard of spending time on email forums. Spotting that the discussion had gone sour, Mark stepped in with the following overview. Before long the feisty correspondence drifted into a more calm exchange.

POLICE EXPERIENCE

Many police officers have seen big cats for themselves and they are trained observers. Several police forces have contingency plans should they be in a position to capture an animal. Humberside police were the first to confirm that big cats are loose in Britain. Gloucestershire police admitted they scooped one off the roadside in 2004 and Yorkshire police worked with the RSPCA to rescue lynx from Yorkshire which were being used for canned hunting (hunting in an enclosed area) which may be a growing problem here according to some police. Oxfordshire police tell the students in their helicopter training course that they have captured three big cats over recent years.

SIGHTINGS, REPORTS AND HARD EVIDENCE

Big Cats in Britain averages about five reports a week, ranging from suggestions of tracks and prints to detailed explanations of a sighting. Are they all big cats? No. Most of the prints we get are dog or fox, and even rabbit prints in the snow. 80% of the sightings are of large black cats. Thinking that they are mainly melanistic leopards or even jaguars, when they are rarely seen in their own official countries, does not make sense. But people are seeing something – not all are mistakes. Sane and sober people are seeing large cat-like animals in the British countryside and the objective should be to try and discover just what people are seeing.

There is some questionable and grainy footage, but not all images are blobs or blurred. We even have police helicopter infrared footage. We do have prints, we do have hairs confirmed by DNA analysis to have come from leopard and from puma; we have had scat (droppings) analysed and confirmed to be from big cats.

Casts are good evidence especially when found on a kill site – a print from a large cat in the British countryside is helpful. It doesn't prove that there is a breeding population, but it goes a long way towards saying that there was a big cat in the area, whether escaped or released from a private collection.

RESEARCHING WITH AN OPEN MIND

Does the evidence back up a large population of leopards here? No, it doesn't. But that is hardly surprising. I do not believe there are a great number of cats (big cats) loose in the British Isles. But complete believers and complete non-believers are not much use; we need researchers who will evaluate the evidence that comes to us, discard it or log it. Complete belief or disbelief in the subject is worthless.

Anyone with a 'Bring proof to me and I will believe' attitude is going to have a long wait. The sightings you see in the press are nothing to what is actually reported direct to investigators and to Big Cats in Britain. Furthermore, the press do not check the verdict of experienced researchers before they publish the pictures of people's suggested evidence. Many big cat researchers are the first to doubt or disprove the photos and press reports doing the rounds.

We should not forget the lesser-sized cats such as jungle cats and leopard cats as an identity which may be being seen, so forget pumas, leopards and lynx for a while – there appear to be a range of cats out there. In addition, designer breeds are causing confusion these days, and one expensive pet was actually shot in Lancashire a few years ago.

BUSTING A FEW MYTHS

Most big cat researchers are not in it 'to prove'. They do it because they have a real interest. They include professional zoologists, pale-ontologists, police and engineers – many of them highly qualified across different fields, whose knowledge is needed to sort the wheat from the chaff.

The sceptics suggest that more mobile phone camera pictures should be snapped, but mobile phones are worthless when spotting an animal 100 yards away – they will not give any detail at all. You-Tube big cat footage is also a distraction – it is difficult to know the origin of any footage and the intent of the person who has posted it.

Finally, a further point about investigating the possible evidence. We have had reports of many sheep kills from several areas of the UK, as have the press elsewhere, and not all of these are the result of a big cat, of course. Several farmers have lost up to 20 or more sheep, others just one. They wish to know if a big cat could have been responsible. Not all of these incidents get reported in the news – some do get referred to us. Many people do not want the publicity, nor do they want the thought of people trampling over their land, even though in our experience that won't happen. These people simply want a quiet bit of advice, a second opinion from somebody with a bit of experience in investigating big cats. And when a farmer who has lived and worked on his land all his life tells me he hasn't seen such a kill in all his years, I tend to take notice. It's a myth to suggest there is no evidence.

Chris Johnston
Location: UK, Lancashire and Exmoor
Website: www.bigcatsightings.com

My own relationship with big cats started back in 1990, while on a farm in Cornwall. Two sheep were mysteriously attacked in a manner that had no explanation, and was beyond the knowledge of the local vet. Shortly after these two instances, sightings of large black cats began to be reported, and having an interest in animals I became captivated by this subject.

As an animal behaviourist I am interested in how the cats' behaviour may have adapted and evolved to this new environment.

TRACKING AND EVIDENCE

I am often asked, 'Where is the evidence of the cats' existence?' It is a valid question and one hard to answer truly. To try and address it we have to look at a big cat's behaviour: leopards and other cats may only be active for short periods, they can sleep and rest for up to 21 hours a day. When they do prowl, in many cases it is beneath the cover of

Right: Chris Johnston with a puma he helped care for at the former Santago Rare Leopard Project in Hertfordshire.

Below: A scrape found by Chris Johnston thought to be a possible territorial scent marking from a large cat. Such scratch markings are produced by the hind legs scratching the soil. The cat is also placing its pads in its own urine so as it walks away it also leaves a trail of scent. This was a pronounced marking which smelt of a cat with no visible scratch marks as there would be from a dog.
Photo: Chris Johnston

darkness, or early morning and late evening, tying in with when their favoured prey may be at their most active. Many researchers do find the evidence but simply do not want to make it public, cherishing it for themselves and others who share the same interest. It took me 13 years to see a big cat in the British countryside – this may mean that as a tracker I am rubbish, but it is more likely to explain just how elusive these cats can be.

EVOLUTION IN ACTION

Our big cats are an island population. At some point in time these isolated cats must have had to inbreed to continue the population. Have they already come to a genetic bottleneck and overcome a shortage of genetic diversity? Are we looking at evolutionary biology in the making, or is it yet to come? To judge by my own and other researchers' work, it is clear that in certain circumstances we may be

Jonathan McGowan with sika deer bones in Dorset.

observing animals which have entered and gone through the next evolutionary stage, because their form and coat colour is not always of the norm. Are these genetic mutations a key to survival and a way of becoming a viable genetic population?

Over the years I have seen the awareness of the presence of these creatures increase to an all-time high, and I am divided by this. Is it good or is it bad? I often wish that things could return to the more low-key situation, as it was in the early years of big cat research, with the cats slinking back into the countryside and the back of our minds.

Jonathan McGowan
Area: Dorset and neighbouring areas
Website: www.theNaturalStuff.co.uk

Most of my research and sightings come from Dorset where I am based. My real interest began in 1984 when I witnessed a puma at close quarters stalking a badger. I believe I saw the same puma on two more occasions. At first I kept my sightings to myself, having been used to people's sceptical nature. Through my tracking and my nocturnal and crepuscular wanderings I have had further sightings since, not just of puma, but of leopard and leopard-like animals, and of lynx. On two occasions I have seen puma kits (each from a different litter) and I have twice seen cubs of leopard. Three other witnesses have reported cubs in Purbeck alone: black ones and grey ones, and puma types.

Dorset seems to be a hotspot like the rest of the West Country, with many sightings a year by credible witnesses, including naturalists, biologists, police officers, foresters, ecologists doing field survey work and by other people who are regularly outside, such as dog walkers, horse riders, car drivers at night, not to mention lampers and poachers. Often, I ask farmers on the off-chance, and I frequently get a matter-of-fact reply: 'Yes, we have them', 'No we don't, but the next farm does', 'My wife sees them', and so on. It seems that more people see cats than badgers in some areas. That's not because the cats have eaten them all, although some have!

THE THREE MAIN SUSPECTS

Big cats are not much of a news story in Dorset any more, as sightings are so regular. The amount of sightings in different areas often on the same day means there are more than just one or two individuals around, even though they can cover many miles, especially at night when they are more active. There is much misidentification of all three large species, but the consistency of witness reports makes the evidence more robust, coupled with the field evidence, and the

*Left: Steep wooded valleys and old quarries – part of the big cat landscape of Dorset?
Photo: Jonathan McGowan*

Below: Jonathan McGowan sets up a baited trail camera at a Dorset location where big cats have been reported.

occasional amateur video footage, as seen on Sky TV's documentary *Big Cat Tracks*, for which I acted as a researcher. For my own observations, chances of photographing the cats have been thwarted by lack of time at the moment of a sighting, lack of light and even the lack of a camera – I am not sitting in a hide with an array of photographic and infrared equipment, but am on the move, tracking in the field.

UNDERSTANDING THE TERRITORIES

To try and map the large species I first looked at all the alleged sightings in Dorset and on the borders of neighbouring counties. I marked them on a map along with all areas of woodland, rivers, roads, herd deer, rabbit colonies, game rearing, badger setts and any other features relevant to a cat's territory. I then searched these areas for evidence and found signs in all locations at some time over a six-year period. Some of the signs were old but most were fresh, mainly consisting of paw prints, tree scratches, spraying areas and remains of kills. Particularly helpful are deer remains that have the characteristics of being eaten by large cats as opposed to dogs or other scavengers. A leopard may kill one deer every four or five days, depending on whether it can keep it from other scavengers. It will not kill in the same location twice a week, in order to keep the prey less alert, or so it seems. I have found many field signs scattered throughout the county, but certain hotspots seemed to have emerged. Signs would prevail every week or two in certain areas, in the form of footprints and scats.

Sometimes it took up to three years before these signs ceased, so one can conclude that the animal had a territory. I looked at possible natural boundaries such as main roads, wide rivers, expanses of arable land without much cover, or large tracts of conifer plantations. To judge other parameters of the territories, I have used people's sightings, and speculation as to how far a large cat would travel for food, water, cover and other members of the same species. Proof that these cats are stealthy and elusive comes from a well-reported incident when six leopards were once caught in traps left out one night in Johannesburg, traps that were meant for one known escaped animal. This demonstrated that leopards can live amidst urban settlements but go unnoticed by people.

I first concluded that in Dorset there had to have been at least eight leopards since the year 2000 because of the number of cubs seen by myself and others during that time, taking into account that two is the average litter, and they can remain as juveniles with their mother for up to two years. These are the ones seen or at least known about. It is estimated that for every reported sighting, there are at least ten unreported. As of summer 2006, when *Big Cat Tracks* was filmed, the police estimate in Dorset was of around six big cats. Looking at the availability of food in these areas and at how many cats they could support, along with all the other info, my own current and cautious estimate is of ten for both puma and leopard, with a top estimate of 20 per species, bearing in mind that cats do not know county borders.

Nigel Spencer
Area: Leicestershire and surrounding counties
Website: www.bigcats.org.uk

THE DYNASTY

Researching UK big cats all started for myself and my father, David Spencer, back in the early 1990s after my father, a university lecturer at the time, had a close encounter with a mysterious creature near his home in Knossington, on the Leicestershire-Rutland border. The cat literally nearly ran into him as he stood in a gateway with his dog. It was the size, look and smell of a juvenile black leopard. Having seen this creature himself, there was no doubt in my and my father's eyes that the so called 'Beast of Rutland' was for real and needed further investigation. Cue 'Operation Panther Watch'! Given that our local Leicestershire Police Wildlife Liaison officer, Inspector Neil Hughes, was a firm believer, we got off to a great start with scores of sightings, even from as far off as Shropshire, passed from the police to us for further investigation. We forged links with John Foden, the late manager of Drayton Manor Park Zoo, and its current manager Robin Roberts. They have been a fantastic source of knowledge on both black leopards and pumas, having the former in captivity. Coincidentally, they have both encountered the two breeds in the Midlands countryside themselves. We have appeared in many regional and national television and radio programmes, including the award winning Canadian- produced *Monster Hunters*, which premiered on the Discovery network worldwide in 2002. It led to an astonishing incident on a Russian cruise ship when my father and mum met the captain and he asked Dad for his autograph, saying, 'You are the big cat hunter in England!' Not quite true, though, as we do not hunt these magnificent creatures but merely try to understand how they interact with their surroundings through visits to locations and by interviewing eyewitnesses. In 2000, I had my one and only big cat encounter while driving only feet away from an unmistakeable puma in rural North Essex.

REVELATIONS FROM ALL QUARTERS

We have had some very reliable and close IDs by professionals on these animals over the last 17 years, including many serving and retired police officers, and even two professional MAFF employees (the former Ministry of Agriculture, now Defra) surveying woodland and reporting to us a black leopard observed over a 20-minute period at close range. Another reputable witness included the solicitor son of a High Court judge reporting a clear sighting of a black panther on his driveway. Even the local hunt has been in touch to mention that they have observed large cats being flushed out of cover by the commotion of the hounds. We have also had several reports of people's dogs being stalked, and of dogs being killed and injured by big cats.

Within the Midlands there is also definite evidence of the odd lynx and then there are the ones that are neither 100% puma nor black leopard, rare in our area but seen frequently in other areas. A hybrid? You could write a whole book on that debate alone! And we have plenty of evidence of breeding here in Leicestershire and Rutland, which after 17 years of receiving sightings would be the only way, short of continual releases, that the pool is being sustained.

As for the future, where we go next really depends on the government stance. There is no desire by Defra to classify these animals, although interestingly they now state on their website that a viable breeding population does not exist, which is slightly more than the early days when they didn't believe in big cats at all.

Of course as soon as you admit to something, the costs start to become your responsibility and you get into complex legal and ecological issues, not to mention compensation for livestock predation, so I can't see the current *status quo* and fence-sitting changing. This may be a good thing for the cats, as if they don't exist they cannot be hunted or controlled legally! With the current explosion in deer populations and lack of large-scale fox control, the presence of a large predator such as the puma, black leopard or lynx can only be good for the British countryside, even if we lose the odd sheep along the way.

Shaun Stevens
Area: UK, formerly Argyll, now Somerset
Website: www.bigcatsinbritian.org.uk

FINDING FELLOW TRAVELLERS

My suspicions about big cats were aroused some 16 years ago. My house at the time was on the edge of fields and woodlands, and we often had deer in the garden. I let my rather cavalier spaniel outside for her nightly walk, only for her to get to the top of the garden, stop, and run straight back into the house shaking. I went outside and heard a low rumble-growling sound. With no lights outside it

Shaun Stevens is caught on camera while checking one of his own remote trail cameras.

was pitch black, I didn't stay around long and shot back into the house. A few days later a big black cat was spotted by a farmer a few miles away. I actually began investigating big cats in 2005 after I stumbled upon the Big Cats in Britain website. I noticed it didn't have a number of the sightings that I knew about in my area, so I emailed a list. I soon became the rep for Argyll and beyond!

I've always been interested in cryptozoology, ever since the days of Arthur C. Clarke's TV programmes and the 1970s magazine series *The Unexplained*. Investigating big cats has allowed me to become a part of this scene and, after all, who can resist the chance of uncovering a mystery?

PUZZLING OVER THE CATS – LARGE AND SMALL

It would be very strange if there were *not* any big cats roaming the British countryside. Throughout past centuries we have records of escaped animals from zoos, circuses and menageries. And those records would be just the tip of the iceberg: many owners would never report an escape, hoping to recapture the animal before it caused any damage to people or livestock. The question people should be asking is: 'What species of animal are out there and in what numbers?

I'm not a great believer in the large species of cat (puma and leopard) having viable breeding populations. To me, the facts don't indicate such a thing. Yes, we have had reports of people seeing cats with cubs, but if we take into consideration the general number of misidentifications on big cats, then perhaps we should await firm evidence of breeding rather than automatically believe the 'mother and cub' sightings.

Now when it comes to the strange black cats of 2–4 foot in length that are often reported, my thoughts do change. I am quite happy to accept that there is a healthy breeding population of these animals. What their lineage is, though, is another matter. Large ferals, hybrids, and a new species have all been put forward as theories and maybe we are getting a mix of all three. With large designer cats increasing in popularity, there is a strong possibility that their genes are also influencing the feral cat population. Add to that Scottish wildcat genes (an animal that in the past has been recorded up to five feet in length, nose to tail), along with escapes of smaller exotic cats like jungle cats, servals and leopard cats, then an increase in the size of these hybrids is not only understandable but would be more or less expected.

Di Francis puts forward a very persuasive theory regarding the possibility of the UK having not just the Scottish wildcat as a native species, but others as well. Her work on the Kellas cats, rabbit-headed cats and the snub-nosed cats is very interesting. However, without specimens to work with, we will just have to wait to put this theory to a rigorous testing.

THE SENSE OF DISCOVERY

My main hope is to discover conclusive evidence of big cats in this country. After all, everyone would like their 'I told you so!' moment in life. But in saying that, proving a puma or leopard is present in our landscape is not that exciting to me. After all, we know how it came to be there – it either escaped or was released. What I would really like to achieve is to point to something more striking, scientifically, about the mystery of our cats. For me, such examples are the possibility of the lynx having never fully gone extinct here – perhaps isolated populations have hung on in the vast expanses of Scotland. Another option might be to discover a different subspecies of wildcat, distinct from the Scottish wildcat, which would explain many of the sightings, especially at the medium and smaller scales. And finally, it would be good to understand these animals from a genetic viewpoint. So, if I could make any of these sorts of breakthroughs, that would do me fine!

GETTING RESULTS OF A KIND

I have had two sightings of big cats: one of a puma crossing the road in front of me, the other of a large black cat, slightly smaller than the sheep it scattered as it ran through a field. My trigger camera

Shaun Steven's trail camera captures a feline animal partly obscured by long grass in the mid-left of picture (2009). From measuring the branch Shaun's scale estimate is as follows: 'If the animal were directly below the branch it would be approx 32 inches. long in body, and about 28 inches. tall. However, the animal is behind the branch and, as such, slightly larger.

pictures of a 3' 3" (nose to tail) feral black cat created much interest amongst big cat enthusiasts and showed there are some interesting ferals around, which could sometimes explain some of the sightings.

Frank Tunbridge
Area: Gloucestershire

OUT THERE WITH THE BIG CATS

Since the advent of the internet a world of knowledge is now at our fingertips. The habits and lifestyles of any creature can be accessed within seconds, with images brought up in graphic detail. No need for many of us to experience often cold and damp wild places to gain these facts. But there is no substitute for personal observation, and the thrill of watching a wild animal or bird at close quarters is unforgettable. Our senses have become dulled as we retreat to a materialistic life and lose touch with the environment around us. When we do venture out, we should not always expect our wildlife to conform to the classic pattern we expect – the denizens of our countryside sometimes exhibit behaviour not mentioned in any book or website.

One of my own first-hand experiences of a big cat was way back, when I was four years old. I was charged at by an angry leopard. Fortunately, the bars of its enclosure saved me from harm, but this frightening encounter became etched in my memory. It happened in the grounds of Regent's Park Zoological Gardens (London Zoo) early one morning when my family were being shown around before opening hours by a friendly keeper whom my father knew. Since that time, my passion for wildlife has blossomed. I have studied, kept, and worked with many and various animals and birds, and at every opportunity observed them in their natural habitat.

Mammals became my favoured subject, especially the large predators which seem to enthral people. I think that we fear and respect

Above: Frank Tunbridge at one of his educational talks on big cats.
Photo: Rik Snook

Left: Frank Tunbridge follows up a winter big cat report and measures the stride of suspected prints with long, needle-like claw marks.
Photo: Tony Dean

them knowing that in their world, on their terms we are powerless and could even become their prey. So we tend to hold them in awe, even if only in our subconscious. The proliferation and spread of exotic species within the UK has also fascinated me, especially as some seemed to flourish while others declined and eventually vanished, sometimes for no apparent reason.

The elusive British big cat became my subject for investigation, and for over 25 years now I have followed up sightings and other evidence of the animals. On many occasions I have skinned the neck area of a deer kill to determine whether a big cat-like predator was responsible for its death, which it often was.

I have seen a variety of evidence over the years, and have had a few close encounters with these cats as well, most notably when I heard a leopard-like cough noise from a marshy area in Gloucestershire, which I was walking over on a footbridge. I rattled the bars of the bridge and then peered down to see the reeds quiver as a large black mammal with a long tail slinked through them. Another striking case was when I followed up a sighting report in a Gloucestershire woodland. Once into the wood I heard two short and sharp cat-like sounds from different areas, as if communication to each other. I carefully moved through the wood but there were no visible signs of the animals responsible for the noise. The two animals kept calling to each other as I passed through the area, but kept out of sight. I sensed they were indicating my location as they moved away, keeping me under surveillance and keeping each other posted on my movements.

IS A BRITISH BIG CAT EVOLVING?

The big cats at large in our countryside are, I believe, breeding, existing on the abundant natural prey available to them. But to determine precisely what they are remains a challenge, and one I hope to help unravel in the near future. Many theories have been advanced as to their origin and their appearance in our midst over the last five decades or so, the most popular, of course, being the 1976 Dangerous Wild Animals Act. It seems reasonable to assume that due to this hastily-assembled piece of legislation, many exotic cats such as leopards and pumas were released into the landscape throughout different parts of the UK. Cats being cats meant that they would readily adapt to a feral life. Carnivores are well versed in the habits of the species that they prey upon, otherwise they would soon starve and perish.

Big cats especially shadow the lifestyle and movement of deer, their preferred prey, but like these predators, the deer have more than one trick to help them survive, and are often too fleet of foot to

'BIG CATS' IN THE U.K — FRANK TUNBRIDGE.

A DESCRIPTION OF THE BLACK TYPE
OF BRITISH 'BIG CAT'- IN 90% OF SIEHTINGS.

EG. — A SHINY, SLEEK, SLIM, JET BLACK,
CAT TYPE CREATURE, LOOKING LIKE
A 'STRETCHED LABRADOR' IN SIZE,
WITH A SMALL HEAD AND VERY LONG TAIL,
CURLED AT THE END WITH A TUFT ON IT.
'WHEN IT RAN IT MOVED LIKE A WAVE,
IN MASSIVE EFFORTLESS BOUNDS. /
QUOTE BY — BOROUGH COUNCIL EMPLOYEE.—
LOCATION— CHURCHDOWN, GLOS 11.30am - MON.16/2/09.

An illustration by Frank Tunbridge depicting the most common
characteristics of large black cats reported to him.

be caught. This means that smaller prey such as rabbits, pheasants and small mammals will often suffice for the large cat.

So what type of cats are they, and how many are there in the UK? The simple answer to both key questions is that we don't know! It seems we have a variety of big cats present, some resembling the standard candidates of lynx, puma, and black leopard, but many not conforming to these options at all. With only a limited gene pool of any one of the few source species, I believe they have hybridised and after several decades of living wild, a 'type' has developed – a British big cat which is well suited to its environment and its food source. Many scientists and zoologists will question this idea, but I have based it on a few important factors, as set out below.

LEARNING FROM THE REPORTS

I cannot speak for other locations, but a high proportion of big cat encounters reported directly to me follow a similar pattern. The animal seen is either 'jet black' or 'fawn' in colour. It is slim of build, roughly the size of a Labrador dog but longer in the body. It has a smallish head and moves in a distinct, flowing and feline way. The prominent feature of many sightings is mention of a very long tail, often with a thicker tuft of fur at the tip.

Following the reports and being as rigorous as possible is necessary and shows a scientific approach. Note what occurs based on observations; form a theory as to what may be occurring; test the theory by further observations and by experiments; watch to see if the predictions based on the theory are fulfilled. These observations are not exclusive to myself, but are based on routine eyewitness reports from the Stroud Valleys area of Gloucestershire.

REPRODUCTION RULES

A cat's urge to reproduce is paramount and will drive an animal to great lengths in its quest for a mate, forcing them further afield if no member of the opposite sex is in the vicinity, and possibly resulting in an encounter with a closely-related species. The outcome of the union between two types of big cat is uncertain. The hybrid offspring may be infertile, but we do not know for sure. Generally, male hybrids are sterile but females are often fertile. Eventually, knowing how nature adapts her wild fauna to suit a changing environment, a 'type' of big cat well suited to its habitat and prey could emerge. Just a cursory look at the semi-feral pariah dogs of the Middle East and Asia will confirm this theory.

I believe this sort of change could happen over a few generations, and a large proportion of the observed cats in Gloucestershire show a close uniformity in the black and the fawn individuals reported to me, especially over the past decade. Lynx-type cats, of which there are lower numbers but consistent observations, do not seem to come into association with the other two types, although they are sometimes seen within the same territorial ranges.

THE ONZA – PARALLEL LESSONS FROM MEXICO?

A reference to the Onza may be worth considering. It is a little known but large cat, looking like a tall and slim puma. It is not fully accepted by science, but according to Richard Green, in *Wild Cat Species of the World* (Basset Publications, 1991), onza specimens have come from the Sierra Madre Occidentale mountain range of Mexico. Like reports from the Stroud Valleys, the Onza has a cursorial build – it is an upright cat with long legs. Slim of body with a small head, it has non-retractable claws (like the cheetah) in paws which are more elongated than usual for a cat. It seems to have evolved for the open, undulating grassland landscapes, and is a more of a running than an ambush predator. It mirrors much that we find from observations of the behaviour and appearance of large cats in the Stroud Valleys.

ALONGSIDE THE FOX

The British big cats' habits are similar to those of our native red fox, only preferring deer wherever possible, but like the fox, a large proportion of their diet, based on my observations of their droppings, consists of rabbits and small mammals including mice and voles. But during winter months I believe the fox itself becomes part of the big cats' diet, when the usual prey is more scarce.

Humans are most disadvantaged by darkness: like a fish out of water, we stumble around without a torch to light our way. Whereas the big cats are masters of cover and concealment when the sun goes down, using every patch of shadow and contour in the landscape. They may not pass the same way for months, but if your patience is resolute they may well return to the same spot sooner or later.

In this fast changing world, any wildness should be treated as a tonic for us all, and it is time that we began to cherish all our remaining wild animals, including the predators, as they all add a richness to the environment and to our own lives. So let's work it out before we wipe it out.

BIG SOCIETY FOR BIG CATS

Reflecting on the range of experience and the work of these leading trackers, I can hear some sceptics crying, 'Is that it? Is that all? How, after all this effort, can the supposed experts have delivered so little?' 'Bring me the bodies!' 'Show me the photos!' they continue to call from sitting in the confines of their cosy offices. But the doubters are crude in their demands. They have not learnt from projects overseas, where painstaking effort is needed to plot wild cats and capture them on camera. A researcher who radio-collared lynx in Bavaria told me that apart from the collared individuals he followed, he'd had, in the heart of their territories, just three glimpses of the animals in eight years. These are wild cats, and maddeningly elusive.

Let's recognise the paltry resources the trackers and researchers are working with. They manage with no university lab and no budget for DNA tests. Any suspicious droppings found must be stored in the fridge at home, if at all. Volunteering and doing things for the greater good has recently been retitled by politicians, branding it the Big Society and claiming it as something new. Outlined above, operated by the dedicated inner circle of researchers, is the Big Society effort on big cats. But like a lot of volunteering, it works better as a partnership. Volunteer labour, however experienced and however dedicated, needs resources and systems to back it up. Public bodies, research bodies and centres of learning might like to consider their part in this partnership, and what they might be missing out on.

RED IN TOOTH AND
CLAW – SIGNS OF AN APEX
PREDATOR

'It's often said that, if alien big cats are real, then why don't
we have good photos, why don't we have dead bodies, why
don't we have captured live animals, and why don't we have
definitive track and sign evidence? But this data is out there
for anyone that's prepared to examine it. Why isn't this more
widely known? That's the mystery.'

*(Darren Naish. 19 February 2006. British big
cats: how good, or bad, is the evidence? www.
scienceblogs.com/tetrapodzoology)*

NATURE'S NEW SIGNS

'He's so matter of fact about big cats being around – I can't get over it!'
said an ecologist listening to Jonathan McGowan's talk at a Big Cats in
Britain conference in Middlesbrough. Jonathan was showing different
field signs of the cats that he finds as he combs the heaths and woods
of Dorset. As we toured the county's landscape in the photos before
us, he confidently explained the various pictures: 'Scat – a bit calcified,
most likely leopard...' 'Footprint, showing direct register, more likely to
be puma...' 'Eaten-out sika deer, on what I think is a territorial route
of a puma...' 'Lynx footprint close to where I found suspected faeces of
lynx ...' And so it went on: prints, hair, poo, tracks, caches of bones,
all pointing to large and elusive felines in the depths of our southern
habitats. Some audience members, those not previously exposed to clues
of the cats, reeled from the culture shock.

During questions, somebody asked about another type of photo
Jonathan hadn't shown: 'Given all your time out tracking, and your
own evidence and sightings, how come you haven't got a photo of a
cat itself?' The questioner's point was immediately intercepted, for
the assembled ecologists were now keen to have their say: 'He hardly
needs such a photo – look at the other hard evidence he's shown.' They

had seen enough to satisfy themselves that a case had been made. I've experienced this myself. I cannot describe the field signs and the carcasses with the precision of Jonathan, but talking through the photos with wildlife professionals, I can see them open up to the proposition of new predators being around. Rather than being laughed out of the building, I am met with curious minds. The vibes suggest there is a case. Yes, they are robust, as I'd want and expect, but overall, the build up of these signs from the field, the actual big cat forensics, gives them hints. This is not the natural world they know and expect: a different force seems to be at work. Back in their offices, these ecologists and wildlife managers are faced with organisational constraints and corporate cultures, the cryptic cats stay off the radar, and colleagues may not be convinced. Asked about big cats living in the wilds of Britain, TV's Chris Packham is up front too: '…they will give themselves away by scratching trees, leaving footprints, excrement and leaving traces of their kills around,' he said to the *Hampshire Chronicle* on 20 January 2010.

A partly-calcified dropping with pound coin for scale near Purbeck. The scat contained hairs which were DNA tested and concluded as leopard.
Photo: Jonathan McGowan

Tracking with Jonathan is an experience in itself. You become a feral person, your vision gets wider, you develop senses never known. 'Act like a deer and merge with the deer and they'll ignore you, and the wild-life will carry on undisturbed,' says Jonathan. I worry he will one day be stalked as a deer in the twilight by the very carnivore he is in search of.

THE GRISLY EVIDENCE

In 2008 Frank Tunbridge and I were advising an American film company. They were preparing a documentary on the 'Beast of Exmoor' and its cousins elsewhere in Britain. They needed hard evidence, tangible signs of the predator at work in our landscape. They knew they'd be pushing their luck to get actual big cat footage during the allotted two weeks, so something like a deer kill with a big cat's hallmarks might be the next best thing. Amazingly, on day four of their visit, and less than two miles from their hotel in Nailsworth, nature delivered exactly what they needed – a roe deer carcass, fresh and eaten out. Gail Cooke fortuitously spotted the gory crime scene and quickly contacted the crew. They had interviewed her just two days before, after her previous 15-minute sighting of a black panther in the area. They rushed to the site that evening with Frank. He examined the carcass under the camera lights while it was still fresh – by morning it might be scavenged and picked over by foxes and badgers. The skin on the carcass had been peeled back and neatly sheared, and as Frank skinned the throat area he uncovered more confirmation – the puncture marks of a predator's clasping bite. The programme led with Frank's dramatic comment as he examined the throat: 'Yes, here - the tooth's gone in'. There were no signs of messy tearing bite marks at the legs and hind quarters, which are more typical of dog attacks, and there were pithy lumps of fur deposited by the kill where incisors had picked out tufts before the carnassial teeth had got to work. Reproduced on these pages, it looked as good a cat kill as you will find.

A TASTE FOR HERBIVORES, ONE AT A TIME

Back in the mid 1980s, Nigel Brierly studied and wrote about some of the sheep kills being found on Exmoor: 'Sheep kills themselves gave me the first important clues that members of the cat family were most likely to be their attackers. Not only in the execution of the kill, but also in the way they had been eaten afterwards.' This and other more detailed descriptions of sheep kills were set out in Nigel's seminal book, *They Stalk by Night*. When I compare his comments with the suspicious sheep and deer carcasses we find today, it all rings true. The same characteristics appear in the carcass we examine, we make the same diagnosis, and still the suspect remains hidden.

When I am invited to check or discuss sheep kills with a farm family, they are usually puzzled. They are suspicious and dumbfounded in equal measure. At the dead of night, an animal has picked out and half-eaten one of the flock. It didn't set the dogs off and often it came and went without trace. Generally, the flock are not spooked afterwards, as might be the case after being terrorised by a marauding dog. Dogs can often

Above: The fresh roe deer carcass found near Amberley in Gloucestershire. The amount of consumption, plucking of hair tufts, peeled skin and hide, and puncture marks at the throat all indicated a likely big cat kill.
Photo: Gail Cooke

Right: A fresh fallow deer carcass found at Ruspidge, Forest of Dean in 2006. The carcass was checked over the following day and found to have been dragged into cover.
Photo: Brian Jones

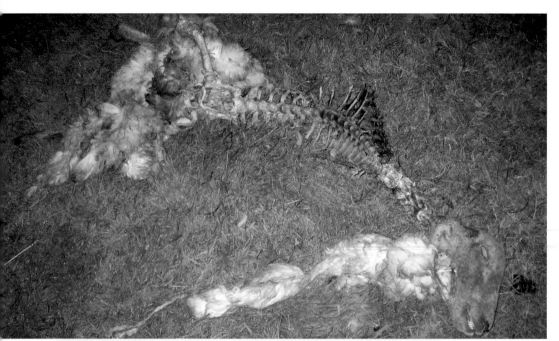

Top of page: Freshly killed sheep at Siddington, Gloucestershire 2007.
The carcass situation illustrates many points of a likely big cat kill and
consumption. Especially noteworthy is the cut and rolled back one-piece
fleece. This amount of consumption over one night may indicate the
involvement of more than one animal. The carcass had been dragged 40
metres through the field from the place of impact before being eaten.
Photo: Gareth Harris

Above: A sheep killed and consumed at Siddington, in the field
next to that in the previous photograph, two years later.
Photo: Phoebe Carter

create havoc, injuring sheep and sometimes killing several. Wool can be torn and widely scattered. A big cat despatches and consumes one animal, cleanly, leaving no other trace. The cat may or may not come back at intervals. Sometimes a more wild strain of dog, or a lurcher, perhaps experienced in poaching, may kill sheep, leaving signs rather more like those left by a feline predator, but they often attack several of the flock while on the rampage. Cats may sometimes get the blame for a dog attack, and the reverse can be true too, but a one-off clinical kill, with consumption occurring at intervals, points to the cat as attacker. The farmer may not recognise what's happening until a pattern emerges, and the predation may stop as suddenly as it starts.

A ewe killed and eaten overnight in Monmouthshire in winter 2010. Marks indicating the impact of the kill and the dragging can be seen in the frost in the bottom photo.

Fortunately, 'prey switching' seems a rare occurrence amongst cats. Why would one suddenly target sheep rather than pursue easier natural prey? Was it a harsh winter? Did the available lambs make for easy pickings? Or is it that there are cubs to feed? Flare ups of sheep kills suspected from a cat seem to be the exception, and usually do not last long. Many farmers have mentioned that they will tolerate the odd loss: 'It's taken one lamb in ten years, and it helps keep the vermin down, so it's fine by me and the neighbour,' is a message I heard from one farmer, and several others have echoed his words. We should appreciate anyone's concern, though, if stock loss is greater or sustained, or if a strategically important pedigree ram is taken. Another question lingers amongst many farmers: how long has the hidden predator been around? How familiar is it with the area, now that it has introduced itself? 'It knows my times and movements about the farm better than I do,' said one farmer, who holds a quiet admiration for the skulking cat he sometimes sees and which he believes has consumed both geese and ewes on his land. But not all farmers think like this, even if they've not had loss of stock. One told me he watched a black panther larger than a German shepherd, with a huge long tail, playing on top of a hay bale. 'He couldn't have been hungry. He wasn't interested in my sheep and they didn't seem bothered by him. I went to get my gun but he'd gone when I came back. I hope I don't see him again.' By their nature, landowners are resourceful and adaptable, keen to learn and to think through situations pragmatically. I have seen them vary their views both ways on the apex cat on their land, with some coming to terms with it and seeing wider issues, others troubled by the animal's presence. Situations and states of mind will differ, because this is for real.

FOLLOWING THE DEER?

When in Exmoor I enjoy the changes in the landscape. Sometimes it can appear soft and rich, while a glance in another direction or a change in the weather can render it harsh and brooding. Its hues and textures contrast with my usual outdoors experience in the southern shires. I scan Exmoor for red deer, large upright mammals which we know are there in good number yet which seem submerged. Somebody will point some out in a far field corner, and I will barely make them out. They blend in to the landscape and I have not yet adjusted to these animals in this terrain.

The high numbers and wide distribution of deer present our land managers with new headaches, as will be discussed in Chapter 8. We have the native red and roe, along with fallow, sika, muntjac and Chinese water deer. A deer stalker in Wiltshire recently despatched a Chinese water deer, yet they are thought to be confined pretty much to the eastern counties of England. He had to photograph the evidence to support his claim. Rough but informed estimates of the total deer population amount to two million across the UK. The situation is, of course, dynamic, with one and a half million a minimum estimate. The number of muntjac has reached 150,000 in England and Wales and is likely to be spreading and growing. To keep a population of such herbivores level, it might be necessary to cull a quarter of them a year. Predatory cats are not going to do our stalkers out of a job, but they do have an important task to help with.

A fair few people tell us of deer kills across Gloucestershire and beyond. They rarely stop to take a picture, but a selection is reproduced on these pages. I often apologise to the squeamish as I click through these photos at talks, but time and again these are the images which people of all ages, male and female, want to focus on – here, they feel, is the sign of the predator. Deer die in winter and are hit on our roads, so we must not jump at every carcass thinking it is the work of the cat. Those reproduced here, along with the sheep kill photographs, have impressed overseas experts, deer stalkers, and even a poacher contact. They feel these pictures tick the boxes for a large feline predator. Examining the evidence directly, *in situ*, is of course a more rigorous approach, but given the impossibility of being present within hours of the kill, these photos may represent some of the best hard evidence available. One of the challenges is to erect a trail camera close to a fresh deer kill, to see if the culprit returns for a second sitting.

Assessing a carcass – signs which may suggest a big cat

The characteristics set out below are indicative. The more of them that are apparent, the greater the indication of a likely kill by a large predatory cat. They are based on consideration of leopard-type, puma-type and lynx-type cats. These points are based on the author's observations of photos and kills, on discussion with farmers and discussion with others with experience of investigating potential big cat kills.

One-off kills and consumption: a big cat dispatches just one large prey animal at a time in usual circumstances

Area of consumption: the prime target for consumption is the under part of the rump end, to access the richer soft body organs such as the liver and heart. Surrounding flesh will then be consumed, exposing ribs

Amount of consumption: a large amount of consumption in a very fresh carcass is a possible indication of a big cat's work. What foxes can manage in three to four nights, a cat can manage in one. Consumption may vary from ten pounds to over 40 pounds in one session if the prey animal is large enough. An adult leopard-type or puma-type cat can eat around 18 pounds or more at one sitting. Consumption of much more than this

Assessing a carcass – signs which may suggest a big cat (continued)

is likely to indicate more than one animal's work. Lesser amounts of consumption should not rule out the cat's involvement as we do not know when it started eating and if it was disturbed. A limb taken away from the carcass and freshly consumed may indicate one of the cats eating away from the main carcass to avoid confrontation

Freshly-killed and consumed carcass: a carcass which has been scavenged – by foxes, buzzards and crows for example – may still have been initially killed and consumed by a cat, but the scavengers' involvement makes a conclusion difficult. If the carcass has been killed and consumed the night before being located, there has often been no time for secondary consumption by a scavenger, and a fox may be wary of the situation and avoid it

Canine indentations: often puncture marks at the throat will be present, indicating the clasping bite of the air pipe for suffocation of the prey. Skinning of the carcass may sometimes be needed to see such marks. Around 4 cm apart is consistent for the canines of adult puma and adult leopard

Nape bites: leopard-type, puma-type and lynx-type cats can also kill their prey with a crushing bite to the back of the neck which serves to break the prey animal's neck quickly. This is less likely on larger prey but may happen in the UK with smaller prey.

Other marks on carcass: the fur and body on a carcass is generally little touched and affected if an experienced big cat has made a quick and efficient kill. The impact is focused on the throat or neck. Incisor teeth marks may be seen above the nose, made by the less frequent method of a cat suffocating the prey with a full facial hold. Sometimes some raking of the claws may be apparent at the shoulder of the prey

Plucking of fur: the cat often licks parts of the fur then picks out tufts with its incisors and discards them. These can often make a neat pile near the carcass. This is done prior to shearing into and consuming the flesh using the carnassial teeth

Stomach and intestines discarded: cats will mostly not consume stomach and intestines. The carnivore is not interested in the content of a herbivore's stomach and the enzymes in the feline carnivore's stomach have difficulty dealing with such matter. Stomach and intestines will be scavenged by foxes, as they are not strict carnivores, being more omnivorous. The stomach remains left aside can be seen in the photo by Andrew Dempsey on page 26.

Tight and precise shearing: the edges of skin and fur show a tightly-cut definition, with no ripping as is the case with foxes and dogs

Fleece and fur stripped away in large sections: the shearing and cutting actions of the cat can leave large sections of the fur or pelt intact but peeled away

Rasping of bones: bones such as ribs may be clean from the rasping of the cat's rough tongue. However, the bones may also appear clean following attention by scavengers

Impact on bones: ribs can be clean-cut like shears, and not gnawed. There may be teeth marks on the bones, such as large canine holes at the ends of bones

Ear removed: often an ear can be removed. This may be from the predator using the ear for gaining some purchase on its prey during the attack and hold. It may also act as a convenient tag for peeling back skin

Dragging: a carcass may be dragged, including into cover, by a large cat, during or after the first sitting of consumption when it takes its fill. Dragging an animal such as an adult roe deer or ewe is a challenge for a fox in particular and is not a trait of a dog

Flattened grass: if the animal is in a pasture, the surrounding grass can appear flattened, suggesting the impression of a large mammal beside the carcass

Distinguishing impacts and consumption by dogs: most dog attacks occur because the dog's predatory instinct is ignited by the chase. Most dogs are well- fed pets and don't normally consume the carcass. If their attack results in a kill it is from biting the neck, ripping the stomach open, or shaking the animal at the neck or top of the head. A dog attack may also leave bite marks present on the back legs where the dog has tried to pull the animal down, as well as possible bite marks on the rear. Some dogs do scavenge on carcasses but usually in lesser or no greater amounts than a fox

ELSEWHERE ON THE FOREST FLOOR

Deer are likely to be a big cat's favoured prey, but other mammals and birds will be in its sights as opportunities allow. People claim to have seen big cats stalking badgers and chasing foxes. Running at prey is not the hallmark of an ambush predator, but fox carcasses are reported. Cannibalism in foxes appears to be restricted to adults eating cubs in harsh times, so a big cat is a prime suspect for a fox kill. Along with a large cat's interest in eating canids, the big cat may view the fox as hassle, an inconvenient neighbouring scavenger and a predator which it could do without. While badgers are big feisty mustelids (members of the weasel family), a big cat may see them as a prey option if one can be cleanly ambushed without risk of injury, especially at times when the food choice is more restricted but the badger has come above ground. Elsewhere the forest floor may also contain pigeon, pheasant and rabbit remains as key components of the cat's diet. These are smaller and less distinct signs to read, but they make ready pickings for an outsize cat. There will be much else besides. A swan carcass is shown amongst the later discussion on wildlife. One lady told me that she and a neighbour watched an old-looking panther go through their gardens several times, heading for the pond stocked with Koi carp. The carnivore's diet is all about seizing the opportunity presented in its territory.

SKULLS, BONES AND REMAINS – REAL, PLANTED OR IMAGINED?

People sometimes suggest that hard evidence of big cats in the country-side might be found in the form of their corpses, bones or skulls. This is

Nikita the black leopard (as described on page 99) showing her canine and incisor teeth, and the hook-like papillae which help the rasping effect of the tongue.
Photo: Mark Fletcher

both right and wrong. There certainly should be some, but they would not be easy to find, or for the novice to spot, and when they were present they could have been planted. A month before writing this, a big cat's claw was dug up to great acclaim – allegedly by a gentleman's dog – in a hotspot area for sightings in southern Scotland. Those who studied the photo in the newspaper felt that the claw was too big for a puma or leopard-sized cat. Again we are left with the double bind: evidence which may be legitimate can be shot down, while an individual who may have a legitimate find is overlooked. As Mark Fraser of Big Cats in Britain often says, the case must be 110% right to be evidence of a big cat. Nothing else gets a look in.

Bodies resulting from road kills are discussed in a later chapter, but it is unlikely that anyone, even a tracker on the case, would stumble upon a freshly-deceased body. Nature cleans up quickly. Remains of other large mammals do not stay intact or recognisable for long. Bones and skulls from big cats certainly would be left, but the likelihood of anyone spotting one, then taking sufficient interest to have it checked and examined are remote. There have been three false alarms with suspected big cat skulls, the most notable occurring two weeks after the Ministry of Agriculture's 'case unproven' verdict on the Bodmin Moor big cat investigation. A skull was picked up in the River Fowey on the southern edge of the moor. After initial excitement, the Natural History Museum's zoology department concluded it was part of a leopard-skin rug: it contained a cockroach egg-case not native to Britain. The media heralded the find as the Piltdown Puss.

SCRATCH MARKS – EVERYWHERE AND NOWHERE

Half the trees in the landscape seem to have scratches, grooves, marks and impressions on the bark. These can have many causes, including deer, squirrels, voles and humans, so looking for signs of a cat scratch on a tree is mainly a lost cause. Watch a cat of any size, from a moggy upwards, and you'll realise that scratching often isn't scratching at all, but just as much a plucking action. This means signs on bark can range from striations from the classic raking down of claws, as well as picking marks from the plucking, and fraying of the bark from the overall scarification. Cats may have a favourite scratch site, for convenience and territory. It may be a lateral branch which is walked on as much as a vertical trunk, either thick or thin. Several eyewitnesses have told me they had seen a cat scratching, but not been able to identify the tree or provide me with photos. I conclude that scratch marks sound good in theory but are nearly impossible in practice to assemble as part of the evidence. Courtesy of Nigel Brierly, we can show one photo here, of where a lorry driver claims he watched a puma scratching a tree trunk in the late

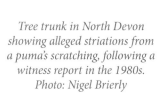

Tree trunk in North Devon showing alleged striations from a puma's scratching, following a witness report in the 1980s. Photo: Nigel Brierly

1980s. With the advent of trail cameras, such a location would be ideal to observe with the aid of a remote camera, in case a territorial cat returned to rake its claws.

THE PUGMARKS – STEPS THROUGH THE LANDSCAPE

I was once looking at the multitude of dog prints across a sandy beach near Bournemouth. Jonathan McGowan and I were playing a game of 'spot the big cat track', a nonsensical exercise designed to check what proportion of prints we'd consider as a possibility (I stress 'possibility') for a cat print in the open countryside, away from obvious dog walking routes. We reckoned that a good 10% of the prints before us in the sand would have got us thinking and scurrying to find more, in case further prints in the area seemed cat-like. We were fully aware of the lesson we were teaching ourselves. In a landscape swamped with dog prints, one can easily be thrown onto a false trail.

To me, a cat's prints are just like scratch marks. Good ones which seem to be textbook examples, and where the witness is certain they saw a cat, come in the category of 'definitely possible', that's all. Checking for prints is fundamental in tracking, and taking plaster casts of likely impressions of a cat's presence is a valuable learning process. Looking around pools, puddles and drinking sources is especially worthwhile and, of course, all trackers love snow. Along with other big cat researchers, I am sent several photos of prints every winter, when people have spotted tracks that excite them. I rarely feel the prints are in the zone of a cat, and it can sometimes be awkward to disappoint people: some feel disheartened, while others argue back. Overall, though, whatever the origin, be it big cat, dog or rabbit (the four impressions of a rabbit's feet sometimes trick people), it is good to see people alert to tracks. Never mind mistakes: everyone makes them, and no one is without uncertainties. I would encourage everyone who doesn't already do so to look at the trails nature leaves around us – it can transport the mind and sharpen awareness.

Above: A small leopard-like print on Portland, found near to a possible cat's den site. A 20p coin shows scale. Photo: Jonathan McGowan

Left: Tracks of an animal which paced up and down against a dry stone wall in the Cotswolds and then leapt over it. Most steps showed direct register and there were no claw marks in any print. A £2 coin shows scale next to the top print.

A lynx print from Slovakia.
Photo: Dan Puplett

Presented on these pages are a few prints which are felt to be 'in the zone' for a big cat, as an indication of what makes trackers stop, think and investigate some more. On the tracks in the snow, direct register is in evidence, where the back foot treads into the front foot's position, knowing the front step made no disturbance, and keeping the animal stealthy. Dogs can do this too, but it is more routine for a cat's locomotion in the wild. We also see a definite lynx track in the snow from Slovakia, and get a helpful worm's-eye look at a leopard's pads. These are conveniently modelled by Khan, an adult black leopard whom we meet in the next chapter. Looking at Khan's overall pads and toes is a prompt to mention that cats are digitigrade (they walk on their digits, as do animals such as dogs and rodents) rather than plantigrade, walking on the soles of the feet as do humans, apes and bears, for example.

On some of the page margins of this book the front and hind prints of a cougar (puma) are reproduced. These have been provided by the US organisation The Cougar Network, who emphasise they have no view of the UK's feral big cats. The prints show the overall roundness of cat prints and the widely splayed toe pads. Puma and leopard prints are non-symmetrical in contast to dog prints which have near perfect symmetry. Here are three other main points about cat prints:

Scale: big cat prints are often not as big as people expect. Look, for example, at the overall scale of Khan's feet, and note that the toe pads sit well within the overall outline. This is the case for all our main candidate cats, leopards, puma and lynx. As the celebrated game hunter and writer Jim Corbett said: 'All animals that stalk their prey have small toes as compared to their pads'.

Splay: toe pads on a cat print are widely splayed. They are usually more spanned out than those of dogs, giving an overall wider and rounder proportion, especially on the front feet.

Above and previous page: The front and the back pads of a black leopard. Note the leading toe evident in the wider front pad on previous page.
Photo: Chris Johnston

Claw marks: do not rule out a print if it has claw marks, unless these are short, thick and blunt. Sometimes in snow or on slopes, or other situations where the cat needs to get a grip, it may display its claws. The cats' claws are longer and needle-like in comparison with those of a dog. In addition, if some of the UK cats do more running and ambushing of their prey, as has been reported by some witnesses in Gloucestershire, might they evolve a need for semi-retractile claws as their own running spikes?

CHECKING THE CARNIVORE'S DIET

When I first met Frank Tunbridge, he had been out tracking and wanted to show me what he'd picked up. He thought it could be lynx scat. Straight away I thought so too: it was light in colour, not like the droppings of any dog or fox I'd seen, and slightly segmented. Its composition seemed typical of a cat dropping – a tight mass of hair and small bones. We checked it in my field guide of tracks and signs to European wildlife (I also use an African version for its tips on leopards) and, sure enough, it gave a perfect match for lynx in size, colour, form and content. I should have photographed it, but to Frank, it was just another possible trace of a cat he'd noted on his general quest, something you become tuned into if you are on the case. Yet with possible evidence in your hand (or in this case a sample bag) you are, as a lone investigator, faced with difficult choices. How should you store it without contaminating your domestic

Wildlife photographer Robert Haynes noticed this suspicious carcass of a roe deer 3 metres up a tree in a wood at Oversley in Warwickshire, as shown in BBC Wildlife *magazine in September 2011. Robert felt it was most unlikely to be a hoax given the difficulty of a human getting access to that point of the tree, in which case it would indicate the actions of a leopard-like cat. There are few reports and photos of carasses up trees in Britain, but given the lack of aggressive scavengers, perhaps a leopard type of cat would rarely need to expend energy on taking a carcass up a tree away from scavengers and disturbance?*
Photo: Rob Haynes/Nature Quest

fridge or freezer? Is it worth getting DNA-analysis if it isn't fresh? Which university or vet should you befriend? Frank tends to do two things with such scat, both for his own satisfaction and to help people learn about the cats. First, it is a perfect sample of possible evidence to show people. There is nothing like passing round a sample bag, with something so real, at the big cat talks. Rather than squirm at the prospect of poo, people love to have the elemental object to see and to smell. Here, right before them, might be a predator's mark offering clues to its lifestyle.

The other option Frank takes with the poo is the 'kettle test'. He waits for it to dry out, then dissolves it in hot water and filters out the contents. This is the diet analysis, in which, at least, fragments of mice and rabbit bones might be expected. Rather than do this in the kitchen, it can be done in the lab. In 1995, according to press reports, a dung sample found near a savaged sheep carcass was found to comprise mainly rabbit. It was tested by a carnivore specialist at the then Institute of Terrestrial Ecology in Aberdeen who concluded it was 'a puma or leopard dropping'.

SNAGGING THE HAIRS

A cat's hair is a pretty small thing to look for in an open landscape, but people do try. Hedges and barbed wire are the main places to aim for, where a cat may have tunnelled its way through gaps on its thoroughfare. The hair of a cat is soft and wavy, the down hair or secondary hair in particular but also the guard hair or primary hair. Even if snagged it could easily float away in the wind. People like looking for hairs because they are tangible signs that can be tested. The cell structure can be checked under a microscope and, if the hair is fresh and has been carefully handled, DNA tests can be done, albeit at a cost, unless you have particularly willing contacts.

So far two hair samples among those offered to labs have turned up trumps. 'This is concrete proof, as far as we are concerned. It is certainly the best evidence by a long way that we've had in Lincolnshire of the presence of big cats'. Those were the words of PC Nigel Lound of Lincolnshire Police when a black cat hair was tested positive for a leopard. 'The core of the hair is not that of a domestic cat. The outside of the hair shows evidence of a scaling pattern that is consistent with an animal of the leopard family,' said Rebecca Webster of DNA Bioscience, quoted in the *Daily Telegraph* in October 2003. An American lab gave a second opinion which verified the result. The hair had been recovered from an old caravan on land owned by Sandy and Julie Richardson in Horncastle. Sandy had gone into the caravan on which the door was ajar. He turned around to see a large black panther just feet away, sitting on a mattress and staring at him. 'It bared its four big yellowy-brown teeth but didn't make a noise.' Sandy backed off and slid out of the caravan. Police came to check the caravan, with several officers and tranquiliser guns. The animal had gone but one of the hairs on the mattress was submitted for the testing. And so it was official: Lincolnshire had its own wandering black leopard.

Sceptics would remind us that hairs are easy things to plant, or simple to acquire from contacts. Yet this does not appear to have happened, and it is negative results which have characterised the odd occasions of hair testing in the UK for feral big cats. Apart from the Lincolnshire leopard, there is or was an official South Wales puma, the Baglan Beast. Tested as a *Felis*, a puma or possibly a lynx, the hair of a large cat wandering out of the forest on the slopes above Baglan, near Neath, was confirmed in November 2005. The animal had been reported several times and was thought to have killed a goat in the area. An off-duty policeman then reported seeing a cat-like animal and officers were able to make a plaster cast of a paw print. Hairs discovered in the cast itself gave a positive DNA test. Local police officer Inspector Huw Griffiths told the *South Wales Evening Post* that the police did not want the animal killed but ideally wanted it captured and taken to a place where it could live out its days happily and safely. 'We had a team up there from dawn trying to track it down but to no avail.' No further official word of the Baglan Beast was heard, but Britain now had a confirmed puma as well as a leopard.

LEAVE ONLY FOOTPRINTS

My local police in Gloucestershire tell the media that there is evidence of big cats breeding. Now they have been joined by Thames Valley Police, who on 16 June 2011, were involved in the popular daily programme *Real Rescues* which was broadcasting stories of police endeavours direct from the control room that covers Oxfordshire and Berkshire. Half way through the programme they had a break from the normal kind of incident. 'Now here's something that will blow your mind,' said Nick Knowles as he introduced the area's Wildlife Crime Officer. They were holding a plaster cast of a large animal's footprint, and Nick Knowles did a good job of explaining the arrangement of toe pads. Not only did it look like a cat's print, explained the police officer, but it had been verified as a puma print by an expert at the Home Office. The print had been one of a track measuring an impressive 300 metres, which wound along a path, around a pond and back again. The trail was fresh. It had been made directly below stalkers who'd been on their high seats looking out for deer. Unnoticed by people watching out for mammals, the cat had come and gone invisibly. The stalkers, on descending, found the tracks and the police came to take a cast. Nick Knowles quizzed the officer about the origins of the cats. On hearing what the 1976 Dangerous Wild Animals Act might have unleashed, Nick Knowles wondered if, given a good lifespan of 15

*The cast of a puma footprint from an Oxfordshire woodland in 2011,
verified by the Home Office. The print was part of a 300 metre track
which occurred directly under high seats occupied by deer stalkers who
discovered the tracks on descending. Photo: Thames Valley Police*

years, the cats were breeding. 'Yes, we have had reports and evidence of
mothers and cubs,' said the officer calmly.

SITTING BY MOLE HILLS

So it can be done. The field evidence can be seen, smelt, photographed,
picked up, tested, double tested, and learnt from. If we prime ourselves,
put the resources in and get people on the case, it's possible. But how can
field signs of the cats be systematically recovered and analysed if there are
no budgets, no formal system of recorders and no follow-up researchers?
And how can faeces or hair samples be analysed at £100 a time and
remote cameras purchased and installed in the quantity needed while

there is no funding and no formal recognition of the subject amongst agencies, wildlife groups and research bodies? Those who demand hard evidence should recognise what has been achieved by just a few intrepid trackers. Meanwhile, waiting for a big cat among the signs it leaves in the landscape has been likened to sitting over a mole hill. It's pretty obvious a creature has been active and in the area, but don't assume it will emerge any time soon.

Nick Morris photographed this cat from a distance of 12 yards near Great Witley, Worcestershire, in April 1992. Described as 'a dark cat with grey markings' Nick spotted the animal when following up a big cat report in the area. When Nick took a second photograph the cat looked up at him and ran off. He returned to the location several times but did not see the cat again. A scale exercise for the photograph has not been carried out but Nick believed the cat was significantly bigger than a domestic cat.

EVERY POSSIBLE CAT –
CLASSIFYING THE MISFITS

'Leopards have a home range of perhaps 40 square kilometres, within which there are hundreds of nooks and crannies where you will never ever find them.'

(Fritz Pölking, Leopards. 2005. Evans Mitchell Books)

'The puma is rarely seen by man. Even where it occurs in goodly numbers it is so elusive that the student must have good luck to observe it.'

(Stanley P. Young and Edward A Goldman. The Puma, Mysterious American Cat. 1946. American Wildlife Institute)

THE ALLURE OF THE PANTHER

Everyone knows Bagheera from Rudyard Kipling's *The Jungle Book*. Commonly referred to as a panther, he is the black form of a leopard. Up close you would notice the rosettes (the leopard's spots) subdued amongst the dark fur. Another black leopard is the panther in the classic story and film *The King and I*. Actor Yul Brynner postured as the King in his palace, complete with the beguiling black cat, a symbol of the master with his subservient beast. More recently a Volvo car advert, running in winter 2010–2011, showed an obliging black leopard bounding into the boot. In the human mind the black panther image is enduring. On a leash with a fashion model or beside the gangster in his underworld, people crave a link to the panther's wild spirit. Locally, in the Cotswolds, two household names from the rock and pop world have had their own cast of exotic cats tethered in the garden.

Another black panther is the dark form of the jaguar, from the forests of Central and South America. Similar in size to the leopard, and equally reclusive and versatile, the jaguar is more thickset and stocky. The jaguar has been likened in build to a wrestler, the leopard to a gymnast. Despite these distinctions, a large male black leopard might be tricky to distinguish from your average black jaguar, especially in low light or from a distance. The natural range of leopards today covers sub-Saharan

Africa, the Middle East, Asia Minor, south and southeast Asia and the Amur valley of Siberia. They are also found in Java and Sri Lanka. Black leopards occur throughout the range, often in more forested environments, but mostly as the odd individual rather than as a population. The significant clusters are in parts of southern Asia.

The two types of black panther possess stealth and mystery and generate strong forces in our psyche. The black leopard has been dubbed the 'Missionary of the Devil' in India, while the black jaguar is currently a strong force in the shamanic world, I am told.

Photographer Mark Fletcher writes: 'This is a small but beautiful leopard called Nikita, bred for filming in South Africa, half-African, half-Indian, and kept in an enclosure of several acres. She seemed very wild to me, yet even fully grown she was not much bigger than a large domestic cat, easily mistaken from a distance but, close up, very much a leopard'.
Photo: Mark Fletcher

Above: A male black leopard's profile. Photo: Chris Johnston

Right: The male black leopard with female cub. The grown-up cub is now at Exmoor Zoo where she helps explain the Beast of Exmoor legend. Photo: Chris Johnston

Shown here is a photo of a black leopard (Khan), conveniently posing in profile, taken at the Santago Rare Leopard Project in 2006. Khan is also shown with one of the cubs from a litter of two. Hints of leopard coloration and pattern in the cub can be seen at this early stage of its life. Another cub from an earlier litter sired by Khan is now an adult female, Ebony. She is around two thirds the size of a standard adult male. Adult female leopards average 88 pounds (40 kg), while the adult male averages 132 pounds (60 kg). We should be cautious in quoting text book size and weights, though, as most types of cat may be bigger or smaller depending on the main components of the diet across their range, and the strategies they need to employ to exploit the main available prey. In addition, the scales above relate to the types of leopard present in open savannah-type habitats, whereas those occupying forested environments can adapt to be smaller. Ebony now lives at Exmoor Zoo, helping to illustrate a splendid information display on the Beast of Exmoor legend. She could readily be described as the low-to-the-ground 'stretched Labrador' which so many witnesses claim to see. Looking at Khan in profile, we can see the sweeping tail, the indistinct head and the high shoulder blades, all features picked out by eyewitnesses.

Another photo (page 99), courtesy of film-maker Mark Fletcher, shows the poise of a more wild black leopard, Nikita. Note the rounded pupil of its *Panthera* eyes as opposed to the pupils of smaller *Felis* cats which form a more vertical slit. Nikita has a body length of around 70 cm, demonstrating why we should not become fixated on a standard scale for a leopard or indeed any other types of cat. Wild tropical leopards from Asia are often small animals, and tropical pumas, too, tend to be small. Our perception of the size of leopards and pumas is distorted by the fact that large ones are more popular in zoos and more obvious in the wild. The ones hidden away, or that live secretly close to man, are under selective pressures to be small.

The different views of black leopards in these photos, the profile of Khan and the form of his wilder friend in Africa, equate to what many people claim to see when they report panthers in Britain. When I checked the sightings and reports submitted to Big Cats in Britain, close to three quarters, in both of the last two years, were of large, black, panther-like cats.

People do sometimes report having heard leopard-like noises without having seen a cat, while others report noises from an actual panther in view. Two separate people in Gloucestershire have reported leopard vocalisations in their local woods, most commonly a snorty cough, and have recognised them from having previously lived in Africa. So if we have reports of animals that look like leopards, move like leopards, sound like leopards and leave prey remains like leopards, then maybe that's just what they are – or at least some of them.

OUR OWN BLACK PANTHER PUZZLE

The leopard's black coat is from a recessive gene. The term used is melanism, and so members of the cat family displaying this trait are called melanistic. A black leopard, for example, can therefore also be referred to as a melanistic leopard. Many species of cats can display melanism, not just the 'black panthers' of leopards and jaguars. A gene mutation has created it and it is not officially known (I stress 'known') to have occurred in pumas. It has been known, however, in ocelots, jungle cats, servals and bob cats, along with others of the 37 cat species. In the next chapter I summarise the case for possible breeding amongst the cats that are thought to be here, and we have statements confirming breeding from police, as reported elsewhere in the book. But if breeding was occurring amongst black leopards, wouldn't we see normal spotted ones in a proportion of the offspring? It seems this does occur for black jaguars but not for black leopards. Bred amongst themselves, the cubs of black leopards are consistently black, as we see in the examples and explanations below.

For three years, biologist Kae Kawanishi led a team using 150 trail cameras in rainforest in peninsular Malaysia's Taman Negara National Park. Their focus was on tigers but they recorded over 100 photographs of leopards. Of course, some were of the same individual, but every photographed leopard was black. Big cat expert and author Fiona Sunquist reported the study in the US *National Wildlife* magazine in 2006. In the article, Kawanashi had this to say about the area's indigenous hunter-gatherers, the Orang Asli, who helped with the camera traps: 'They know every animal in the forest. When we asked them about the various cats, they recognized clouded leopards, tigers and black leopards, but no one recognized a large spotted cat. To the Orang Asli all leopards are *harimau kumbang*, or black leopards.'

Fiona Sunquist makes the following deduction from this important experience in Malaysia: 'Historical reports and hunters' stories from a century ago record that as many as half of the leopards in the Malay Peninsula may have been black, but as Kawanishi has just discovered, black leopards now seem the norm in that part of the world. The reason might be as simple as camouflage or as complex as disease resistance.'

Douglas Richardson is a mammals expert at the Highland Wildlife Park. In his book *Big Cats* (1992) he explains the breeding on of black leopards by referring to work by Robinson[1] in 1970 and Richard O'Grady[2], the then director of Glasgow Zoo. In his account of the permutations in leopard breeding and offspring, Richardson states: 'A black leopard only carries the code for the black pattern, since if it possessed that for a spotted coat it would not by definition be black itself as the spotted trait will always dominate'. Douglas Richardson cites consistent ongoing breeding of black leopards at Glasgow Zoo during the 1970s to confirm this. In contrast he refers to the breeding of black jaguars at Marwell Zoo and Chessington Zoo which both produced mixed black and spotted

1. Robinson, R. 1970. *Journal of the Bombay Natural History Society,* Vol. 66, 423–429

2. O'Grady, R.J.P. 1979. *Proceedings of the 4th Symposium of the Association of British Wild Animal Keepers,* Vol. 4, 32–41

Photographer Mark Fletcher writes: 'This is a large African male leopard that lived in an enclosure of several hectares in Namibia. He was a local leopard who had been captured and needed looking after, and could not be reintroduced as he was habituated to people. He appeared in the 2010 'Secret Leopard' documentary for BBC 2's Natural World series. Even in Africa, finding and filming a wild leopard outside of the few famous leopard reserves would be unthinkable, an illustration of how elusive leopards are.'
Photo: Mark Fletcher

litters, as melanism in jaguars is not governed by a straight recessive gene. In addition, *The Leopard in India*, a key book on Asian leopards by JC Daniel, revised in 2009 by Natraj books, explains the consistent black offspring when both parents are black.

Reports of leopard-sized cats with spots in Britain are few and far between. The first one I have ever received was sent to me earlier this year (2011) but it fitted the size of something like an ocelot, about 85 cm long in the body. An ocelot's home is the centre and northern half of central America. Its spots are sometimes banded and flowing, but an observer would certainly call it spotted. A similar- looking cat is the margay, a notch smaller and occupying a similar geographic range. Cats seeming to match ocelot and margay descriptions have been reported in small numbers over recent years in Britain, and the smaller leopard cat is discussed below. With their striking markings they are all coveted and seen as desirable for captive collections and domestic situations. Larger spotted cats of the size of leopards and jaguars are an extremely rare feature of the sightings documented in the UK. There is a view that spotted cats are better camouflaged for a range of environments and thus would be more cryptic than black panthers but despite this, the sightings reports only suggest that larger cats with rosettes amount to the occasional vagrant individual.

My thinking is that the form of the black cats reported tends to fit leopards much more than jaguars, and given the dearth of spotted-cat sightings, the black panthers are predominantly leopards (*Panthera pardus*) for if they are breeding they are remaining black. A neat report of a leopard-like black panther is recorded here from Claire Blick of North Devon, together with her helpful illustration which gives a feel for the animal's appearance and movement.

Claire Blick explains her encounter with the black panther in North Devon, which she later illustrated: 'I was taking a walk along an old

Claire Blick's illustration of a black panther she encountered near Braunton in 1999.

railway track near Braunton on a lovely sunny evening. No-one else was around and it was all quiet. After 35 minutes, I turned to return home and as I did so, a large black cat came out of the bushes about 20–30 yards away. I stood in shock for a few moments, realising it was a cat and not a dog by the way it moved in a snake-like stalking pose and because it had a very long tail that touched the ground then curled up at the end. I became a little scared and decided to walk a different way home to avoid going towards it. I instinctively knew not to run as it may have drawn attention to me, although it must have known of my presence. It took no notice of me. It was glossy black, the size of a Labrador, with a small head and brown patches on its hind quarters. All I could think was: 'It should not be in this country!' and that it was powerful enough to kill me in an instant. Since then I have only walked alone in open spaces like the beach, near me. It was such a beautiful animal.'

CAT'A MOUNTAIN – A LION, A PANTHER AND A PUMA

If the black leopard is a cat of much mystique and many talents, so also is the puma (*Puma concolor*). Its variety of names is confusing, too. Take your pick from a lengthy list, including painter, catamount (cat up a mountain), panther (in eastern US states), mountain lion or cougar (in western US states). Its geographical distribution indicates its versatility, as its territory ranges from deserts to mountains, from wilderness to suburbs, from the tip of Chile in the south to the far reaches of western Canada in the north. The eastern fragments of the population in North America cause intractable debate. Are they traces of the original range which was decimated when settlers arrived and took a liking to the pelts? This would make it a leftover subspecies, the eastern panther, deserving protection. Or is this a dispersed array of wandering pets and releases with no official status? According to official judgement, the latter view holds sway at present, but there are grassroots groups who study the eastern populations and beg to differ.

The different names and identities of this cat reflect its connection with many cultures through the Americas. I largely stick to puma throughout this book, but it is interchangeable with mountain lion and cougar. The risk with using 'puma' is that many people conjure up a black cat in their heads. It seems ingrained, maybe from the leaping black images emblazoned on the sports equipment of that name. The curious identity of the cat takes another twist as, despite its scale being equal to that of the leopard, it is *Felis* rather than *Panthera*, for it cannot roar.

Within Britain, the 'fawn-coloured' cat which eyewitnesses report resembling a puma – long, low, with high haunches and a rope-like tail – seems a solid case for the presence of *Puma concolor*. This category

A puma carries her newborn kitten in the Rocky mountains, Montana. (These are captive animals.) Note the characteristic brown spots of the puma kit.
Photo: © Daniel J. Cox/NaturalExposures.com

of sightings, about 20% year on year, seems simpler to classify than the black panthers. Some people recognise their sighting as a puma, cougar or mountain lion, others look it up and deduce 'puma', while some just report a cat unknown to them that fits the puma description well. Unsurprisingly, given the basic similarity, the occasional person speaks of a 'lioness' but describes a puma. The difficulty in the distinction of the two is illustrated in the apparent photo from Cornwall reproduced in this section.

The most celebrated case of a possible wild puma in Britain came in Cannich in 1980 where a female puma, 'Felicity', was allegedly trapped by a farmer. The suggestion was that given her tame temperament, she'd had a captive upbringing but had found her way into the trap after living feral for a year. The case turned out to be a publicity stunt by a tabloid newspaper which had offered a reward for the capture of one of Scotland's wild-living big cats. When the Highland Wildlife Park picked up Felicity from Cannich, according to the Park Director of the time, Eddie Orbell, she was 'quiet and purring and obviously hand-reared. That evening, returning to the Wildlife Park, I was stroking her and sensing no aggression at all.' It appears the story of Felicity was a bad hoax, for she was seen the night before 'capture' travelling north in the back of a car up the A9. The exercise was meant to show the existence of big cats roaming in Scotland, for here was an apparently loose puma lured to a baited cage-trap in a hot spot for sightings. The saga of Felicity did illustrate a wider point about pumas in Britain though: an unregistered one had been found, no questions asked, well after the clampdown of the 1976 legislation. Felicity lived a further five years at the Highland Wildlife Park and now remains on public display, stuffed as an exhibit in Inverness Museum.

To look at the colour and form of a puma through an eyewitness account, we can again turn for help to Claire Blick, who with her son watched what they felt was a cert for a puma in North Devon in 1994. Her account and illustration on the following page help to give a sense of the animal's jizz.

DARK CLUES TO THE PUMA

The puma might seem a more straightforward cat to consider, but there is a twist we should explore. Back in the 1980s, as the big cats were being reported through Exmoor, Nigel Brierly, who was central to the ongoing local study, noticed an important trend. People would report a black panther-sized cat, but making a puma, *Felis*, sound. Nigel first toyed with the idea of mutant, outsize feral cats, but later settled on dark or black pumas as the most likely cause. Until recently I thought nothing of this explanation. My assumptions for people reporting dark cats which might not actually be black were based on the following thinking:

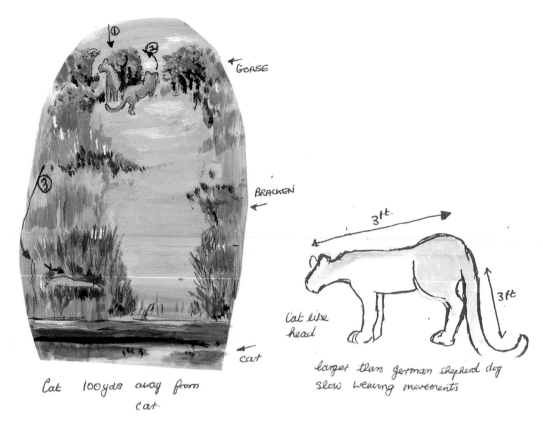

GORSE

BRACKEN

cat

3ft.

3ft

Cat like head

larger than german shepherd dog
slow weaving movements

Cat 100yds away from cat.

Claire Blick describes the situation which led her to illustrate the apparent puma which she encountered: 'My son Oliver and I were driving slowly down a narrow lane where we stopped in a gateway. My son saw the cat first because it moved from a sitting position (1) in a clearing between gorse bushes away from us. At first I thought it was a young lion, but then noticed that its hind quarters were higher than the shoulders and realised it was a puma. It was at least six feet in length, including the tail, and a beautiful rich orange-to-gold colour. I noticed the bracken was a similar colour. We stayed for over ten minutes after it disappeared (2), thinking it was gone. It appeared again nearer, about 30 yards away (3) and its smooth back was just visible above the top of the bracken. Just then a car came behind and we had to move off. I often wonder just how close it would have come to us.'

Backlighting and low light: most animals and objects, of whatever colour, will be silhouetted and look dark in low light conditions and against a back light.

Wet fur: I've twice noticed a fox in the field next to me that looked black on first sight. As it got closer to view and my cats made grumbly noises in response, I realised its fur was wet. It had not dried off from a plunge through the local stream, and looked impressively dark and different.

Hearing and seeing different cats: I felt people in Exmoor might have seen a black cat, maybe just a large feral, or possibly a black leopard on the same beat as a puma, but within the same day or night heard a puma scream.

Any of these explanations, especially the first two, may still account for false diagnosis of black cat sightings then and now. However, in the past three years, a strand of the feedback from eyewitnesses in Gloucestershire has been bugging me. We also now get black cats, seemingly panther-sized, making puma-like calls and screams. Not only that: we have had four reports of a big black cat seen 'running like a cheetah' (the witness didn't feel it was one) or doing a 'jack-knife run', with front and back legs crossing in the galloping movement. I have searched the internet, checked my leopard books and asked leopard-expert friends abroad. This does not seem to be a leopard's movement. 'Physically impossible,' was the response of one specialist who works with leopards daily. It may not be a leopard's locomotion, but it is just how a puma can run. The case developed on one of my farm visits beyond Gloucestershire when I chatted to the farmer. He'd had ewe kills and other signs of a visiting cat. He had seen the cat on his land through binoculars and thought it more like a puma, only it was black. I wasn't persuaded of a black puma diagnosis from a one-off sighting, but asked him if he ever heard animal noises he might not recognise. As he did not know the sounds of a puma, I told him of a common one, frequently described as 'like a woman being strangled'. 'No kidding,' he declared. 'Last year I heard what I thought was a woman being attacked in the wood in the valley below. I was worried and phoned the police, but when I checked there was nobody about.' As he made me a cuppa in his kitchen I played the cats' sounds on the internet in his study. The puma noises included sharp coughs and throaty purrs, and at the sound of the puma's harsh and shrill scream he rushed in exclaiming, 'That's it! That's exactly what I heard!'

These different accounts had opened my mind to the prospect of black or dark pumas, so I decided to dig a little deeper. The literature is mostly closed on the case for dark pumas. Any book mentioning it refers only to one actual specimen in Brazil from 1843. 'The whole head, back, and sides, and even the tail, were glossy black, while the throat, belly and inner surfaces of the legs were shaded off to a stone gray,' says the report of the shot animal. This is indeed clear, but one specimen over a giant land mass, well over a century ago, isn't much to go on. Yet black panther-sized cats are reported across North America today, not in great numbers but consistently. I agree with the view that they are most likely escaped or released black panthers (leopards or jaguars) or even wild black jaguars north of their central and south American range. Another smaller candidate is the otter-like dark brown cat, the jaguarundi, creeping beyond its Central and South American home. This is less likely as it is only the scale of a large domestic cat. But why rule out the puma from these sightings? Why assume every report of a dark or black cat is one of these out-of-place candidates, when there is a native cat the same size to consider? Amongst over 50,000 puma in North America, naturally and normally ranging from grey to brown and from slate grey to rusty red, maybe someone should take a closer look? True, there are no black puma specimens other than the Brazil case, but the case is open, not closed.

A PUMA SEARCH IN GOD'S OWN COUNTRY

To delve further into the case for dark pumas we move to the east side of Canada, deep into the forests of New Brunswick. In 1972, Bruce Wright published his analysis of the puma population in the northeastern US states and the east of Canada in the landmark book, *The Eastern Panther: A Question of Survival*. He accumulated hundreds of reports of pumas in the wild where they were thought to be largely absent following the settlers' impact on the eastern side of the continent. Wright's approach was entirely professional and systematic, for he was Director of the Northeastern Wildlife Station in New Brunswick. He was well connected and well respected: his view counted amongst peers in the wildlife, forestry, and game sectors. Even without a dead specimen, his painstaking reports of people's clear and vivid explanations pointed to a case for scattered local populations of pumas.

Wright's findings on the residue puma population were significant enough, but he made a further revelation. Between 1951 and 1970 he collected 20 reports of black cats seen at close range and fitting a puma description (he used the eastern North American term of 'panther', but meant 'puma'): 'Two were watched through rifle scopes, one for ten minutes. The evidence cannot be disregarded.' Wright considered the reports and ruled out the distraction of released or escaped black leopards and jaguar, wet cats and cats against a sunset or sunrise. 'Jet-black all over' and 'Black as midnight' were amongst the emphatic descriptions. He concluded his examination as follows: 'This leaves me with no alternative but to accept the eyewitness accounts at face value. I now believe there are a few black specimens of the panther in eastern North America.'

Wright's reasoning for black pumas in the region was a plausible one. The extreme north-east of the puma range, where his studies were based, accommodated a puma population isolated for over 100 years. It was that geographical section where the black animals were most commonly reported. Wright assumed the puma population had experienced a mu-

Illustration of black puma by Robert Hines. Originally produced courtesy of the North American Wildlife Foundation.

tation, sometimes allowing melanism to express itself. With due respect to the pioneering man, I would suggest that there may be another cause. Had this closed-off section of pumas, living in thick forest, adapted and evolved, with some individuals coming out dark? Either way, we cannot ignore these findings, given the array of large black cats reported in Britain and the parallel conditions we may have to the New Brunswick case. Whatever the biological cause, has it been at work here too? And have some witnesses who falsely perceive pumas as naturally black, as many do, seen a dark one after all?

THE INCIDENTAL LYNX

There are puzzles with the identity of most of our apparent cats, but not, it would seem, with the lynx. Present in Britain until at least the 6th century A.D., the once-native alpha cat already knows its way around. When people mention their sighting of a lynx they often give it a secondary status, and frequently seem apologetic. 'Are you interested in those too?' they sometimes say, as if the lynx is optional and hardly counts. When captive lynx, such as from zoos, are filmed for TV, a favourite trick is to get them to earn their meal. A lump of meat or a chicken is tied up above them, as high as 15 feet, and the lynx must snatch it down. The rearing cat makes good TV, but out in our countryside, it can be seen doing the same. 'I watched it leaping up and catching pheasants,' said a drystone waller in the Cotswolds. 'It springs after the grouse,' said a forester in southern Scotland. Other Gloucestershire witnesses have reported lynx sitting atop a quarry surveying their farmland or sprawled out catching the warmth of their garden cold frame.

A Eurasian lynx in the Dinaric Mountains of Slovenia conserves
its energy (A captive animal). Photo: Miha Krofel

Elsewhere in the Cotswolds, the wife of an A-list celebrity phoned her neighbours to ask if they'd had a lynx escape, as she'd seen it wander around the outbuildings. She is not the only megastar family to have encountered a wandering big cat. Over in Hertfordshire, at David and Victoria Beckham's 'Beckingham Palace' home and estate, they allowed their friend the TV chef Gordon Ramsay to raise two sheep on the land in preparation for his 2007 *F Word* series, which was emphasising healthy home-grown local produce. One of Ramsay's lambs never made it to the menu, though. It was found mauled and filleted, wild-carnivore style, on the estate's lush pastures. The Beckhams' own Rottweiler dogs were not to blame, according to the vet's examination. This meant something might have scaled the perimeter fence, and black panthers had been reported in the vicinity. The programme ended with a mystified celebrity chef, but Ramsay felt the area's big cat sightings may have been linked to the killing.

The Eurasian lynx (*Lynx lynx*) is discussed more in Chapter 8, as are the tactical questions faced in the debate on whether to bring it back officially, as parts of Germany, Switzerland, Italy and Austria have done in recent times. Its current range spans from much of Scandinavia through central Europe, and also includes Soviet Central Russia, Asia Minor, Iran and Iraq. It is an upright, gracile cat, with large paws and powerful legs, designed for rocky, woodland and scrub conditions. Rabbits, hares and deer are its main target prey. In much of its natural range, its yellowy-brown fur will thicken in winter, but its dark spots are usually in evidence. Its tufted ears are designed to enhance its hearing, while the reason for its short tail is apparently unknown. Its body length can be up to 130 cm. Like the leopard and the puma, the lynx stays largely out of sight. 'By the time you see the lynx, it's seen you many times,' goes a Polish saying. Europe's other lynx, the smaller and more heavily-spotted Iberian lynx (*Lynx pardinus*) is officially critically endangered, with only around 250 remaining in the wild across its range, mainly southwest Spain and southern Portugal. These are fragile numbers. Road kills have been bad enough through the core habitat in Andalucia, but a previous culture of snaring the animal, and a low density of rabbits compared with what we are used to in Britain, have been the main reasons for its decline. In response to the crisis, the Lynx Life initiative is humanely-trapping juveniles and translocating them to areas where rabbits are helped to colonise key habitat. Young from the litters of captive animals are also released into the wild after being acclimatised in large-scale habitat enclosures. These costly efforts, plus awareness-raising (such as through the memorable cartoon film *El Lince Perdidio*) are the sort of action that's called for when helping the most endangered cat on earth.

Back in Britain, celebrated reports of lynx on the loose go back as far as 1825, when the great social commentator of the time, William Cobbett, the author of *Rural Rides*, reported seeing a 'catamount' in the grounds of Waverley Abbey, but described it is a lynx rather than a puma. Perhaps we should not doubt a man of such high repute?

In 2000 the late Quentin Rose was asked by the police and RSPCA to recover two unlicensed lynx in West Yorkshire, where the owner had stated they were due to be released for hunting. In May 2001 London Zoo staff were called to a reported lynx seen loose in a garden at Golders Green. A woman had seen a spotted cat on her garden wall. 'We get numerous calls at London Zoo reporting big cat sightings and so far all of them have proved incorrect – it usually turns out to be a large domestic cat,' said Ray Charter, Head Keeper of Big Cats at the time. 'So you can imagine my surprise when I bent down to look under the hedge expecting to see a large ginger tom, only to be met by a much more exotic face!' After several attempts to catch the cat with a hand-net in the open area, it was finally contained in a smaller area under the steps of a nearby flat. The Zoo's veterinary officer sedated the animal with a blowpipe. On examination it was found to be a female Eurasian lynx, approximately 18 months old. Its origin was unknown, but it went to the zoo as Lara the Lynx.

In 2006 the media confirmed stories of a lynx shot in Norfolk in 1991, and a photograph of the dead animal backed up the original story. According to the *Daily Mail* of 22 March 2006, the police report obtained by the *Eastern Daily Press* said the discovery of the dead cat was made when a search was carried out on a gamekeeper suspected of killing birds of prey. The police officer involved stated: 'At the start of the search in an outhouse, which contained a large chest freezer, I asked him what he had in the freezer, and he replied: 'Oh only some pigeons and a lynx.' On opening the freezer there was a large lynx lying stretched out in the freezer on top of a load of pigeons! He had shot this when he saw it chasing his gun dog.' According to the report, Defra was informed and staff believed the cat had escaped from illegal ownership or a zoo.

Another lynx incident was reported to have occurred at a former wildlife park in Derbyshire which bred Eurasian lynx in the late 1970s and early 1980s. Wikipedia mentions activists releasing several lynx into the wild from a now-closed zoo in Derbyshire. An attempt to recapture the animals may well have been made, but a lynx was reported dead on the A6 a few weeks after the incident, according to the local press. In theory, in a situation like this, a small mixed-gender stock, even of just four to six animals, could lead to an ongoing generation viable for around 30–40 years before the incestuous inbreeding would cause chronic genetic weakness or sterility. However, if there was interaction with other feral lynx from other sources, perhaps others released or set free by parties unknown, the population could possibly be genetically strengthened and might persist. A college lecturer contacted me with his report of the following sighting in the Peak District from September 2006: 'The lynx I saw was exceptionally close as I nearly ran it down, and it walked round my car allowing a very close-up view of the animal. Of typical size, with distinctive facial markings and ear tufts, it nevertheless had what seemed to be a longish shaggy coat that gave it a somewhat scruffy look for a cat. This was no doubt a happy adaptation given the harsh Derbyshire winters.'

OUR GENERALIST KING CATS

The above round up suggests that the majority of larger cats settled in the UK are leopards, puma and lynx or their derivatives. These are the great generalists. They are amongst the most adaptable and resourceful cat species around. The geographical range and varied terrain they inhabit shows them to be all-purpose. If we had more specialist species we would know it – they would be seen more and we would notice their effects. The cheetah, for example, would be seen making bursting and looping runs to trip up its prey. If any of the great cats were to settle unnoticed into our landscape it would be the leopard, puma and lynx. They can also take to the trees when necessary, while the leopard is positively arboreal – it likes trees. So these cats may spend large portions of their time underground or above ground, resting and out of our way, and not in our plane of vision. I asked Frank Tunbridge to find me a quote on the invisible leopard from the writings of game hunters Jim Corbett (north India) or Kenneth Anderson (south India) through the first half of the 1900s, thinking their tracking and jungle experience would be helpful to refer to. Typically this set Frank thinking and he conjured up his own soundbite based on bitter experience: 'A fleeting shadow at dusk, a grey patch of mist at dawn. Big cats have played hide and seek with man for thousands of years, and nothing's changed.'

THE HIGHLAND TIGER

Before we move on to other suspects, we should take a look at Britain's official wild native cat. If I see them at zoos or wildlife parks I make a beeline for the Scottish wildcats. People sometimes pass them by, remarking how like domestic tabby cats they appear in scale and markings. Give yourself time to pick up the wildcat's vibes, though, and you'll see how wrong this assumption can be. The wildcat is rightly named. It is totally 'other' and genuinely ferocious. We are not part of its world: the distant Cheshire Cat has nothing on this creature. 'I admire its cussed spirit,' says Mike Tomkies, the author of acclaimed books on wildcats. He lived alongside three litters of them and – almost – became the first person to tame one.

The elusive Scottish wildcat caught on a trail camera in 2010. Note the distinctive dark dorsal stripe and the thick blunt tail.
Photo: Kerry Kilshaw, WildCRU

An emblematic cat it may be, but the wild cat has long been off our radar. Now with around 400 left, it needs our help. Originally found right across Britain, its numbers declined over the centuries due to human activities such as deforestation and persecution. The beginning of the 19th century saw it still hanging on in the Highlands, Southern Uplands, northern England and Wales. By 1860 it was gone from all areas apart from the Highlands. Now it is confined to pockets like the Cairngorms and western fringes of the Scottish Highlands. One of these outposts is the most westerly point of the British mainland, the Ardnamurchan peninsula, north of Mull.

On a recent visit into the far west of Ardnamurchan, the woman serving me tea at the community centre told me she'd seen something special. She had recently spied a mother wildcat, and was sure it had kittens. She'd been lucky to see the shy cat, and it was great news about the young. Scottish wildcats are now one of Britain's rarest mammals and may be in serious danger of extinction. It is the local effort, the local excitement I saw in Ardnamurchan, which will help our little alpha cat. Many farmers and gamekeepers are rallying to the cause, for they have the skills to steward its habitat. Local pet owners are being asked to vaccinate and neuter their cats, for interbreeding with feral and domestic cats dilutes the genetics and creates hybrid animals.

The cause of the wildcat is one we can all support. Trail cameras are now installed across some known hotspots, and as reclusive as the cat may be, it sometimes triggers off a picture. And in case you are wondering, the answer is 'yes': I am envious of the cameras and the concentrated effort being made to study this animal. There will be things we can learn for big cat research along the way, but helping our own great little cat must get priority. The Scottish Wildcat Association, Highland Tiger and the Cairngorms Wildcat Project are three initiatives working to make a difference. Check out their essential websites to find out more.

LESSER CREATURES?

Like many with an eye for wildlife, Frank Tunbridge takes a careful check of any bodies of road-kill animals. A fresh deer prostrate in the gutter could serve as bait for the trail cameras, while roadkill could offer the Holy Grail itself, a big cat's body. He once picked up a fox-sized black cat on a roadside near Cirencester. It was late at night and raining hard. The sodden carcass was big and heavy as he picked it up, but he quickly judged it to be a large feral, so he threw it into the long grass and drove on. It probably was a (very) large feral, but I wish he'd kept it to see. It is in the small- to mid-range of cats, black and other shades, where odd things may be occurring. This may or may not muddy the water in relation to the big cats, but I suggest we need to open all the doors before us to see what quirks of evolution, hybridisation or mutation may be occurring within feral cat populations here, for this may not just be happening amongst smaller-sized cats.

FERAL DIMENSIONS

Most feral cats are no bigger than domestics, but some crop up which are genuinely mega, like the above-mentioned cat found by Frank Tunbridge. The owner of a truly grand feral-domestic once wrote to Big Cats in Britain, submitting details of her former cat and sending a photo too, which she agreed to having printed in this book. So meet Fairfax, and if you're the next door neighbour's dog, 'Be afraid'. His owner, Daphne Hilsdon from Buckinghamshire, told the mighty housecat's story:

'About 20 years ago I owned a black cat which came from feral stock. He grew to four feet long, weighed about 30 lb and was almost as big as a Labrador. I am told by the vets that occasionally (it's not frequent) a feral tomcat will grow to this size, and it's almost always a black or a grey tom. I am attaching a photo of him on my desk; my other cats were the size of the radio behind him. He stood about 19 inches at the back, 4 feet from head to tail (we measured him). Local people called him the Exmoor beast - he hated dogs and would attack them. His bite was about 2 ½ inches across at the fangs, from memory. His name was Fairfax, after the commander in the English Civil War, Sir Thomas Fairfax, who was known as Black Tom.'

Fairfax, the outsized feral-domestic. A reminder of another type of big cat we live alongside.
Photo: Daphne Hilsdon

Fairfax is an extraordinary specimen and he begs many questions. Was there a hint of jungle cat or something else in his make-up? Was he exhibiting giganticism? And, crucially, how many others were and are there like him? Sadly, one way of learning is to check more roadkill.

THE JUNGLE CAT AND ITS FERAL COUSINS

We meet the jungle cat (*Felis chaus*) up close in Chapter 10, thanks to my own family's experience. People report them at the talks I give and others seem to be reported around the country, mostly from people not using the label but giving a passable description of one: banded legs, a short thick tail, and slightly tufted ears. Dead ones are known to have been found in Hayling Island and, as shown in the stuffed example here, from Shropshire. Head-to-body length can be up to 75 cm. Also called the swamp cat, it is found in 25 countries from Egypt in the west of its range to IndoChina in the east. It may have arrived in Britain from doing its duties on Asian ships, but more significant is its breeding role. It is crossed with a domestic cat to form the chaussie, which people pay good money for. But how many chaussie-like cats may have formed in the wild from a loose jungle cat? And we know that jungle cats can come in black: they can be melanistic. We should not point the finger at the jungle cat unless we're sure, for who knows the various strains present in our ferals, the cats, numbering several hundred thousand, which can be found amongst our docklands and urban fringes and from barns to hedgerows. Do some of the larger ones sometimes come with a hint of *Felis chaus*?

Let's return briefly to the wildcat. The cat shown dead on the sack in the photo here is a separate wildcat species, *Felis lybica,* the African wildcat. It was verified as such by the curator at the former Cricket St Thomas wildlife park, and it can come in a dark shade, as here. The picture was taken in South Molton, Devon, in 1996 by Nigel Brierly. The cat was three times larger than his own domestic cat. According to Nigel such cats were kept locally. We know the problem of the Scottish wildcat interbreeding with domestics and now, it seems, its bigger African counterpart may have been strutting its stuff down in Devon.

NO LONGER THE CUDDLY KITTEN – LESSONS FROM THE BENGAL CAT

When a Bengal cat was found dead on the road near a pub in Wiltshire in 2007 the local paper heralded it as 'The Beast of Swindon'. No fewer than five different people phoned the pub suggesting it was theirs. Bengal cats are domestic-cat size, and they are mainly fairly docile. Early-generation ones can be feisty, may bother neighbours' cats and be scratchy to owners. As small and benign as they are, Bengal cats 'get out', either pushed out or of their own accord. If not befriended elsewhere, they can, just like other cats, fend for themselves. So if cats the size of Bengals can try their owners' patience, what might it be like to keep a full-grown puma or a black leopard?

Left: A preserved Jungle cat (male), found dead at
Richard's Castle near Ludlow in 1989.
Photo: Dr Karl P.N. Shuker/Fortean Picture Library

Right: A dark version of the African wildcat found on the
roadside in South Molton, Devon, 1996.
Photo: Nigel Brierly

Left: Asian leopard cat shot at Kingsley, Frodsham, Cheshire, November 1981.
Photo: Fortean Picture Library

Right: Amur leopard cat found stray in London in 2011.
Photo: Galloway Wildlife Conservation Park

The source of the Bengal is a domestic crossed with the Asian leopard cat (*Felis bengalensis*), with its pale-brown coat and dark blotches and bands. Like the jungle cat, the leopard cat can slip away from captivity. Specimens have cropped up in the Scottish Borders, in Widecombe in Devon and on the Isle of Wight. Another from Cheshire is shown in this section. In 2011 an Amur leopard cat was found stray in Chiswick, perhaps evading the base where it was to be used for Bengal breeding. Someone handed it to Battersea Dogs and Cats Home who passed it to the Specialist Wildlife Centre via the Heathrow Animal Reception Centre. It was identified as an Amur leopard cat and is now on display at Galloway Wildlife Conservation Park.

REAL MISFITS AND THEIR IMPLICATIONS

So should we automatically assume 'leopard, puma, lynx' for our big three cats? Do they only fit these neat labels? We should certainly first consider the key options presented by science and keep it simple if we can. Individual cats differ and people could make mistakes in the detail they report, so even just amongst the main three, various tweaks will show amongst the cats' features. We should, though, be true to the detail of the sightings and recognise the complications, for the oddball cats keep coming up.

A recent example of a misfit cat occurred in Pembrokeshire. Southwest Wales has been a stronghold for big cat reports and sightings and in January 2011 it was Michael Disney's turn to be astonished. A Pembrokeshire County Council staff member, his close-up sighting six miles north of Haverfordwest was widely reported in the press at the time. Here is an extract from his report of the sighting, including his struggle with the ID: "The most striking thing about it – apart from the fact that it was a big cat on the loose – was that it had distinctive brown markings on its head. I immediately stopped my vehicle and stared at this animal. It had a large, cat-like head, muscular build and was approximately three feet tall. I have made various searches on the web but not really seen anything that I could say, 'It was definitely one of those'. I am beginning to think that it was a 'mutant' type of big cat.'

Michael Disney's uncertainty over the panther-sized cat he saw applies to plenty of other witnesses, and it plays on the minds of those who record the sightings. Just what can we assume the range of cats is? Is it too easy to clock them as leopard, puma and lynx? One of the oddities which occasionally crops up is a white blaze marking. I am aware of five witness reports of clear sightings of large black cats with white blazes: four were on the chest, one on the side. This is a significant feature for an observer to pick out. Chris Johnston's illustration of such a cat is shown in Chapter 3, while in 2009, several national newspapers published a photo of an alleged black panther at New Denham in Buckinghamshire displaying such a white chest marking, There was no scale on the photo which made it difficult to judge. Are these cats just a black leopard displaying some colour morph, or are they an indication of something even more unorthodox?

NATURE'S COCKTAIL – HAVE WE GOT HYBRIDS?

When different cats meet they may either keep away from each other to avoid a scrap, have a scrap, or mate. Due to the range of descriptions in the UK which don't conform to known cats, some of the investigators have wondered about hybrids, and some of the eyewitnesses suggest this too, after agonising over what they've seen. Various websites, including Messybeast, explain some of the notorious felid hybrids which have been produced. They mainly comprise the weird and bizarre, for instance: the lion and the tiger making a 'liger', the puma and the leopard creating a 'pumapard', which showed dwarfism in some specimens, and a puma-ocelot, 'l'ocelot-puma'. Several others are listed on Messybeast. Many of these hybrid exhibits are more like captive freak shows than creatures which could evolve in the wild, capable of finding their niche and stalking their prey.

The 'mutant cat-like animal' discovered by Jonathan McGowan in August 2006 in Dorset. Its body was just over four feet long and its tail nearly the same length. Photo: Jonathan McGowan

People who consider hybrids in the mix of UK big cats suggest that there may have been a combination which does work and produces offspring with vigour, given the pressure for the low population base of cats to spread their genes. The hybrid advocates recognise that offspring from most mixes would in most cases be infertile or weak, suffering from, for instance, deformed spines. The options may be greater from the smaller-range cats discussed above, and then the matter of possible giganticism or the occasional outrageous mutation arises. A specimen which begs such questions is shown in Jonathan McGowan's photograph in this chapter, taken in Wiltshire. Jonathan stopped on the roadside, went to the decomposing body and was shocked by what he saw – an unrecognisable animal, most likely feline, four feet long in the body. 'Look! A lion!' said some startled passing cyclists as Jonathan inspected the flattened beast. Jonathan took two quick photos and was due to pick up the mouldering animal on his way home later that evening. He missed his chance for a spectacular autopsy, for on his return the body had been removed. There are many tantalising questions surrounding the classification of our vagrant cats, and hybrids is another on the list.

ADAPTATION THROUGH SELECTION PRESSURE – HAS IT BEGUN?

The prospect of adaptation in the UK's cats has already been raised in relation to pumas and it is hinted at elsewhere in the book. Leopard and puma, living in different habitats across the globe, vary across a range of forms and shades. They would seem, then, more than capable of achieving 'adaptive advantage', having found that adaptation allows them to survive in our landscape. Characteristics such as colour variants in their coats and a more cursorial, upright form to make longer runs at prey are examples of such possible adaptations, and some witness accounts seem to report these traits. This thinking is neatly explained in the following passage from Chris Johnston:

'Do we have our own British big cat? I don't mean vastly different from any other big cats around the world living in their natural habitat but slight subtle changes in their genotype and phenotype (observable form). If I use a black leopard as an example, all black leopards in Britain would have been released from different sources at different times, over decades, and this would have helped in a small way in creating greater genetic diversity but at some point inbreeding would have had to occur in the species.'
'Would this introduce health problems as a result of deleterious recessive genes and could a viable breeding population ever exist? The Amur leopard is trying to hold on in its natural range with

numbers varying around 50, this population is inbred but still survives. The Florida panther (the puma subspecies in Florida) faces the same fate, again numbers are critical at around 100 in the wild and inbreeding has resulted in some genetic deformities. As a result of isolation new species are formed, as can be observed in the clouded leopard. Genetic research has shown that clouded leopards living in isolation on Borneo and Sumatra are genetically different from clouded leopards on the mainland and have been classified as a new species. Could this be the same for black leopards geographically isolated and living in Britain?'

'Studies show that the clouded leopards on Borneo and Sumatra were isolated 1.5 million years ago and have had a much greater length of time to evolve than any black leopard inhabiting Britain but, without the evidence, who knows if the changes might already have begun? In one year from Exmoor I had reports of tan, red and grey pumas all in the same geographical area. Depending on its location in its natural habitat the puma comes in many shades of brown, from light tan to a red and grey. It would be unusual to find pumas with so many different colour morphs in the one area. Is this a result of a small puma population in Britain trying to create genetic diversity throughout the species, as has happened with the king cheetah?'

ALL FROM THE 1976 ACT? OR A CENTURY OF NATURALISING?

We will never know for sure how our vagrant cats came to be. Is there one source stock or several? Is it more about escapes or releases, or have a mix of circumstances fused these cats together in our outdoors? Cats are Houdinis – some will wander and sneak away if they can. Many situations, from circuses and zoos to domestic confinement, are likely to produce the odd wandering cat finding the leak in the system.

When interviewed on the UK's big cats for *The One Show* in 2010, I was given my script of questions by the thoughtful producer. One of them, for which I was not really prepared because I don't see it as pivotal, was: 'Please explain the origin of the cats from the 1976 Dangerous Wild Animals Act'. 'Can I also mention the 1981 Zoos Act, which clamped down on ramshackle zoos?' I asked. 'And what about ongoing unlicensed ownership – could I mention that?' There wasn't time. Viewers were to be fed the standard assumption that most big cats loose in Britain stem from releases after the '76 Act. This may be quick and easy for the media and it may be partly right, but it cannot be that simple. The Act may have triggered a big cat exodus into the wild, but I suspect that this was one of several such episodes.

The hastily-prepared Dangerous Wild Animals Act was a response to concerns about exotic animals being kept in domestic conditions. Wild cats of all descriptions, including pumas and tigers, had been reportedly walked in public, restrained with nothing more than a leash that you might use for your puppy. The Act gave these cat owners three choices: to pay for a licence (currently over £1,000, before insurance costs) and have a yearly check of the animal's compound by the local council; deposit the creature with a zoo or wildlife park; or have the animal put down. Quoted on the 1976 Act in *The Field* magazine in 2000, the late Quentin Rose said about big cats: 'I was working at Windsor Safari Park at the time, and we turned away hundreds'. And of course, another option may have occurred to people after the Act: to nudge one's beloved pet into the great outdoors.

A young puma is exercised in Kensington Gardens in 1974.
Photo: David Gear

A photograph shown here is of a juvenile puma being exercised in Kensington Gardens. David Gear, who took the photo, said that the Royal Parks police dog kept well back from the young animal. David learnt that the puma lived with the owners in their Chelsea flat. This was two years before the 1976 legislation. At that time, pumas and puma cubs were being advertised in *Exchange & Mart* for about £200. A zoological supply company operating up to the early 1970s apparently offered lions, tigers, pumas and panthers. Pumas, for example, can grow up tame if habituated from young, but ongoing costs, the need for responsible and secure conditions as required by the Act, along with a big cat's temperament under stress could all test the resolve of an owner.

Helping a large carnivore into the wild is hardly something you would broadcast to others. Several big cat researchers pick up whispers about such instances and I am no exception, knowing of possible cases across different regions. Sometimes the same gossip from different sources corroborates the tale, and sometimes several cats at a time may have been helped free, which may allow the potential to breed, as discussed above with lynx. The most specific and public admissions on freeing cats came in the following scoop by the *Yorkshire Post* on 29 January 2000:

'A former lion tamer has admitted he released a panther and a cougar into the countryside near Sheffield in the 1970s. Leslie Maiden, who once owned more than a dozen big cats, said he released the animals off the A57 Snake Pass in Derbyshire. He also said people in Sheffield had released big cats on the moors. 'I released a panther 26 years ago on to the moors on the Pennines at Snake Pass,' Mr Maiden, of Cradley Heath, near Dudley, West Midlands, told a BBC regional news programme. 'It was miles from anywhere. It was a couple of days after releasing a cougar,' he said… Mr Maiden added: 'I've always been an animal lover. But people came to me with the animals saying they would have to put them down. I had no option.' Fellow big cat owner Lewis Foley, 61, who kept the animals at a menagerie with Mr Maiden, disclosed that a friend of his in Coventry had set a panther loose in Nottinghamshire in 1974. Mr Foley said: 'He knew about the new laws and didn't want it put down.' Friends in Sheffield also set big cats loose on the Pennines, he added.'

In many parts of Britain, people in wildlife and zoo circles will speculate on who had cats, who had collections stashed in the outbuildings and which eccentric character kept caracals, golden cats, or bigger. Delivery drivers speak of a reclusive owner who collected 'pointy-eared exotic cats' at his country house in Gloucestershire. Where did they go when the property exchanged hands on his death? Does this explain my local jungle cat, or am I making a leap too far? There is debate about whether captive cats could readily catch their prey in the wild, or whether they would seek out human occupation once out on their own, associating humans with food supply, having been fed all their lives. While escaped pet cats have been quickly recaptured in several instances (including, it is thought, tigers) going feral is not that much of a challenge for a cat. While a cat coming from captivity may not have been taught to ambush and pick apart a deer, it would possess the skills and instincts to live off ever-present small prey like mice, voles, rabbits, pheasants and pigeons. These would not present a problem for any self-respecting cat to catch and consume.

Another potential source of roaming cats is the circus and the menagerie. On the Fairground Heritage Trust website, Dave Page makes the following points on travelling menageries:

'The advent of the travelling menagerie had more to do with cash for curiosity than any quest for understanding, and showmen realised there was a good living to be made in the exploitation of the exotic. Improvements in the sophistication of foreign trade, added to by the arrival of the British Empire, meant that animals of all kinds were involuntarily finding their way to Europe… In the 18th and 19th centuries, the only chance people who lived in villages and most towns ever had of seeing live wild animals was when a travelling menagerie visited their area… it is not unreasonable to conclude there were many animal shows on the road from the 1700s to the 1900s… Viewing animals in their cages, elephant rides and feeding times were all very well, but most people were there for the excitement of seeing the big cats and the trainers that risked their lives with them.'

Importers and dealers for menageries and collections were based in ports at London and Liverpool. They used contacts and agents across the world. With Malaysia's colonial history, it may well have been a key source of black leopards for the UK.

THE EARLY VAGRANT CATS

The earliest reported sighting at one of my talks was from 1931, in the Forest of Dean, by a lady's parents who watched a puma-type cat on a verge in the Forest. Others, though, can be found dotted around in archives and newspapers. In October 1816 a lion escaped its parked-up menagerie and attacked the horse of the Exeter Mail Coach at Winterslow Hut near Salisbury. Workers from the menagerie recaptured the lion after it fought off and killed a mastiff dog and passengers fled into the nearby Pheasant Inn. The mail coach was only 45 minutes late arriving in Exeter and the incident was celebrated in paintings by A. Sauerweid and James Pollard.

The *Daily Express* in January 1927 reported three lynx trapped and shot in Invernes-shire District. One was verified at London Zoo and they were assumed to have escaped a menagerie. In the 1930s the Royal Engineers were called out to shoot a black leopard near Blue Bell Hill close to Maidstone. Some reports speak of the owner of a large private zoo nearby acknowledging that it had escaped.

Wartime may have made keeping large carnivores particularly tough. Money and supplies of meat, in particular, would have been tight. Consequently, private collectors may have faced difficulties holding onto their large cats.

In *The Surrey Puma* by Roman Golicz, the author points out that within two and a half miles of Bushylease Farm near Crookham village, which a puma was known to have visited (see Chapter 10), there was an open space used by circus acts during the 1950s and 1960s for winter-

Right: Illustration of a puma re-capture in Surrey, c. 1900, after a puma escaped from a house in West Horsley
From C. Stephenson, 'A Puma Hunt in Surrey', in The Wide World Magazine, vol. XI.
Courtesy: Fortean Picture Library

Below: A puma living in a domestic situation in the USA, featured in the recent American documentary on house-bound exotic animals, 'The Elephant in the Living Room'. Photo © Michael Webber

ing their animals. The author concludes: 'The most likely origins for the Surrey Puma and the lynx are surely to be found at this site, involving unregistered animals whose escape went unreported for obvious reasons.' Elsewhere in the book, Golicz notes the number and variety of reports of possible large cats in Surrey and its hinterlands from the 1950s to the early 1970s. These include the log of alleged sightings – 'the puma day book' – which contained 388 individual entries from September 1964 to November 1973. Not all the reports fitted puma descriptions and some seemed to have supplementary clues suggesting a mistaken identity.

In Australia and Britain it is known that American World War II pilots brought over live pumas as mascots, to make their military insignia come to life. Sources quoted in the Australian literature speak informally of a location in Victoria used as a repository for the live pumas that their masters did not wish to destroy. We may ask if the same thing happened in middle England. Big cats like pumas and black leopards have also been used as guard animals – in Australia for some of the settlers' mines and in England for scrap metal dealers in Sheffield, where they deterred staff from discarding items over the fence, to be collected and sneaked home after a shift. Once again, one wonders what happened to these tethered beasts on their retirement?

A mass tracking party goes in search of the Shooters Hill Cheetah in southeast London in 1963 after a policeman claimed to have seen a cheetah take its prey into a wood by the roadside. Perhaps the animal heard them coming?
Photo: Fortean Picture Library

*Exotic cats held in domestic environments can create local disputes, as illustrated here in 2006.
Photo: Mathew Frith*

THE CURRENCY OF CATS

Moving on from these reports from the past, it might be naïve to assume that no releases or escapes happen today. A cheetah escaped from a wildlife park in Cambridgeshire in 2008 and was quickly recaptured, but not before demonstrating that zoos can still have problems with their fences. But what about the unlicensed ownership of big cats? It could well be happening given the scale of the trade in exotic animals and the wildlife trafficking which evades the governance of CITES, the Convention on International Trade in Endangered Species of Wild Fauna and Flora. The illegal wildlife trade often focuses on prominent individuals who use networks of agents across countries and can quickly supply creatures ranging from rare reptiles to cats. Because captive animals are not covered by CITES, these dealers and smugglers have used false zoo labels as part of their tactics. Wildlife trafficking is reckoned to be one of the most profitable illegal trades, and there will be strong incentives for some people living amongst prime wildlife habitats to provide wild fauna from their locality.

One particular off-duty police officer once told me of his own big cat sighting from his home in Gloucestershire. He mentioned that his role with the police was training in firearms. As part of that position he was updated on the register of animals that managed to find their way out of confinement. He stressed that we should not be surprised if the occasional big cat did a runner, for over time the list of vanised animals contained 'anything and everything'.

The interest shown in keeping exotic pets in previous decades lives on, although the desire to build a leopard compound in your garden might not find favour with your neigbours, as the newspaper hoarding shows on page 129. A recent award winning documentary from America, 'The Elephant in the Living Room' illustrates the infatuation people have with keeping captive wild creatures and looks at the implications of doing so.

Even the above-board ownership of exotic cats in Britain makes interesting reading, giving us a flavour of current trends. Here is a snippet on a survey undertaken by Shaun Stevens for Big Cats in Britain in 2007:

> In 2007 Big Cats in Britain published the results of my 2006 Freedom of Information requests to local authorities regarding the number of wild animals being kept by the general public under the Dangerous Wild Animals Act. Police files were uncovered by contacting the various police and government authorities. There was me thinking I could email all the requests in a couple of days. Big mistake! But after a lot of research, three months of work and over 600 emails and letters, the information we received was eye-opening. The key results revealed the following animals kept by licensed private owners in England, Wales and Scotland in 2006: 154 big cats, including 12 lions, 14 tigers, 50 leopards, plus 500 assorted monkeys, 50 crocodiles, and snakes, ostriches and the like – here was the confirmation that plenty of weird and wonderful exotic creatures live in domestic situations, and one can guess that many more might do so without a licence. The subsequent press release was picked up by Reuters and flashed all round the world, leading to news reports in places as far away as Mexico, Tibet and New Zealand. To be in print worldwide was extraordinary, and shows the interest in this subject.

THE GENETIC FLOW

Does the origin of the cats matter? There are a variety of mega-cats here, with effects which are good, bad and indifferent. Surely that's what counts now? But maybe the origins do matter if they can tell us something about these animals and help us think about the future. Let's take the pumas as an example. If they have bred and then ebbed and flowed in numbers from a limited source, we might face the situation in which Florida finds itself now. The Florida panther (*Puma concolor coryi*) is sadly in trouble. This flagship species once roamed all of the southeastern United States, but now the remaining population is isolated in South Florida where its habitat is shrinking due to over-development. It may be a challenge to hang onto the weak genetic strain of this subspecies of puma. There are

now just 100 or so individuals left, so when some get smashed on highways, it really does matter. Captive breeding is part of the drive to save this distinct brand of the puma, and more highway underpasses have been created to make safer territorial routes. Another key action was taken in 1994, when eight female pumas were captured in Texas, the nearest wild population (but of *Puma concolor stanleyana*), then quarantined and radio collared before being introduced to south Florida to allow interbreeding and strengthen the genetic stock of the residue Florida panthers. The process is called genetic introgression. There has been a more reproductive puma population in Florida following the exercise.

On the face of it, an accidental puma population in Britain might provide a parallel to the problem in Florida and the fragility of the animals' status there, but does it in practice? Perhaps not, for two main reasons. Firstly, the population may have been intermittently topped up with new individuals, adding to the genetic mix; and secondly, the founder population may have been from different sources anyway. So we may have had ongoing genetic introgression by default. And genetically-diverse populations may also have developed for melanistic leopards and for lynx. These are the great unknowns with our big cats. Have they genetic health or not? In what ways might they adapt their behaviour and form? And might any kind of mutation have occurred? Are the populations on the up or down, or regulating themselves? And, in time, would characteristics develop amongst the populations which were worthy of a subspecies status? We won't know until we look into it.

If by now you are confused with the candidates for our big and our medium-sized cats, then join the club. I wonder if we will ever satisfy ourselves about the types and the lineage of the cats in our midst. Even when we get more and better photos to help identify one or two, this will not provide 'the answer'. And one black leopard found dead on the roadside or identified conclusively on a trail camera won't mean that all the other dark panthers fit the bill. Once we do have more close-up evidence, though, we may be in for a shock.

BLOBS IN THE DISTANCE – A FEW SNAPSHOTS

If we want to have close-up photographs of Britain's cryptic big cats, then there will need to be more people on the case with trail cameras. It is a mistake to think that people with mobile phones and pocket cameras will achieve clinching photos of some of the most elusive animals. This rarely happens in these cats' main host countries.

The most conclusive pictures are those involving moving footage, as this is tougher to contrive and the scale and the movement can be better judged. The main examples of moving footage come from people filming in their back gardens or on their property, having seen a cat, expecting

CAT SPECIES – COMPARISON SIZES
Indicative adult weight and size ranges spanning female and male

The table below is based on various literature and web sources and has been discussed with UK zoologists. It is offered as a guide to show proportional scales of the UK's officially present and main candidate feral cats. Note that both adult leopards and pumas in some environments, including forest locations, can be smaller than the scales indicated here, as the opening text of this chapter explains.

Cat type	Scientific name	Adult weight (kg)	Head and body length (cm)	Tail length (cm)	Height at shoulder (cm)
Domestic feral cat	*Felis catus*	3–6	40–55	25–35	30–35
Scottish wildcat (European wild cat)	*Felis sylvestris grampia*	3–7	45–70	21–30	25–40
Jungle cat	*Felis chaus*	6–14	60–75	35–38	35–38
Lynx (Eurasian lynx)	*Lynx lynx*	17–30	80–130	11–24	60–70
Puma (cougar, mountain lion)	*Felis concolor*	36–103	96 195	53–78	60–70
Leopard (black panther)	*Panthera pardus*	28–90	91–191	58–98	45–78

it again, and having equipment to hand. Examples of such achievements include:

Rhosemary Rhodes' filming of a big black panther on her land in Bodmin in 1993

William Rooker's film of the slim and upright cat on his land in Cambridgeshire in 1994, dubbed the 'Fen Tiger'

The Wirral cat, on a Cheshire golf course, but filmed from a garden in 2003, thought to be a puma or an Asian golden cat

Other good quality moving footage of what appear to be panther-like animals include:

Adrian Hodges' 1992 footage of a black panther walking in Worcestershire countryside near South Littleton, taken while he was birdwatching (see page 151)

Ray Taylor's footage of a black panther in a China clay quarry, filmed in 1999 and re-scaled as a large adult leopard or jaguar-sized cat

Sky TV's *Big Cat Tracks* has been broadcast several times in recent years, showing footage of a large black cat in Leicestershire and a black panther on Dorset downland, both re-scaled as significant in size

Inverclyde: A puma-like cat walking on a road at Inverclyde, Greenock in 2007, available on YouTube

Left: A cat carrying a rabbit in its mouth, photographed by Selwyn Jolly at Morvah, Cornwall, in 1988. Re-scaling it using the wall measurements showed it was 91cm from head to rump.
Photo: ©Nigel Brierly/Fortean Picture Library

Right: A cat sitting on a rock, photographed by Tim Young at Zennor, Cornwall, in 1988. The photograph was taken at a distance of 200 yards. Re-scaling of the photo indicated that the top of the cat's head was 3 feet from the ground.
Photo: ©Nigel Brierly/Fortean Picture Library

There are several other passable clips, including one made during a balloon trip over Exmoor, in which a bounding leopard-like cat keeps pausing for breath as it is flees from the noise of the air balloon. Others show panther-scale cats walking confidently (or, in some cases, going like a rocket) across farmland. Other grainy glimpses of possible panthers can be seen on YouTube, including sightings from Hertfordshire, Herefordshire and Shropshire. In total there are more stills and videos than people imagine, and while many of them are not scaled or can be debated at length, they combine to give more clout to the case. A few more are set out here which may be of interest.

Left: Phil Buck photographed this 'panther-sized cat' in Oxfordshire in 2005. He and the landlord of the nearby pub had seen the cat in the vicinity several times but had kept it quiet to avoid the animal being harassed. Once the animal was no longer being seen, the photo was displayed at the Masons Arms pub.
Photo: Phil Buck

Above: A photograph claimed to have been taken in Cornwall in 2007, showing what appears to be a puma-like cat. Some people suggest this is a lioness in the African savannah. The photographer does not wish the location to be identified, but Google Earth shows the landform and vegetation to match the alleged location in Cornwall. Photo: Frank Tunbridge

Above: Chris Swallow captured footage on his mobile phone of this cat scenting in the railway embankment scrub and then walking along the rail head at Helensburgh in Scotland in 2009. A Royal Navy dog handler, he was at a friend's house overlooking the railway when he saw what he at first thought was a Labrador dog loose on the line, which he thought he would need to help. He was 30 metres away at the time. On realising it was a large cat he ran to the car for his mobile phone and managed several seconds of footage. He gauged it to be an intermediate-size cat, much bigger than a domestic mog but not a five-foot-long panther. Scaling the animal is possible from the railway track width (143.5 cm) and one rail engineer calculated it at 74 cm head and body length, confirming PC Swallow's hunch. The footage taken in July 2009 was widely shown in the media at the time. Photo: Chris Swallow with stills provided by Mark Fletcher

Left: Carol Cowley watched what she feels was a panther chasing something in long grass, during a dawn walk on the Sussex downs in July 2011. She managed to photograph it emerging at the field edge, then left the area immediately, not wanting her Jack Russell to be vulnerable. Sussex big cat researcher Charlie Bones felt the animal was 'the real deal' after visiting the location and assessing the animal's scale, which he felt was over two feet long in the body. Photo: Carol Cowley

HOW MANY CATS AND WHERE DO THEY GO?

'For him the dirt track is just one segment of a convenient path leading toward localized prospects of what he wants and needs: food, water, mating, and comfy repose. Having travelled along the roadside under cover of darkness, at first light he turns off and melts into the woods. I arrive with all my questions and notions, about half an hour later. By then he's gone. What remains are his pugmarks, impressive but transitory.'

Monster of God: the man eating predator in the jungles of history and the mind. David Quammen, Pimlico, 2005

COUNTING THE INVISIBLE

I was caught off guard. A national newspaper, one of the broadsheets, had heard I was preparing a book on the UK's big cats and wanted to know more. 'People just don't know about these cats around them, but need to,' said the correspondent. 'What are the numbers? That's what we all need to know,' the journalist went on. 'Quite right!' I thought. 'Good for you for wanting to look at the bigger picture.' It is exactly the right question, but it's also an absurd question, not that the journalist would know. I was tempted to fudge my reply but decided to play it straight. I told her that even with some radio-tracked animals to give us an indication, we could then only extrapolate and make an informed guess and we were a long way from that stage. But the journo wanted something tangible and was clearly dissatisfied. The conversation was deflating – a respected daily paper felt a book was badly needed, but implied mine was of little use. Hard facts and real numbers were needed and little else would do.

Stating a firm number of big cats currently roaming the UK is such a stab in the dark that it risks undermining your credibility. But it's worth contemplating because of the issues it throws up, issues that go to the core of the subject. At a national meeting of Big Cats in Britain members in 2007, I helped to run a session on 'How many cats?' The participants split into three groups to argue the case for the numbers they felt might be present of all types and sizes of exotic cats living wild in Britain. The task was to assert and to justify not just the panther- and puma-sized animals but the likes of jungle cat and leopard cat too. Nobody thought that there were no big cats, so we agreed that people would select one of the following groups: the lowest group went for 0–50 cats (about six members), the middle group decided on 50–500 cats (most of the participants were in this group) and the highest group skipped a stage, confidently declaring that it would defend the proposition of over 1000 cats. The four members of the 1000+ group were not just anybody: they were seasoned pros. A couple were the ones who went out tracking most often, in the night, in all weathers, on their own as they wanted no noise, and they were the ones who'd been most rewarded. Between them, I guessed they'd seen the 0–50 argued by the first group. If you asked some of them why they hadn't got photos they would laugh, and remind you that they were out tracking, not armed with clever equipment. At the meeting, each group had half an hour to prepare its case to justify the chosen number before each group presented their case to the whole gathering. In the final discussion we asked if anyone had been persuaded to change their view. Among the few that had, the revisions were upwards, with a couple from the 0–50 group feeling they had been too cautious. Here is the gist of the arguments each group proposed:

Summary of views on numbers of feral exotic cats living wild in the UK,
Big Cats in Britain conference, Tropiquaria Zoo, Somerset, 2007

0–50 big cats

- No breeding
- The same animal seen many times by different people, featuring in several sightings, giving the impression of greater numbers of cats
- The cats not widely distributed in Britain. Restricted to a few areas
- Just a handful of actual panther-type cats and of puma-type cats, supplemented by an assortment of lynx, jungle cats and others

50–500 big cats

- One cat featuring in many sightings (as in the 0–50 group)
- Breeding happening in places, but limited
- Breeding may not result in ongoing viable populations
- Breeding may be uneven and some areas and regions may have few cats and limited or no breeding

1000+ big cats

- The cats well-distributed, with territories established throughout many parts of Britain. There may be clusters unevenly distributed across certain regions making up a meta-population of each type of cat

- Breeding has become a routine pattern of the cats' behaviour
- Areas of good habitat and plentiful prey can be used by different cats
- The cats in some locations and counties are not well logged as there are no proactive investigators to whom people can report sightings
- Occasional further releases are topping up the breeding population and adding to genetic variety and health

There is a rider to this debate about assessing the hidden cats. One of the 1000+ group, Shaun Stevens, has now scaled back his estimate. He now feels the figure is far lower. Shaun's go-getting approach for evidence and photos has been stifled at every turn. His trail cameras have delivered a bigger-than-average feral cat and the top section of a larger-looking unidentifiable cat, as reproduced earlier in the book. But the prize panther eludes him. I appreciate Shaun's change of mind, even though I disagree with him. I have combed the secret valleys of Gloucestershire following the scent of the cats, and I have laid the camera traps: I know the frustrations. The great game hunters who wrote of their exploits, like Kenneth Anderson and Jim Corbett in India, had their patience tested as they pursued giant felines and lay in wait to despatch the rare man-eater cats that were troubling communities. As well as relating to the ways of the cats and merging with the jungle, they knew that cunning, resourcefulness and waiting, exactly as exhibited by the cats themselves, was part of the art, part of the mindset for meeting the predator.

A view over Gloucestershire commons, hills and valleys. Big black cat sightings are reported on the common in the foreground, the valley below, wooded hills in the middle distance, and woodland along the Cotswold scarp slope immediately to the left of the view. Could these areas be the range of one big cat or could several different ones have been seen?

THINKING LIKE THE PREDATOR

The trail cameras we use today are part of the waiting. Much easier and quieter than a night-time vigil, they are a remote lens in the landscape. With just a few dotted around, we hardly give ourselves a chance to find the roaming cats, but the cameras are a great aid to our learning and thinking. Hand-sized contraptions, tied to a tree and aimed at angles to observe what passes, they have a better chance when baited, and lavender oil, valerian-hops oil, cat nip or perfume can all be drizzled onto moss or bark to provide an inviting waft, designed to draw animals in. The dropping from a domestic cat can also be used to alert a fellow feline. For edible bait, Frank has smeared dog food into bark to tempt any wild carnivores and to make them hang around. Dead rabbits have been strung to branches and I've twice recycled road-kill deer carcasses. The bait must make the animal linger and be hard to snatch away. Another trick is to set cameras near pools, springs and streams, allowing a water source to be the natural bait. The trail cameras are our best chance to study and snap the cats up close, something we could rarely, if ever, do in the wild, where a roaming cat remains a smudge in the distance if you see it at all. Most modern trail cameras provide still photos or video clips, and the moving footage may be better. It shows the animal's intent and behaviour, and any still photo is open to accusations of tampering.

Frank Tunbridge sets up a trail camera under a major road bridge where he tracked a possible cat in Gloucestershire. He later found people disturbing the camera and so removed it after a few days.

The cameras are now integral to the sleuthing but they bring other rewards. They are part of a wider process of tracking which forces you to think like the target animal itself. Where's the best water source? Where do you cross a deep stream? Which are the efficient routes through the land, by day and by night? Where are the vantage points in the landscape? Where is the ambush cover? Which are the limbs of a tree to scale and from which to survey the land? What might be setting off the birds' high-level warning calls in the wood? New features and new dimensions appear in the landscape when you assess it like a giant cat, a crepuscular stalker. You do the cat's own watching, thinking and roaming.

Tucking away the cameras at optimum points is an exasperating process. Even knowing the very field where a cat has been thought to strike at sheep, there can be no obvious entry points, or those that are may be conspicuous, risking damage or theft to the equipment. One or two cameras out on a farm might seem to give you a chance, but arriving to install them, the realisation dawns: the field dimensions, the array of hedges, the lengths of stream and many scrubby corners can seem like a chasm into which to tuck away a remote pair of digital eyes.

Earning landowners' trust is a key element of tracking cats. The link with a farmer becomes an important partnership, with different perspectives on where the predator would range, what might have made unusual calls and why livestock or horses are acting out of character or becoming shy of familiar field corners or gates. Enjoying the camera results and wildlife clips with farming families, other landowners, gardeners, and wildlife experts becomes a special time. The cameras expose surprises, an array of wildlife doing its own thing, each in its niche. I've seen bounding March hares stretched out like deer, strutting and moon-walking herons, vixens calling their cubs, the occasional bat shimmering past and the tiny bright eyes of mice, reflecting back at me as they spring in the pasture at night. There are ubiquitous comedy pheasants peering at the lens, badgers' bums, foxes' tails, and rabbits munching away in every other scene. Three times I've enjoyed watching the surprised reaction of farmers on seeing deer they had assumed were not on their land. Delightful though these creatures may be, caught in their secret world, they are all potential prey for the new alpha cat. Where there is something to eat there is something to eat it. Not yet on my cameras, a random needle in a gargantuan haystack, I'm sure the beast is there. Surely it's only temporarily away? Or maybe, just maybe, Shaun is right.

THE CAT IN ITS TERRITORY – TANTALISING SIGNS

To understand a photo it helps to know the context. The one offered here shows a cat in stubble in the Wiltshire countryside near Swindon. I can hear cautious cat tracker friends writing it off as a 'large feral' or be-

*The long-bodied cat in 12-inch high stubble in north
Wiltshire, photographed by Wilf Ashman in 2007 and seen
later in further stages of growth.*
Photo: Wilf Ashman

moaning the lack of scale. The scale is certainly imperfect, but it lies in
the stubble, much higher than usual, for this was 2007, the soggy summer, when half of the southwest of England seemed afloat. With water-
logged and fudgy ground, the stubble was cut higher and much later that
year. It measures a foot where this cat appears, so we have an animal of 15
or 16 inches at the shoulder, long in the body, clearly feral and stealthy,
and seen several times on the same territorial route. 'I've watched it grow
up,' says Wilf Ashman, the deer manager who took the photograph, a
seasoned pro who is well known in the area for his experience and advice
to young people in the game industry. He urges them to be subtle and
discriminating in their approach to game shooting. He has ably demonstrated his stalking qualities by photographing a cat he was ready for, way
out in the fields, something few people have managed. 'It's not a normal
feral cat. We've got those around the place and this is different and bigger,' says Wilf.

He has seen it five times in four years, as a juvenile and now as a 'five-
foot-long black panther.' 'Its tail now touches the ground as it ambles.
Its body sways as it walks, like a women's hips,' he observes. 'Every time
I think about shooting it I'm too busy with the binoculars, working out
what it is.' I asked him where he felt the territory was. He spoke of friends
and contacts who see a similar cat three miles south, and another five
miles west. But is it the same one? 'Who knows?' he asks. 'Some of my
stalking friends can't understand how they are out as much as me, all

hours, in high seats, and never see a big cat like some of the others claim. But it doesn't work like that.'

A roe deer buck in north Wiltshire consumed within six hours of being dispatched by Wilf Ashman in the evening and recovered by him early the next morning. Photo: Wilf Ashman

He has watched the cat stalking a fox, and he has seen the results of its eating habits. A freshly-consumed roe deer marked the route of the now-adult panther. We can see the roe buck carcass photo reproduced above. A cat didn't despatch it, Wilf did. He shot it through the heart at 10.30 one summer evening – the exit point can be seen in the picture. The deer petered out into the wood so Wilf decided to return in the morning in search of the carcass. He got up early, reaching the body at 4.30 a.m. But a night-time visitor had beaten him to it. The photo here shows what he found. Ignore the mark at the neck – Wilf was preparing to remove the head before he realised that a photo of the predator's work would be useful. Nothing at the rump end remained, all was consumed in the six-hour window, cleanly and with the cat's tell-tale razor shearing. 'It would take foxes four days and nights to get it like that,' he said.

MELTING INTO THE VALLEY

This is the cue for Coryn Memory of the Stroud area. She describes her experience of several big cat sightings below. The local newspaper reported

Photo: Gloucestershire Media

one of her accounts alongside a stock photo of a snarly black panther. Coryn is keen to stress that although she watched what she believes is the same cat on six different occasions, at no time did it resemble the fang-bearing beast depicted in the paper. Coryn's sightings are important. She has seen what appears to be a territorial route, and she has examined much of it thoroughly. She has noticed gaps in hedges and crossover points at the canal, the railway, and the cyclepath. She's considered likely bottlenecks for a cat moving through the valley, the nooks in the landscape essential for the route from A to B. What Coryn has seen may soon become shared and better known, and help us appreciate more about the life of our king cats. Here is her account of the experience:

'I have seen a black big cat on six occasions over an 18-month period in 2009–2010, in the fields near my house. It was roughly the size of a leopard, and had a very long tail. Although it could have been a leopard, I cannot say for sure what actual type of cat it was. It appeared to be on its way somewhere and followed the same trail on all six occasions. During the snowy period of January 2010 my sceptical neighbour saw the cat walking up our road and into the field; it stopped to sniff my son's motorbike and when her dog barked it ran off into the field. Personally I am fascinated by these beautiful creatures and feel that they have as much right to live in our landscape as any other wildlife. They are clearly an established part of the British countryside and I believe they should be left alone. Historically they have posed no threat to humans and as their prey seems to be deer, rabbits, etc, shouldn't we be glad to have a predator which will help to control these animals? Study them and research them, yes, but also offer them protection.'

If more of these animals were as obliging as Coryn's observed cat, we'd have a better chance of occasionally peering into their lives. Some impatient commentators suggest it should be possible to tail the cats, given their routes and their signs. But this assumes full-time dedication to the cause. It is optimistic to assume the cats are wholly consistent and any tracks and signs are mostly traceable – mostly, they are not. Like the Scarlet Pimpernel they are masters of concealment. The plotted routes of radio-collared cats abroad show their habits: they twist and they zig-zag about in their range. They can be away from particular parts for weeks and months, and when they do pass back it may be as a brief flash in the darkest hours.

LIFE UNDER COVER

In much of their lifestyle the cats are troglodytes. They dwell under straggly fallen trees, in rock fissures, hidden pipes and tunnels, in abandoned cars. They will know the lay-up sites and the denning areas on their beat, and they will have several options. They work by scent and smells, of others and their own, along with the occasional call. They rest and sleep for most of the time, preserving their energy. They will be up and active for just the odd few hours.

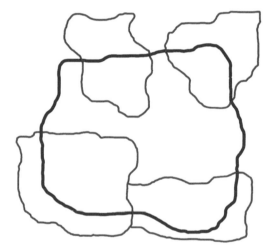

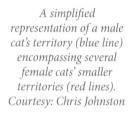

A simplified representation of a male cat's territory (blue line) encompassing several female cats' smaller territories (red lines). Courtesy: Chris Johnston

The cats are loners. Once juveniles have left or been pushed out from the mother at around 18 months, they are singular in their lifestyle. They avoid encounters with fellow felines, as scraps will be dangerous to them. Their eyes, nose, teeth and claws are their tools and the means of their survival, not to be put at risk. The territorial wandering is about securing the right to mate, taking opportunities presented by the prey and ensuring an equilibrium of energy. Strength must be conserved for hunting, stalking and the crucial ambush, the few metres' spring at prey. Efficient routes across the land are key. The predator cannot guarantee its next refuelling so must minimise effort at every stage. Conserving energy may also mean there is no need to stash a deer or other larger prey up a tree. Why waste the effort if there are no scavengers to see off? A male's range will extend over several female territories and the boundaries of each will be scented and marked. The male is drawn to a female by the distinct smell of her scent when in oestrus, or at the sound of a call to mate. This kind of call is the most penetrating of the cats' vocalisation. Exmoor Zoo told me they could hear Ebony, their female black leopard, at a range between 150 and 500 metres, depending on wind conditions, but something we cannot detect is the frequency vibration, which may be picked up much further by any cat in range.

Our text books on the cats are yet to be written. If ever they are, the rules of the territories will be fundamental to our knowledge. It is the key question: what drives the cat to move as it does, when and where, and to keep away or interact with others? Of course it is likely to follow the deer, to lurk where water birds congregate in winter, to lay-up near scrub overrun with rabbits and to forage on freshly-cut summer pastures, where the mice and voles are exposed. But does it do this while tolerating other cats, because sharing the range makes no difference? Or would it see them off, wanting its lone living space? Does a cat here need to put effort into defending a territory, as in the tough conditions in some of the cats' ranges in Asia or Africa, where boundaries are often tightly demarcated and prey is precious? We can only speculate how territories may work here, but the UK cats may not be so possessive of their patch – the stakes may not be so high.

SPREADING THE GENES

A sightings report will sometimes tell of more than one cat, mostly two but occasionally three, and once, to me, of four around a carcass. People speak of calls being made between two co-operating cats, and sometimes of a mother with young. There is one crucial factor implied by this sort of account: a breeding population. 'The pointy-eared ones were going at it all day on my neighbour's land' said an Exmoor farmer to me once, referring, I presume, to copulating lynx. Many witnesses are ultra-guarded when reporting cats seen with cubs. Locations remain top secret: people feel extra-protective of what they've seen. During 2010 I was informed of three separate cases of what were accurate descriptions of puma kits, from three separate counties in southern England. Jonathan McGowan once watched what he believed were puma kits playing on heathland in Dorset. His evocative sketch of the boisterous youngsters is reproduced in this chapter. He was photographing raft spiders on the heath, and aware of the backs of mammals ahead of him, sunken in the scrub. He assumed they were sika deer, common grazers of the area's acid-loving vegetation, but in a three-second rush, he saw two feline youngsters tumble together, spring up, and melt back into the dense furze.

Amongst the range of accounts of two cats seen together, here is one from Somerset, as described in the area's paper, the *Midsomer Norton People*, in August 2010. The paper relayed a large black cat sighting, after which a number of people came forward with further accounts from the area. One of those who made contact was Robert Stokes, who said he had seen two giant black cats in woodland near Litton during a walk with his daughter in March 2004. Mr Stokes said that if it were not for the fact that his daughter also saw the two cats, he would not have believed it. 'When we saw them, they were chasing deer. I saw the first one and said, 'That looks like a puma or something!' Then, lo and behold, about 15 metres behind it was another, exactly the same. If we had not been together I would have started to doubt what I had seen. We were not brave enough to follow them but a few days later we went back and found a skeleton of a deer.'

Jonathan McGowan's illustration of his fleeting glimpse of puma kits playing on Dorset heathland. Courtesy: Jonathan McGowan

Apart from police forces stating that there is evidence of cats breeding, and people claiming that they see the very act, set out below are some of the factors that provide the case for breeding.

THE CASE FOR A BREEDING POPULATION

The quantity, geographical extent, and continuity of sightings, year upon year, over four or five decades, suggests more than a small and isolated population of large feral cats failing to interact and to mate. The average lifespan of a big cat in the wild is usually assumed to be around 12 years.

Mating observed: actual mating is observed and heard, and mating calling sounds are reported. Over the years such calls have been consistently more commonly reported in the winter months in Gloucestershire. Mating is a serial activity over more than one day. It could be argued that it is surprising that such activity is not more widely observed or heard, although people are naïve to the sounds of cats, and the activity would occur more at night and remotely. Observing mating cats may also be subject to low levels of reporting amongst witnesses.

Individual cats observed as looking pregnant or appearing to be lactating due to swollen teats. Very few instances of such observations are on record. I know of three.

Cubs and kits are reported, albeit irregularly (puma young are 'kittens', other cats' young are 'cubs'). People's reports of young cats seem mostly accurate and most informants seem particularly cautious and emotionally affected when making such reports.

Two or more cats reported together: as noted above, reports of more than one cat together are made in low proportions but as a continuing feature of the sightings. Two cats together could mean male or female meeting up (the male can be up to a third larger in size); a mother with one juvenile; two juveniles still together; or two sub-adults still co-operating before life in their sole territory. A mother may tolerate a daughter in her territory according to observations of the cats in their official countries.

Amount of consumption of a carcass: research reports suggest that consumption of 18 pounds is possible for a leopard in one sitting and up to 41 pounds for a large puma. These are upper-range figures for larger-than-average cats. Individual cats and an area's populations of cats will vary depending on key prey species. Cats taking large deer as a key part of their diet will therefore tend to be larger than those predominantly consuming rabbits, hares and smaller deer. Farmers have reported eaten-out sheep dispatched and completely consumed overnight, and freshly-eaten deer have been found with significant and sometimes whole consumption in one night. Scavenging can occur and add to a large carnivore's initial consumption, but the number of wholly- and near-wholly consumed carcasses reported and seen suggests that, on some occasions, more than one cat has fed from the carcass.

Clinically-despatched prey is a taught behaviour: the carcasses of large prey killed and partly consumed show the hallmarks of large predatory cats. In the wild, mothers teach their young to hunt and dispatch prey, so the efficiency with which the prey is captured suggests taught behaviour. However, this possible pointer to breeding is not clear cut, as escaped and released cats from captive origins would have to deploy hunting skills to survive, although in such instances they may stick to smaller prey which they could instinctively catch, rather than ambush larger and more specialist prey such as deer

THE PLOT THICKENS – IN A DIFFERENT HEMISPHERE

It would seem that the cryptic cats are not just in Britain. Far away in the Australian bush, another set of mystery felids roam. And they are not just in the outback…

'I thought the talk about big cats was bullshit,' said Australian hunter Kurt Engel. His brash quote comes from the celebrated case in Gippsland, Victoria, in 2005. Kurt is the only person to publicly admit, explain and photograph the shooting of a very large cat in a land where they are not meant to be. Alas, he says he kept the tail but floated the body away in the river, although he claims that he quickly realised his error. We are left with his plausible photo of the freshly-dispatched body, his detailed testimony and a DNA analysis of hair, recording *Felis catus* – domestic cat. I'm not wholly convinced by the analysis, but a weird mutation such as this has certainly been considered by researchers amongst the explanations for unofficial panthers.

We can read a full account of the Kurt Engel incident, and see the strung-up carcass, in the riveting book *Australian Big Cats*, published in 2010. Across Australia the scale and the distribution of reported sightings, incidents, and kangaroo and livestock kills is surprising – there may be some clusters and hotspots in parts of Victoria and New South Wales, close to more settled areas, but 'evidence' of various sorts comes from many other parts of the great landmass. Even Western Australia, where there is less of a population to notice out-of-place creatures, has its accounts.

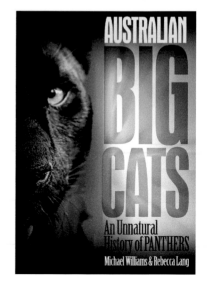

Theories for the origins of the Australian cats include early circuses and menageries, the guarding animals of miners, puma mascots of US airmen and more recent escapes and releases. Much of this chimes with the ideas about the cats' origins in the UK and, just as in Britain, the Aussie reports go back decades, suggesting that this is a far from recent phenomenon. The candidate Australian cats are mainly similar to ours, but the authors are tentative: they prefer to leave the case open on identities. But while cats masquerading as black leopards and pumas, or similar, may be around, the lynx seems absent from evidence and reports – Oz is a long way from any source stock.

So there are some fairly orthodox notions about what the cats are, but the plot thickens. Australia is distinct in its marsupials and its iconic carnivores like the recently apparently-extinct thylacine and the long-gone marsupial lion, *Thlacoleo carnifex*. Surely these cannot account for some of the alleged glimpses and tracks? Well, if you're into cryptozoology, there are some livestock kills and witness accounts which have raised suspicions of ancient creatures like these being in the reckoning. Overall, it's a chasm of a continent, impenetrably rugged in places. Maybe there are still some surprises, but I'll stick to something I know a little about. The cats alone are sufficiently interesting to me.

A REDNECK RESPONSE?

Unlike in the UK, I don't detect that there are many camps of people with sympathy for the big cats of Australia. Rural Oz is famed for being redneck and it seems the cats are pretty much regarded as alien carnivores, menacing the livestock and the indigenous wildlife. It's an understandable reaction, although kangaroos and rabbits must offer the cats abundant scraps as a mainstay of their diet. The Australian bush is already sufficiently wild and challenging for most Aussies' tastes – a new apex predator isn't that welcome, it appears.

A Smashed Roo' – the eaten-out carcass of a swamp wallaby (Wallabia bicolor) at Arcadia in New South Wales, Australia. This location yields 5–10 sightings of big cats a year and other suspicious kills are reported, according to researcher and author Mike Williams. Photo: Samantha Yazbek

Despite the demands of farmers for action and follow-up to their reports and their livestock losses, several inquiries in Australia have been inconclusive or, for the farmers, too half-hearted. Nobody – no organisation, no bureaucrat, at national or state level – wants to get proactive on big cats. It is easy to turn the blame onto dogs and dingoes, shrug off the stories and keep one's head down. Some officials in land-based organisations have been interested and have informally reported the evidence but, as in Britain, nobody rocks the boat.

The accounts from Britain and from Oz are independent yet similar in so many ways, from the animals seen to the field evidence and the human reactions. Perhaps this international corroboration is evidence in itself.

THINKING AHEAD

Back in Britain, should we think about the whole picture and consider what's happening amongst our mystery cats, as the newspaper reporter asked? How widely are the cats spread, to what extent are they breeding and, crucially, will the numbers be viable in future, decade upon decade? Straight away, though, we are thwarted by not knowing the basics. To have a feel for this overall picture we would have to know something about any clusters of populations, the numbers of breeding females, and transient cats which might go within and beyond the clusters. In 2000, *The Field* magazine interviewed the late Quentin Rose, a wild animal consultant who knew much about big cats, advising farmers and the police. At the time, Rose suggested that, based on his assessment, there were 100 cats of all different types, which was about as informed as you could get. *The Field* magazine's March 2000 issue proclaimed his 'A Hundred Big Cats Living Wild in Britain' on its front cover. Quentin Rose also predicted numbers would rise sharply once breeding began, according to mammal and predator population dynamics. We may be in this expansion phase now but, this is finger in the air stuff. As Trevor Beer points out later in this book, the cats could regulate their numbers and cub mortality is mostly high. There is no substitute for studying the animals themselves, as daunting a task as that may be.

Some scenarios to think about are set out below. Take your pick, depending on the numbers you might consider plausible:

Big cats wild in UK – possible scenarios

None: no big cats living wild

Few: a few escapes or releases, now feral. Low numbers, uneven distribution. A temporary issue

Breeding but unviable: breeding is occurring, topped up with occasional escapes and/or releases, but there is no genetically healthy population base to sustain breeding into future decades

Breeding and viable: breeding is occurring, topped up with escapes/releases. There may be sufficient genetic diversity in the population, due to the different origins of the source stock resulting from different releases

FOLLOWING THE TRACKS

So who is right? Tropiquaria's Shaun Steven, who now thinks the cats are here but thin on the ground in isolated areas? Or others, like me, who agree that yes, they are thin on the ground, but who believe that they are spread across many pockets of Britain to make a meta-population? If we want to get a handle on our cat situation we know the methods to adopt. We need to set loose researchers, people with more time and more cameras. They should be equipped to ramp up the efforts of intrepid people like Frank Tunbridge and Jonathan McGowan. They could be armed with resources for the daily work of monitoring sample areas. There are plenty of high sighting-density sites to select. Just some of the known routes, the suspected woods, the old railway lines and the streams could be closely tracked, flooded with cameras, and key local people kept involved, to watch out for and report a cat and its signs, knowing that the effort is above board and responsible, being made both for the good of the cats and to give us a grasp of the bigger picture.

We do not think Coryn's cat lives alone in Gloucestershire: if it does, it can reportedly change colour, appear bigger and smaller and delight and scare people miles from each other over the same weekend, on both sides of the wide River Severn. It would be nice to know where Coryn's cat goes, and whose territory it avoids, or steps into, when it's out of sight.

Adrian Hodges filmed this cat, which was widely reported as a large panther, from a distance of over 350 feet near South Littleton in 1992. Photo stills by Mark Fletcher

HIDDEN WILDLIFE – WHAT COUNTS IN THE ECOSYSTEM?

'The wild predator controls the population of his prey and thus automatically safeguards himself… No prey species has ever become extinct as a result of predation, whereas instances are on record where the destruction of a natural predator has upset the balance of nature…'

(Kailash Sankhala, 1925–1994, India)

THE PREDATORS AND THEIR PREY

In December 2010 a large cat was reported on Fort William golf course. Three separate sightings came from the greenkeeper, the club steward and a playing member. The club commented in the local *Lochaber News* newspaper: 'It was a dark brown/black colour, with a long tail. The tail was the same length as its body. It was about 18 inches to two feet tall off the ground. We've had dogs running about on the course before but this was certainly not a dog – nor a fox, a deer or a pine martin.' Not only were there three independent sightings and suspicious prints seen in the bunkers, the possible effects on resident wildlife were also noted by the club in their comment to the local paper: 'We've always had a lot of hares, not rabbits, round the course but suddenly we're not seeing any at all. It has really got us wondering. Normally there are two or three hares at every hole, especially at this time of year.'

Elsewhere in the book a golf course groundsman reports several mute swans predated on his course, coinciding with a big cat sighting. Such predators are likely to take swans and hares, the latter being a mainstay of pumas' diet in some parts of the Americas. Should this potential toll on our local wildlife bother us? I have met many farmers who assume the cats are mainly after the rabbits, foxes and deer on their land and who have welcomed this, but if the menu extends to swan, hares and maybe some ground nesting birds, should that change our outlook – should we be cautious about the effects of a large carnivore on our established wildlife?

Martin Noble, a mammals expert and a former wildlife adviser with the Forestry Commission, believes that the UK big cats' role as a predator

A male puma starts to drag a mule deer it has despatched in a large habitat enclosure in Montana, US.
Photo: © Daniel J. Cox/NaturalExposures.com

in the ecosystem is the most important ecological consideration, as he stressed in the following comment: 'Although now retired, I worked for the Forestry Commission as a wildlife ranger in various parts of England for 33 years, the last 20 years of which were spent as Chief Keeper in the New Forest. During that time I interviewed in excess of 40 people who alleged to have seen one or more big cats. Some of these observers were fellow New Forest Keepers whose abilities and powers of recognition I would not question. At present the animals seem to exist at very low densities but I am convinced that, over time, numbers will increase, territory sizes will reduce and the cats will perform the very useful role of controlling deer populations in our woodlands in an efficient and, above all, economic manner.'

My own simplistic assumption is that the bulk of the cats' diet in most places in Britain would be rabbits, mice, pigeons and pheasants, along with deer, in particular, where they are present. In addition, it is reasonable to assume that foxes, as the co-habiting and next largest predator, would be predated by big cats – these predators are generally hierarchical and intolerant of others which might compete with them. In Gloucestershire, people have reported seeing big cats in pursuit of foxes in three separate incidents, and two other informants have reported eaten-out fox carcasses in areas associated with recent cat sightings. I suggest that nobody would consider these main prey items as of great consequence, and many people would see the natural control of these abundant creatures to be helpful. One person who has given in-depth consideration to the cats' potential diets and their interaction with local wildlife is Jonathan McGowan, who studies the cats in Dorset, and is featured in Chapter 4. Writing in *ECOS*, he set out the following thoughts about the cats' behaviour and prey:

> In Dorset the warm heaths seem to be more suitable for leopards, as they have much scrubland with very thick cover in the way of bracken, gorse and rhododendron, as these are the areas where I tend to find a lot of signs. Most hunting areas tend to be near water, and several sites are drinking areas for deer among purple moor grass which forms dense, high tussocks – the perfect ambush site. The puma also uses this area and in two of my study areas I believe there are at least two species of cats co-existing. These areas are the richest ecosystems and are centred on estuaries and heath bordered by high chalk downs. There is a plentiful supply of prey: thousands of migratory birds such as sandpipers, godwits, curlew, brent geese, shelduck, pintail, teal, and mallard, and large amounts of egrets and herons, of which the latter have been predated on quite extensively. Also swans have been taken and dragged a few hundred yards from the water's edge to be consumed under cover of bracken. In these areas are large colonies of rabbits, badger setts and lots of foxes. Amongst the flocks of Canada geese I have found signs of predation by both foxes and cats. There are also large colonies of black-headed gulls, where I have also found signs of predation. Within the area are high sea cliffs holding breeding colonies of kittiwakes, guillemots and razorbills. The cliffs themselves have natural, but mainly man-made quarrying caves for Purbeck stone, providing the most secure of breeding dens. The chalk downland surrounding the heath and harbour bays hold plenty of hares, roe deer, many badgers and rabbits, and game bird rearing. In addition there are numerous amounts of rats, mice and voles…
>
> (Big cats in Dorset: the evidence and
> implications. *ECOS* 28(1) 2007)

The trail camera awaits passing wildlife…

So, from various observations, perhaps our big cats are behaving much as we might expect them to – acting as an apex predator, doing their job in the ecosystem. Sometimes they may predate species we are concerned about because they are in decline or charismatic, but mostly they appear to be targeting the plentiful generalist wildlife, especially rabbits and deer, which need control across many areas because of their concentrated grazing and browsing pressure on sites of wildlife importance and on agricultural areas.

But how about the fact that the cats are alien – should that worry us? Looking across the UK's array of foreign wildlife, we need to distinguish those species that are damaging and invasive (maybe such as mink and signal crayfish) from those whose effects on their neighbouring nature seem negligible, neutral, or even positive. From the various comments above, maybe the cats fall into the neutral to positive category, so it is hard to feel that their non-native status matters, while for lynx it is a wholly undeserved label. Big predators can, of course, sometimes take farm livestock and our beloved pets. Under what circumstances and at what intervals is that happening, and could it increase in future? And if our fears were realised, what management measures could we put in place to assist farmers and lessen the risk to domestic animals, helping us to live with large feline predators? Tentative suggestions are offered below and in the penultimate chapter.

Left: This swan was known to have been taken and consumed within half an hour at a fisheries lake in Wiltshire. Part of the remains were found on a willow branch overhanging the lake.
Photo: Daniel Elliot

Right: A fallow deer found by Wilf Ashman in north Wiltshire. It was still warm so had been recently consumed. The surrounding grass is flattened, neat plucking of hair tufts can be seen, an ear has been torn off and the stomach contents left.
Photo: Wilf Ashman

Left: An eaten-out badger carcass found in the winter frost by Wilf Ashman, less than a week after finding the fallow deer carcass close by, as shown here.
Photo: Wilf Ashman

Right: Remains of a fox in Gloucestershire discovered when a witness followed up a big cat sighting and unusual animal calls.

These is an obvious twist to the 'aliens' tag, in that a good deal of what we suspect is the cats' prey is non-native. There are currently more deer in the UK than at any time in the last thousand years. The estimate is 1.5–2 million, and the rapidly spreading muntjac is especially fond of munching our woodland flora, while Jonathan McGowan notes how sika deer are a target for the cats in Dorset. With rabbits and pheasants being non-native (in case we've forgotten), it seems harsh to brand a top predator, a natural aid to the urgent national deer cull, as something that's dubious due to its overseas origin.

OUT OF OUR CONTROL?

Some of my professional work takes me into mainstream nature con-servation. I'm in touch with all manner of people, from government agencies to the main conservation charities, who help manage wildlife, formulate policies and care for nature reserves and amenity sites. These people are part of my peer group and I have great admiration for them. When it comes to big cats, though, I've learnt to keep my distance. I quite understand their reticence on the subject: they don't need the likes of me, a social scientist, telling them that there's more to Britain's wildlife than they know. The prospect of leopards, pumas and lynx, or some other ex-otic felines, living free and even naturalising in Britain is inconvenient. It questions their authority and it messes up the picture of wildlife which they know and study. I am stereotyping, of course, and plenty of people working in wildlife and related disciplines have relayed cat sightings to me and like to keep in touch. But, in general, big cats still seem too awk-ward for people in wildlife circles.

One individual who is firmly rooted in the wildlife industry is Ian Bond, Hartlepool Borough Council's ecologist. He is a recorder of big cat sightings in the north of England, and well-known amongst colleagues for his interest. His book on northeast England's big cat sightings, *Path of the Panther*, was published in 2011, and offers a helpful overview of the possible situation in a region, albeit a region that's apparently far less active with cat reports than others. Here are Ian's thoughts on how practitioners in the wildlife sector view the big cat phenomenon:

> I have been writing up sightings of big cats in north east England for Northumbria Mammal Group's newsletter for around ten years now. In addition, through my work as a local council's ecologist, I work closely with wildlife professionals from various bodies such as wildlife charities and private consultancies. None of these organisations, to my knowledge, takes any stance on whether or not big cats might be at large in the north east. Of those people that have discussed it, views range from those few who have actually seen one,

or know of someone who has seen one whom they believe, to the polemicists who actively dispute the cats' existence. For most, the fence seems to be the most suitable reference point to which to align themselves, although the slightly sceptical view is still comfortably in the ascendancy.

But the numbers stacked up on either side of the argument are irrelevant. One indisputable sighting means that there is at least one big cat out there. I'm surprised there isn't more of an overt interest amongst conservation bodies, given the rather dramatic implications of big cats being present for anyone interested in wildlife. Presently in the north east, perhaps there just isn't enough evidence available for it to be on the radar of wildlife bodies. And even if it were proved that the odd escaped animal was around, it wouldn't be perceived as an issue (a benefit or a problem) by many people in the wildlife sector. I don't think that this will change until it can be established that there is a viable population of big cats – however, even I am not convinced that there are sufficient cats out there. Should we ever get to that position, I expect that the various organisations will trot out platitudes about the threats of alien species to our ecosystems, whilst downplaying the danger of the cats to people, though I suspect that most individuals in those same organisations will secretly hope that the cats are left to roam.

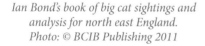

Ian Bond's book of big cat sightings and analysis for north east England. Photo: © BCIB Publishing 2011

I accept much of Ian Bond's view, especially about the fence sitting. But I would add that wildlife bodies don't know what they don't know. They have little experience in handling big cat sightings compared to some of the investigators described in this book. With their own websites and calling cards, and well-established links in the local media, many of the investigators are the primary contact for big cat queries in their area. Many wildlife bodies will be oblivious to this, so it is understandable that they may feel big cats are little more than a quirk.

The vibes one gives off are important. Some witnesses may detect that wildlife bodies could be doubtful of a layman's big cat sighting, and so may be reluctant to converse with them. I know of two cases where informants, very confident of what they had seen, received a brush-off from a wildlife charity when they reported a big cat. I am told that some staff at wildlife organisations did not believe the public's reports of otters for several years, when the otter population began to recover and spread in the late 1980s and early 1990s. These accounts were dismissed as mink. While a small proportion were mink, many were indeed otters, and wildlife bodies should have put more faith in ordinary people's powers of observation and recognition. Hearing reports of out-of-place animals from non-experts needs a patient approach, which may not be the strong point of some scientists. In *Stalking the Ghost Bird*, US author Michael Steinberg describes how witnesses of the thought-to-be extinct ivory-billed woodpecker gave up reporting their sightings to science academics and wildlife groups in and around Louisiana. They found the responses patronising and sometimes hostile, and resorted to keeping the reports amongst themselves until more appreciative researchers sought them out.

Like Ian Bond above, I have met several seasoned conservation staff, and others in forestry and related land-use disciplines, who have had an unexpected glimpse of a big cat in Britain. In nearly all these cases, the individuals wanted an off-the-record chat. Unfolding their stories, they often suggest it is a taboo subject and one can sense it is beyond their comfort zone, yet they also wish to reflect on the predicament of having seen some 'non-existent' and rather special wildlife. These moments with practitioners feel like secret society confessions. Despite being experts in their line of work, big cats have presented them with something beyond their learning, training and expectations. It is shocking and intriguing to them in equal measure. Is it any wonder the topic is often shunned by the very professionals to whom it could mean most?

SIGN TACTICS - ILLUSTRATING THE INVISIBLE

There could be one other impediment to wildlife bodies' interest in big cats – the fact that they own some of the cats' territories. All of the main nature conservation bodies manage land, either as owners and tenants, and have a number of reserves covering different sorts of habitats. Some of these are low profile, and mainly have specialists and researchers nosing around, while others are much busier and better known, with signposting, decent-sized car parks and even visitor facilities. The information and interpretation at such sites is often impressive – I always direct my kids to the signs and panels to get some basics facts on where they are visiting. But are all these signs painting the complete picture of the wildlife that is present? Adding that a leopard or mountain lion might occasionally pass through the site is far from easy. It would risk provoking a full range of reactions from the visiting public, from outright enthusiasm to deep alarm, and derision from the sceptics. Signing the occasional presence of cats could also attract unwanted attention – might some people loiter with intent for very dubious reasons at night? And, above all, health and safety concerns would kick in from a landowner's point of view – any organisation having the public on their land in any numbers might worry about liability, unless of course the cats were classed as 'natural' and part of the mix of wildlife you might experience at the site.

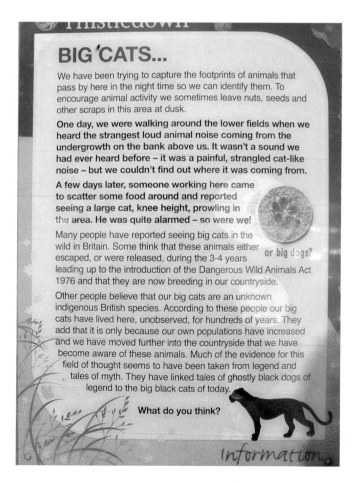

The 'big cat' sign at the Thistledown farm and green camping site in Gloucestershire.

The psychology of signs is complex. A warning tone makes a big impact but an incidental 'You might like to know…' style is intriguing rather than alarming. The information panel on big cats at Thistledown, an inspiring environmental farm and campsite in Gloucestershire, is just such a gentle sign. Reproduced here, it describes people's claims of large cats seen in the area, but invites the reader to form their own opinion on the matter. There has never been a moment of panic amongst the scores of weekly visitors and campers at Thistledown, once they have had a chance to digest the big cat sign. People do not ask for refunds and storm off. If anything, some of them talk and think about the issues. The managers of Thistledown have considered being more up-front with their big cats image, wondering if it would be a positive draw to their customers if handled sensitively. Meanwhile, the softly-softly approach clearly works in this pocket of Gloucestershire's wildlife estate, and may serve as a lesson to others on how honest to be about their unofficial predators.

In fairness, there is one wildlife site where a passing panther gets an official mention: Trimdon, a linear woodland reserve in Teesside, reflecting Ian Bond's influence. There is no right or wrong approach here. We should not bludgeon our wildlife bodies into formal big cat policies or a corporate view on signs. Like the rest of us, they need time to think this through.

NATURALISING OR A MOMENT IN TIME?

According to Christopher Lever, in his seminal and recently-updated book, *The Naturalized Animals of Britain and Ireland*, these are the factors which influence the success or failure of an introduced species in becoming naturalised in a new location:

- A suitable habitat and climate
- A vacant ecological niche
- An adequate supply of acceptable food
- An absence of predators to which the introduced species may be unaccustomed in its native range.
- Fecundity
- A sufficiently large founder stock

Different parts of this book tackle most of Christopher Lever's criteria, indirectly at least. We cannot be definitive about the question of naturalising, but I have argued that the main cats here are untroubled by the terrain and conditions in which they find themselves and by the nature with which they co-exist. This is partly because they are generalists rather than specialists. The cheetah, for instance, as a rangeland, gracile cat, running down its prey, would have more precise requirements and might struggle in many parts of Britain.

I suggest that our big cats pass Christopher Lever's naturalising test with ease. Their vintage may well span several generations, but we cannot know their future viability, because we are unsure of their precise distribution and numbers and their genetic health. Until we investigate, we are left scratching our heads when it comes to these important questions.

RESEARCH ON THE DOORSTEP

In March 2011, during a talk on big cats in a Gloucestershire village, one woman mentioned having walked the previous week along the River Severn with a friend. They noticed a swan's wing, torn and snagged high in a tree. As they scanned the branches they saw other swan remains perched in the adjoining tree. They had not taken photographs, but nobody doubted this lady's account, as she was known by many in the gathering. Unless dedicated researchers become available to make a quick response and examine and photograph such potential evidence, it will be missed along with all the rest. A researcher could have found nothing but, equally, could at least have captured a helpful photo, suggesting the work of a large feline which can take to the trees. Without people readily available to call on, we will remain limited in our efforts to fathom out the cats.

With my ecology friends taking such a tentative view on big cats, I feel they are missing out. They may be passing up some remarkable research possibilities.

Even the fundamental questions we need to ask about our clandestine cats offer challenging and rewarding projects. How can field signs of the cats, like this possible swan kill, be systematically recovered and analysed if there are no budgets, no formal system of recorders and no resources for researchers to follow up reports and check the suspected evidence? How can hair samples be analysed at £100 a time, and remote cameras be afforded and installed in the quantity needed, while there are no resources and no formal recognition of this subject amongst agencies, wildlife groups and research bodies?

The research questions we might draw up are many and varied. They cover the essential information we should discover on these cats, from their behaviour, numbers and distribution to questions about their future, their viability, how they are adapting and their possible effects on other wildlife. My list below is a back-of-the-envelope effort but points to the exciting scope:

Breeding: what are breeding patterns and is breeding seasonal? Which species are naturalising – all the main three suspects of melanistic leopard, puma and Eurasian lynx? What are cub survival rates? How might the cats regulate their numbers?

Viability: what is the viability of these populations into the future? Which mix of species, if any, could create hybrids with any vigour, and even breed on to form a consistent type, as Frank Tunbridge and others have tentatively suggested?

Territory issues: do big cats with no pressure on their food availability need to defend a territory? Would territories for unstressed cats be more adaptable? Would they be smaller, with prey not so precious?

Species interactions: how do the different species interact? Do they need to be aggressive in holding their territory, when prey is so plentiful? Might territories be less defined, with no stress on the cats in finding prey?

Species adaptations: what adaptations might occur in species, including in form and colour? Have dark pumas evolved, for example? Could the different species develop their own traits for the conditions confronting them in Britain, and could a British subspecies of melanistic leopard and of puma occur after many generations of breeding?

Diet and prey: what is the diet analysis of the cats? What do they prey upon in different regions, especially in locations with no deer?

Effects on deer: how do big cats influence deer behaviour, and what are the ecological consequences for our habitats and native woodlands of deer altering their movement patterns, grazing and browsing?

I know at least two university departments in Britain who have considered exploring the UK's big cats. One day, somebody will be brave enough to provide a budget and take on the challenge and the baggage which surrounds the subject. I suggest that group of researchers will enjoy the moment and all that follows.

Dr Sandie Sowler is an experienced UK ecologist who has lived and worked in southern Africa over the last 35 years. She is well qualified to identify a leopard and shares the view that we need to research the feral big cats here, in order to understand them and make decisions regarding their future. Below, she explains her thinking on the need for research, advice and outreach on big cats:

RESEARCH, EDUCATION AND COMMUNITY OUT-REACH – LESSONS FROM SOUTH AFRICA

In mountainous districts in the Western Cape in South Africa, leopards occur and camera traps have revealed their presence close to semi-urban areas. They are endangered and officially protected but legislation is unpoliced and many farmers consider them 'vermin'. Sheep- and cattle-rearing country occurs between the mountain ranges and the fear from conservationists is that the 'vermin control measures' of stock farmers are causing a genetic bottle neck, preventing leopard movements between mountain blocks, thus resulting in their isolation. From experience it is very rare to see these leopards even though their occurrence is confirmed a matter of a few kilometres away from towns. Their impact is minimal on everyday life, even among the farming communities, yet people are aware of their presence because of academic research, outreach work and regular reported sightings. A recent talk that I attended on leopards of the Western Cape and their persecution by farmers was full to bursting. The mountainous areas where they are still to be found are home to a variety of leopard prey species including baboons, small buck and rock hyrax. South African research is ongoing and the leopards' distribution, home ranges, habitat preferences and prey items are known, at least in part.

Leopard country in the open landscape of the Western Cape. Photo: Sandie Sowler

THE NEED FOR SURVEY WORK, NOT SPECULATION

Here in the UK we can only speculate on the species of large cats present, their distribution, their home ranges, their breeding success or anything about their prey or food that sustains them. If we knew with more confidence the species of cats, we may be able to extrapolate something about their biology from what is known in the parts of the world to which they are indigenous. However generations of animals which have survived and bred in a very different climate and habitat to their ancestors are likely to have different behaviour, foraging patterns, food and could have a markedly different ecology. Knowledge of what species occurs and their current distribution in the UK, obtained through use of monitoring and surveillance techniques, positioned by ecologists with an understanding of the likely movement patterns and habitat requirements of the target species, should be prioritised as an important starting place.

Regional anecdotal information and information, including from police records combined with the presence of suitable habitat for lying up and denning, would help to prioritise where to position camera traps, sand spoor trays and other appropriate equipment. From this baseline information of what and where, research projects to study the basic ecology of these species can then be developed. A full understanding of their biology is imperative if we are to understand the implications and risks for both people and wildlife in the UK, as well as to understand what management measures (if any) might need to be put in place. Such research could help indicate what benefits they may provide, perhaps through vermin control including rabbit and deer control and the overall role they are playing in the temperate ecosystem that they occupy. Far from being a 'problem', they may present solutions, especially in parts of the UK where deer populations often have an adverse impact on the biodiversity of upland regions. It will also help to inform discussions relating to their future management.

INCENTIVES FOR RESPONSIBLE LAND MANAGEMENT

In some parts of the world where large members of the family *Felidae* are a part of everyday life, community-based projects have resulted in local benefits through ecotourism. A project set up in the Western Cape in South Africa is educating farmers about their leopards, the dangers and ineffectuality of poisoning and trapping (including the impact of poison bait on many non-target species, including domes-

The first farmer in Eastern Cape to be audited for the Fair Game scheme shows the benefits of the Fair Game branding as his mohair clip goes to auction. This farmer used livestock-guarding dogs with his flock to avoid threatening the lives of predators.
Photo: Sandie Sowler

tic pets) and provides those farmers who sign up to non-lethal means of protecting their flocks and herds with premium prices for their meat by marketing an environmentally conscious and ethical 'Fair Game' trade concept. Farmers are encouraged to use flock guardians and metal throat guards to protect stock from predators.

Although the 'big cats' of the UK are not indigenous to these islands they are here, living amongst us, and we should turn to the native countries of these species in order to learn how to monitor and control populations along with realising the dangers of using non-target lethal measures that can have a damaging impact on both our own indigenous species and on domestic animals.

THE EURASIAN LYNX – BACK TO THE FUTURE

At the 2009 Labour Party conference, the Environment Minister of the time, Hilary Benn, surprised everyone with part of his keynote speech. He declared his enthusiasm for reintroducing the lynx into Britain. Party conferences are times when Ministers make headlines with daring proposals, but nobody had seen this coming. Lynx reintroduction was well beyond even the radical fringes of the government's own agencies. A couple of years earlier I had been invited to chat to some Natural England staff about how they could warm people up to bringing back the lynx, tentatively and as a discussion topic. When the idea reached the senior circles of the agency, though, it was quickly stamped on. But while seeming radical to corporate-minded conservation staff, lynx reintroduction remains a live issue. The topic was debated at a major conference in 2009 organised by the visionary conservation group Trees For Life along with many other bodies exploring the re-wildling and restoration of Britain's habitats. A main message from the event was that bringing back lynx is entirely feasible from an ecological standpoint – Scotland and other parts of the UK have enough suitable territory and conditions, especially woodland, rabbits and deer. It is the human standpoint that has to be resolved. Any such venture involving a species new to people and perceived as dramatic should not be foisted upon communities. People in the very places that might be the focus of a reintroduction project should be deeply involved, so that they can share in making it happen, ensure that pitfalls are designed out and be the ones who make the most of the benefits. The reintroduction of an animal like the lynx should only occur with local people's understanding and backing. It would, of course, need a partnership of key bodies, including wildlife managers, but the local people's wishes should be central to the thinking.

So although farming and game groups would be crucial to bring on board and even lead any initiatives, lynx might be regarded as a predator with which we can safely co-exist. Unlike the other unofficial cats, its membership of our fauna is not an issue – it is a once-native mammal and our habitats have experienced it in the past. The lynx could be a visionary link with other contemporary countryside policies: areas could be branded as Lynx Country, to reflect their wildness and boost their potential in terms of green tourism, wildlife experiences and outdoor adventure. The Harz Mountain region in Germany used just such an approach to good effect when reintroducing the lynx.

The Harz area of Germany uses the reintroduced lynx to promote its wild and scenic landscapes to visitors.

David Hetherington's pioneering research in recent years has pointed to the feasibility of reintroducing this charismatic cat – see, for example, his 2006 article in *ECOS* 27 (1), The lynx in Britain's past, present and future. According to Hetherington: 'We know from bone evidence recovered from limestone caves that the Eurasian lynx once roamed Britain from the south coast to the north coast. These bones now tell us that the species survived in North Yorkshire until at least the 6th century A.D. Cultural and linguistic evidence further suggest that the species was being hunted in the Lake District during the 7th century A.D. and that the Gaelic inhabitants of the Scottish Highlands were still observing its movements into later medieval times. These faint traces of Britain's lost cat are significant in that they point the finger of blame for the species' extinction, not at natural climatic processes which occurred millennia before, but instead at the activities of humans. Under these circumstances, there is an ethical argument for considering reintroduction.'

Recently I asked a big cat investigator if we needed to bring back the lynx, given that it is widely reported in the UK anyway. To my surprise he was keen on formal lynx reintroduction. He suggested it would allow the animals to be radio-tracked and give us an understanding of their movements and thus a gauge of their territory and of behaviour, something we can otherwise only ponder. To those who are inclined toward bringing back the lynx it makes the experiment doubly exciting – an exercise in predator reintroduction at the level of whole ecosystems and a way into exploring big cats already here. What would the newly-released lynx meet on their travels and even breed with, perhaps, as they adapted to their new environment and established their territory? Suddenly the hidden cats already here, and a new quota, released with good intent, seem to join up. There would be no conflict and no regrets from a formal lynx project. We would learn of the lives of this new population and, possibly, some deeper secrets too.

Tourist establishments in the Harz mountains of Germany are using the reintroduced lynx to help promote the area to visitors. Photo: Harz National Park

THE TOOTH AND THE TRUTH
- WHO IS IN THE KNOW?

'When I first told my then teacher, the late Aldo Leopold, that there were still panthers in the forests of New Brunswick he was as incredulous as everyone else. Later, after we had examined the evidence, his first words were: 'We must not tell anybody'. This reaction was typical of perhaps the deepest thinker the wildlife field has yet produced.'

Bruce S. Wright, The Eastern Panther – a
question of survival.
Clarke, Irwin and Co., Toronto. 1972.

THE CLOSED LID ON A CAN OF WORMS

A few years back I read of a cat sighting from Scotland – I didn't file it at the time, although I recall the basics. It came from an off-duty soldier who encountered a big cat in the wilds of the Scottish landscape. His response was to turn and flee. As he did so, he found himself weeping. He said he was crying not because he was frightened but because of his predicament. Yes, he was scared but, more to the point, he found himself totally unprepared and untrained for that moment. It was simply not a situation he was used to, and the whole encounter was distressing for him. I am glad he was so honest. I think his reaction points to wider issues about our authority over what we know and understand, about the limits of our professional confidence and our comfort zones. When I'm in the company of professional colleagues and contacts who know their wildlife, or have responsibility for some aspect of countryside management, I sense their unease with the notion of big cats being at large. To them it is off limits, something of another dimension. They have no experience or mandate, and absolutely no grasp of the topic. It is something best left alone.

Some people feel the authorities are hiding things about big cats. They believe that central government departments like Defra, or the relevant English quango, Natural England, know about the cats but keep quiet. What is certain is that there is no proactive work being carried out by these bodies. They have no budget allocation and they've given themselves no mission to explore it. Any hard evidence passed their way might be inconvenient, to say the least.

Claire Blick, whose illustrations feature in this book, lives in North Devon where she has seen several big cats. She has the following to say about the animals and the role of public bodies:

> The big cats fascinate me. They are beautiful, magnificent animals and I admire their stealth and cunning. Yet my emotions are mixed: first, great affection for the puma which I saw in local woods with my son in 1994, as in my colour sketch. It seemed curious about us and I was curious about it, especially when it came towards us, almost hidden in bracken. Had I been able to stay, I would have got out of my car to greet it! Second, I am a little afraid of the black cats – maybe it is their colour or the 'unknown' factor. Some appear to be like textbook black leopards, others not quite right for leopards because of their form and scale, including some that appear to be too big. I think government should acknowledge the existence of these cats and carry out proper studies. The cats should be protected, and information boards erected in remote areas and forests where they are seen, alerting people to the possible presence of cats and offering a guideline to safe behaviour on meeting one. Meanwhile, I stay frustrated at the pretence from authorities that big cats do not exist.

I know other people like Claire. They feel that government is evasive, a cheat, even, in staying so low key on big cats. But should we be desperate for a ministry or quango to get involved? Maybe not. There can be unintended consequences when government sticks its nose into things. Policies can sometimes prompt a chain reaction, or force actions which many people wouldn't want, or clash with other good intentions. For these very reasons it may be wise for government to stay quiet on big cats. Doing nothing is not necessarily a cop-out, or a sign of a lack of interest – it can be a calculated response.

Another way of operating in public bodies is to take low-key action as needed, but to keep it quiet and stay under the radar. This approach can prevent people from asking questions, spreading rumours and – the ultimate annoyance – making pesky Freedom of Information requests. If no paperwork is done and nothing filed, the F.O.I. request will be useless and will yield nothing. I have been briefed at close quarters on some action taken on big cats and this is exactly how it was done. I would challenge anyone to suggest that it should have happened differently in those conditions. All parties – the landowner, the main adviser, the public bodies involved – acted sensitively and responsibly for the sake of the humans and animals concerned, both the people and the pumas.

PASSIVE GOVERNMENT

If you ask government bodies what they do about big cats you will get some rather plodding answers. For the record, here are the official positions of the main bodies, as of 2011:

England
Defra and Natural England:

> We receive occasional reports from members of the public of alleged 'big cats'. However, none of the sightings of 'big cats' have ever been confirmed and the evidence of all the sightings we have been asked to look at has either been unsubstantiated or has been attributed to other causes. From time to time big cats do escape from zoos or other collections and are usually recaptured very quickly. We are confident that there is no breeding population of big cats in this country.

Wales
The Welsh Assembly Government:

> The Welsh Assembly Government's Rural Affairs Department has responsibility in respect of big cats in relation to damage or potential damage to livestock. If deemed appropriate, we will investigate reports of alleged sightings and attacks by big cats on livestock in Wales, and all reported sightings are recorded on a database. To date, there has not been any evidence proving the existence of big cats in the Welsh countryside. Officials approach investigations with a completely open mind and all incidents are taken seriously and investigated thoroughly.

Scotland
Scottish Natural Heritage (SNH)

> SNH has no direct remit for escaped exotic cats which would normally be the responsibility of the Police or the SSPCA. Our main interest in any such cases would be to determine 1. whether the presence of a large, predatory species was detrimental to the conservation status of any protected species in the area and 2. whether the presence of a non-native species introduced other potential issues, for example disease, which may impact on protected species. We have not, to date, collated any data on incidences.

So there we have it: the cut and dried official responses. Perhaps there was no need for this book after all. If we take government's word, scraping together even a chapter would be tricky. I understand why government is unshakably quiet on the issue and keeps its head down across departments and agencies. My only quibble is the wallabies analogy – if we kept getting reports of wallabies, relentlessly and from all corners of the land, a few crumbs would be found somewhere amongst public funds for research to explore the situation and to inform anything we do. We don't have unremitting accounts of wallabies but we do of big cats.

Natural England log any reports of non-native wildlife and, if pressed, will send out staff to check an incident which might involve a big cat. They will, therefore, do one-off checks but they do not stay on the case. Figures held by Natural England from 2005–2010 showed more than 100 sightings of non-native and unidentified animals reported by the public in England since 2005. Of these, 38 were reported as 'big cats' from actual descriptions or from field evidence thought to indicate a large feline predator. The log is unremarkable and is full of statements to the effect of 'no tangible evidence'. The officer responsible maintains that: 'If they [big cats] are there, the numbers are so small that any risk of people encountering them is pretty small and any risks they present are somewhere approaching zero.' That may be how a government representative declares it from a distance but as I write this, Frank Tunbridge and I have heard from four people who believe they have encountered them in the past two weeks. Natural England's 38 reports over five years can be matched by Frank's own Gloucestershire logbook in five months.

Government did get a bit more interested in 1995, when MAFF, then the agriculture ministry (now Defra), did a short investigation into the alleged 'wild cat-like animals on Bodmin Moor'. Five livestock deaths were studied, field signs checked and any photographs inspected. A sum of £8,200 was spent and 26 staff days deployed. No verifiable evidence for the presence of a big cat was found. The case was quickly closed. This wasn't so much an inquiry as a peep round the corner with a quick retreat before anything interesting arose.

RASH INTERVENTION

It is easy to browbeat government bodies, but people should be careful what they wish for. In 2010, a German newspaper headline read: 'Hunters given permission to shoot marauding panther'. It referred to four independent sightings of a black panther over ten months, after a large black cat was thought to be roaming around the borders of Belgium, France and Germany. 'Officials in the western German state of Rhineland-Palatinate on Wednesday gave hunters permission to shoot an escaped panther that has been on the loose near the Belgian border for almost a year,' said the paper. Here in Britain, Frank and I had four sightings reported to us in a day in January 2011, but none were of a

*A farm in Bodmin erected this sign during the Ministry of
Agriculture's 1995 inquiry into big cat sightings in the area.
Photo: Chris Johnston*

'marauding' cat. Before we press our own government to act, we should
consider what is judicious, in preference to the hasty 'reach for the gun'
response seen in Germany.

Public bodies in Britain, in my experience, are usually responsible
and thoughtful and I hail from a life in a former countryside quango.
But they can slip up: in 2002, one particular district of the Forestry
Commission prepared a so-called policy on big cats which was actually
nothing of the sort. It simply exposed the author's prejudices: 'Shoot on
sight if safe to do so,' was about all it had to say. The policy only reached a
draft stage, before any wider accountability might have kicked in.

PARLIAMENTARY CAT CHAT

How about politicians, the people often exposed to the raw arguments
and the special pleading? Where do big cats rate amongst their priorities?
The former Liberal Democrat MP for North Cornwall, Paul Tyler, pushed

for the Bodmin Moor study and wanted more thorough work by government. Checking through Hansard, a long exchange came in February 1998, when the then Mid-Norfolk MP Keith Simpson raised the matter of big cats with the junior agriculture minister (Parliamentary Secretary to MAFF) of the time, Elliot Morley. Tewkesbury MP Laurence Robertson (still holding the seat and my own MP) also joined in, referring to alleged big cat activity in his part of Gloucestershire. The conversation between these parliamentarians seemed enlightened. Keith Simpson noted the reluctance of any one bit of government to get a grip of the issue, suggesting that different departments and ministries were playing pass the parcel. Simpson wanted to 'consider how we can best evaluate any evidence of the probability of big cats living in our countryside'. Setting the scene, he mentioned that Norfolk police were receiving at the time an average of two big cat sightings a week. He mentioned local concerns about attacks on sheep and possibly horses, and posed the question: 'How should we regard the sightings of big cats in mid-Norfolk? It could be merely an extension of folklore going back to the 18th century. Perhaps Old Shuck or Black Shuck, the mythical large dog which roamed our Norfolk landscape looking for his master all those years ago, has returned to haunt his descendants – perhaps, but unlikely. Perhaps it is merely a question of farmers looking for compensation on a scale the likes of which they have never seen – perhaps, but unlikely… Even if one accepts that in the majority of cases, people have genuinely mistaken large domestic cats, dogs or foxes for big cats, there is still an element of probability that, at least in some cases, there may be a big cat explanation… So what is to be done? How do we best establish a rational method, at national and local levels, to monitor the sightings of big cats and to evaluate the evidence scientifically?'

Elliot Morley gave a reasonable response in my view, illustrating the dilemma for government: 'The Ministry takes these matters seriously. There are a number of big cats in zoos, circuses and in private ownership and it is not impossible that some of them may have escaped or been illegally released into the wild… The Ministry is aware that a total of 16 big cats have escaped into the wild since 1977. They include lions, tigers, leopards, jaguars and pumas, but all but two animals were at large for only one day… the two that stayed at large for some time were a leopard and a puma. The leopard managed to avoid capture for seven days, after which it was cage-trapped… It is impossible to say categorically that no big cats are living wild in Britain, so it is only right and proper that the Ministry should continue to investigate serious claims of their existence, but only when there is a threat to livestock and when there is clear evidence that can be validated.'

For the 13 years since this parliamentary dialogue, we have had variants of these statements from official bodies, excusing action and expenditure. This is a testament to the cats themselves for maintaining a low profile in what they do. Perhaps we should not get too bothered about the role of government? Are the cats simply demonstrating that they can naturalise without undue impact?

As we've already seen, these enigmatic cats crop up in Australia too. The Liberal MP for Hawkesbury, south of Sydney, gave a long account of his experience on the subject to the State Parliament in 2008. In his impassioned speech he set out the case for a viable population of big cats in the area and concluded his case with the following suggestion:

> I do not believe that we need to spend millions of dollars of taxpayers' money going out and hunting these creatures down. The stealth-like nature of these creatures will restrict the possibility of them even being located in this hostile environment. However, we must take the responsible action of alerting all residents who live in proximity to this unique and largely uninhabited area of the potential risk not only to animals the size of a normal family dog – the usual size of prey of such animals – but also children. Many people will remain sceptical of the presence of such an animal... I suggest it is far better to err on the side of caution in this case and simply advise people of the possible risks that face when living in or visiting the remote areas of Hawkesbury.

It is clear from these extracts that politicians can see the issues and possible actions: education, outreach, research and advice top the To-Do list. These are the no-brainers, modest steps that would be affordable and could make a difference, giving help to the few people whose lives do get distracted by big cats. Governments will naturally baulk at new schemes to compensate for lost livestock. More bureaucracy and new opportunities for people to bend a system for dubious claims are never welcome. If we had chronic and sustained episodes of sheep kills I would urge government to rethink this, but thankfully, for now, the odd flare-up of suspected sheep kills rarely becomes protracted. I realise nothing can compensate for years invested in nurturing pedigree stock, but if insurance claims need to cover the monetary value of dispatched animals, why worry thinking about predators which are not officially here? The culprits might, after all, have been dogs.

CONSTABULARY DUTIES

In contrast with the position of government, the police cannot distance themselves from cats. Exposed to bewildered people wanting advice and explanations, they just have to roll their sleeves up. Several police forces collaborate with the local big cat researchers in their area. The relationship often works well and acts as informal and often free subcontracting for the police. It ensures that people get experienced advice and a body of knowledge builds up in the area, retained in one place.

The Gloucestershire constabulary can be more matter of fact on the subject than can Frank and I. 'Big cats are breeding in the Cotswolds,' they stated to the ITV documentary *Heart of the Country* in 2006. 'We take reports of big cat sightings seriously and we believe that there is evidence of their existence in the county,' they told *The Citizen*, Gloucester's main daily paper, in December 2007. In Dorset, interviewed on Sky TV's documentary *Big Cat Tracks*, a police Wildlife Liaison officer suggested there were around six black panthers in the county. He wasn't asked for numbers of puma-types and lynx. The police in Humberside were one of the first forces officially to recognise big cats as a reason for livestock kills and in County Durham, former Wildlife Liaison Officer Sergeant Eddie Bell became well versed in the issues, having himself seen a puma. He told *The Field* magazine of '60 reliable sightings out of 280 in the region' from 1986 to 2000. In Scotland the police can be equally rational. Commenting on the concerns of panther sightings in the Loch Ness area in spring 2011, a Northern Constabulary spokesman said, 'The police do take such reports seriously. Clearly there is a public safety issue and a welfare issue for the animal concerned… Where there is credible information that there may be a large animal in a specific area then we will work with our Scottish Society for Prevention of Cruelty to Animals to try and recover it through the use of humane live traps.'

There is one other job the police have to do with big cats: clearing dead ones off the road. A retired senior officer once spoke to me on the phone to report a dead puma he'd seen on the central reservation of a dual carriageway south of Oxford, between North Hinksey and South Hinksey. It's an intensely busy stretch of road and, other than at the dead of night, a lane would need to be closed to clear anything significant from the central reservation. No, he emphasised, it wasn't a Great Dane or a deer, it was a mountain lion-type of cat. His wife had seen it too, as the car crawled past in slow-moving traffic. He assumed that many other motorists would have noticed the highly inaccessible carcass too. He was reporting it, thinking that it would be useful to somebody who studied these things. After a frenzy of phone calls it was agreed that Steve Archibald, a big cat researcher in Oxfordshire, would check it out. He spent half his Saturday searching the knife-edge verge along the central barriers as traffic flew past. He found nothing, and requests for information went out via BBC Radio Oxford, but to no avail.

In 2004 one county police force took the pragmatic decision to mend a car's damage themselves, rather than let the driver struggle with an awkward insurance claim. The driver kept quiet in return. In

Top right: Sadly, pumas sometimes get knocked down on highways in North America as here in Colorado. Chapter 6 mentions the underpass-crossings being established in Florida to help minimise such incidents. This animal was killed instantly when it ran into the vehicle and the vehicle itself sustained damage.
Photo: Steve Mestdagh

Right: A highway sign in the US alerts drivers to possible road-crossing by pumas.
Photo: Andrea Bearzi

NEXT 10 MILES

this particular instance, the road was shut for three hours on a Sunday morning due to 'a road traffic accident involving a dog'. Frank Tunbridge happened to be travelling that way on the day, and can vouch for the closed road. There was a witness to the case, as there have been elsewhere. Other detailed reports of road kills seen but presumed cleared by officialdom come from Gloucestershire, Leicestershire and Essex, and a mystery, apparently feline body found by Jonathan McGowan on the back roads of Salisbury Plain is shown on page 121.

It is at RAF Fylingdales, in the heart of the North York Moors, that we have Britain's own Roswell moment on big cats. This time, though, it wasn't an alleged alien in the basement of a US military base, but an outsize cat in the vaults of a British one. Retired staff from the establishment have apparently talked about 'a body on the table' and a witness outside the base reported a puma-like cat carcass being trundled off in the scoop-arm of a tractor. This was in 2004, when two sightings of big cats are alleged near the base within seven days. Both were said to have been road traffic casualties in the vicinity, one of which is reported to have involved a Ministry of Defence vehicle. Paul Westwood of Big Cat Monitors investigated the case but found replies and information hard to come by. Both the county and the MOD police seemed reluctant to talk. He got a response of sorts, when he visited the site: personnel at the perimeter gates told him of a big cat being hit by a bus. But this was at odds with all other gossip on the case. The MoD have plenty of things to keep quiet about and here was another.

COMMOTION IN THE SHIRES

In May 2011 the nation's media all laughed at the toy tiger that fooled Hampshire police. Following reports from the public of a possible white tiger slumped in a hedgerow, police scrambled a helicopter and were ready to shut off the nearby M27 if the animal were to bolt away. The stuffed object rolled over in the helicopter's down-draught. Police were unable to confirm the toy's owner... This whimsical case should not mask other occasions of helicopter deployment on big cats, for it has happened in several counties over many years. Here is just one, from 2006. In October, Essex police revealed that several members of the public had independently reported seeing a 'puma-size' big cat in Weald Country Park, Brentwood, and there were reports of a deer having been killed. The country park was closed for a day and a helicopter watched overhead. The police also asked the public to come forward with any further information. Here again was an example of multiple sightings over a short timescale, with a public facility closed and police surveillance brought in. A big cat, it seems, had wandered into an amenity area of suburban England, created mild panic and shut the place down for a day.

In November 2006 the Leamington and County Club, a golf course in Warwickshire, had so many sightings of a big black cat wandering the fairways that it erected a notice in the clubhouse, alerting members to the situation. In this case there was no alarm, just a cautionary message about golfers needing to be on their guard. Again, here was traditional British life having to react to a big cat's innocent intrusion. In autumn that year, Powys police in Wales warned people in Taly-bont and Bont-goch, near Aberystwyth, of seven reports of a big cat in the surrounding hills. A police spokesperson stated: 'It is very important that no-one tries to shoot this cat if they do come across it: they may not kill it outright and an injured animal can be more dangerous'.

In 2007 it was the turn of the police themselves to be out with fire-arms. According to the *Harlow Herald*, police marksmen were deployed and a 21-officer search was carried out after two policemen spotted a big cat near their Hertford station. They reported seeing a large feline-type animal on a building site and a three-hour search ensued. They called in experts from a local wildlife park to stun the animal if it was seen. A po-lice spokesman stated: 'Our firearms unit, including officers with rifles, surrounded the site as a back-up in case the animal got out of the building site.' The animal was not seen again, and the force gave a reassuring mes-sage to the public: 'There are no confirmed records of anyone ever being attacked by these animals, the reason being there is no shortage of small natural prey available to them for food, and they have a natural fear of man.' There is nothing extraordinary about the above selection of reports. Yes, they are all instances of local people, the media and police feeling con-cerned by the possible actions of what seems to be a predator in their midst. But other golf courses, other police forces, schools and local councils have taken action elsewhere and issued letters of alert about big cats. All of this because of an animal, unknown and, it is thought, unpredictable. Except, of course, that the animals are predictable – just as in their official countries, they avoid the commotion they are causing. They do what's natural to them: they go to ground. We will no doubt have plenty of repeat performances of these scenes, much fuss and much anguish over a cat on the loose or a 'marauding panther'. We can panic if we want, but we could also learn. We could take time to study more about this animal going on its way, doing its own thing yet capable of sending us into convulsions as it does so.

SURVEYING DEER BUT WATCHING PANTHERS

As I have hinted above, Freedom of Information requests are mostly shots in the dark. Maybe, though, I should be less dismissive, for in January 2009 one of them hit the bull's-eye. It asked if Forestry Commission staff had seen any big cats on their thermal cameras while

Deer survey catches big cats on camera

Officials say sightings are 'reliable'

The Gloucestershire press reports news of the Forestry Commission's sightings of big cats. Courtesy: Gloucestershire Media

carrying out deer census work. In wildlife circles in Gloucestershire, it was known that this had occurred in the Forest of Dean, so it was an obvious question to ask, but were there records to prove it? The Forestry Commission duly admitted that they had indeed seen a big cat in two of their previous deer census exercises in the Dean, done every three years. The answer caused just about the biggest rumpus on big cats in the UK to date. There was widespread media coverage, plenty of behind-the-scenes chat in policy bodies and the Forestry Commission staff concerned were busy with interviews for a month. The whole furore was a useful marker: it served to indicate just how distracted with big cats a body like the Forestry Commission could become if it allowed itself to be. The Forestry Commission spokesperson played down the sightings as likely releases or escapes, and suggested they were rare occurrences. *The Sun* newspaper gloried in the news, claiming its readers had been right about big cat sightings all along. Its headline declared: 'The Tooth is Out'…

A COVENANT WITH
THE CATS

'We harbour a primordial animal memory in our being. Although largely inaccessible, its shadows dwell in our instincts, just as they stir in our dreams and fears. Sometimes they can be sensed in the beating of our hearts, or in an unexpected encounter with wild creatures…'

Graeme Gibson. The Bedside Book of Beasts. 2009. Bloomsbury

THE INQUIRING MIND

In summer 2009, during one of my family's short breaks to Exmoor, I was pottering around the village of Winsford. It is a charming and sleepy place, where you wouldn't expect to be surveyed about anything. Suddenly, though, three young women confronted me, clipboards in hand. To my surprise they were asking questions about the 'Beast of Exmoor'. Before I announced my own special interest I awaited their questions and the context for them. They had chosen the subject for their Duke of Edinburgh Award scheme, which required a field visit and a written-up project. Their questions were spot on. Had I heard of the beast of Exmoor? Did I believe in it? What would be the main sorts of evidence, other than a sighting? And what were my views – was it a good thing or a bad thing? They politely listened to my extended response, and I was encouraged at their commitment to a slippery subject. I found it all heartening, of course. To me, this confirmed the potential of big cats to get people relating to the landscape in different ways. Furthermore, these young people had chosen the topic for themselves and were seeing all its dimensions. I missed one opportunity in their survey, though – I should have introduced them to the proprietor of a village shop nearby. He and I had previously got talking about the 'Beast', as he and his wife had had a close sighting of a black panther up on the hill one morning. He knew locals for whom the cats were now regarded as just part of the scenery, an additional animal to the Exmoor ponies and the red deer. I wish I'd quoted his revelation on big cats for the survey: 'They must be breeding,' he'd declared.

The black leopard enclosure at Exmoor Zoo explains much about the area's history of big cat sightings.

Back in Gloucestershire, a young guy of 17 reportedly came close to a panther while lamping (shooting rabbits by torchlight) in the spring of 2011. At first he felt shaken up: he'd nearly bumped into the animal which had been watching him in the night with golf ball eyes. He returned to the spot and recounted the event to Frank Tunbridge. On meeting Frank, he immediately became more alive to the issues. He learnt key tracking tips and took charge of a trail camera set up in the thicket where he had met the cat. He felt positive about the panther. Presumably also hunting the rabbits, the animal had just watched him before turning and slinking off when the young man unwittingly got close. In the following month he read up on big cats, checked the local landscape on Google Earth and made long cycling trips around the area's many woods, searching for signs and scouting for evidence. The encounter with the panther had fired something in him and had made the countryside come alive. He now had another motive for studying the world around him.

I could add many such examples, but maybe these ones make the point. I don't pretend it is easy, and I will go on to look at the potential hassles and the awkward side of the cats, but if, like the young people above, we wake up to our big cats, we may find the experience transforming. They can encourage us to look afresh at our surroundings, to see a land where predator-prey relations are being played out. There are many ordinary but still notable things that we miss right before us – like the signs and smells of nature – which an awareness of wild predators can help us discover in the landscape. And maybe there are some extraordinary things, too, that could delight, surprise and scare us, if only we knew about them. What, if anything, do we owe these clandestine cats? What relationship do we wish to strike up with them? And how can we help maintain the general lack of aggression that they seem to display to humans? What is the covenant we should establish as the big cats come into our reckoning?

THE WILD EDGE OF GLOUCESTER

A lot of people enjoy their big cat experience, as we've already seen. But that's not always the case and for some, alarm bells can ring. I've experienced this myself. I've had two direct moments of worry which have offered some perspective and knocked the edges off any sense that the cats are wholly good news. The first came back in 2006, when Frank was showing us a local walk where he'd seen a cat of unknown origin. It had been a restful evening stroll with my family when we heard a distinct and penetrating half-howl, half-bark.... . My son (who was six at the time) was literally shaking with fear. As he gripped my leg I could feel him trembling and the rapid thump of his heartbeat pounded against me. He was truly panic-stricken. I became frightened myself at his near-hysterical state. I did my best to calm him as he stuttered: 'What if it's stalking us?' Meanwhile my daughter (nine at the time) clambered up a spoil heap towards the sound, thrusting her stick and hollering: 'Where are you then, cat? Show yourself!' I was equally worried by her reaction, thinking her bravado a touch provocative. The animal stayed hidden. We trod cautiously back through the site to the comfort of the car.

The noise which had triggered our reaction was not from an animal we knew. It was not a threatening tone, just an animal, close by, stating its presence. The site Frank was showing us was a wasteland on the edge of Gloucester, scruffy but fascinating. It linked to a woodland nature reserve on one side and, on the other, fringed into a sweeping wet meadow along a curve in the River Severn. It was dusk on a balmy summer evening and Frank had seen a fox-sized cat several times in the past month. It had been attracted to the squeaky ball he threw for his dog. Frank said the cat stayed, watching, about 50 metres away. Foxes will quickly flee but this animal remained curious, keeping an exact distance, edging forward when Frank retreated, backwards when Frank advanced.

Returning home that night, I recalled the shock, the palpable fear I'd seen in my son. How had it come to this? Here we were in soft southern England of all places, on the edge of our local town, totally familiar to us, and my kids had had the fright of their lives and were now on their guard from a supposed big cat living wild. I was ashamed of myself – surely this madness had to stop? What was I putting my family through? Well, I'm glad I refrained from a ban on big cats in the household. Now, four years on, when I watch my son out walking, I see him confident and alert in the outdoors. He may be football-mad, an avid viewer (much to my disgust) of *Top Gear*, but a self-made boy scout, a forager and tracker is developing before me, without the need for specialist courses and expensive camps. Similarly my daughter, now a teenager engrossed in Facebook, is also (mostly) at ease with nature, happy out walking, still messing in streams and carefully noting the birds in the garden. We are all capable of this, of anchoring our minds in the natural world, but there are different cues for each person and each family. The big cats helped it happen for us. They make the discovery of tracking, and listening out for nature's night-time noises, that extra bit real.

Back at Gloucester's urban edge, at the spot of the mystery calling cat, I saw the animal for myself a few weeks later when showing the site to Jonathan McGowan, on a visit from Dorset. First, it was just a glimpse from around 100 metres. In the dim light it had the form and brush-like tail of a fox, but something wasn't right: the movement was more feline. It walked on, then crouched and deposited a poo. It was then off on its way, merging into the dense riverside meadow. Jonathan rushed to pick up the scat. It was certainly that of a carnivore, full of small bones and hair. There were no fox-like twisty ends. It was segmented. It smelt of cat. Nothing now suggested we'd been watching a fox. All our separate views of this animal – Frank's description, the sounds, and now the hard evidence from the dropping – pointed one way. We'd been studying a jungle cat (*Felis chaus*). On reflection, I make no apologies for having my family freaked out by a modest jungle cat, officially at home in the swamps and grasslands of Asia. An unfamiliar mammal call, staking its claim to a patch of land, is just that – unknown, and sounding bold. No way were we in danger, but no way were my kids to know that.

It was two years later that I next felt a tinge of anxiety from a big cat's possible presence. Again it was in the quaint county of Gloucestershire, but this time I was encamped in my own house and garden…

OUT OF MIND, BUT ON THE DOORSTEP

I don't regard my immediate surroundings as the haunt of big cats, despite the adjacent open fields and golf course. Quite illogically, I feel exempt from the attentions of the very animals I study. There are plenty of rabbits and pheasants in the area, but we rarely see deer, just the occasional muntjac or roe. I saunter on the golf course, birdwatching and walking the dog, regarding it as off-limits to big cats, unlike much of the surrounding parts of Gloucestershire. But my complacency was shattered in January 2009. News broke that no fewer than four staff of Tewkesbury Borough Council watched a black panther at close quarters at the edge of the course, just five minutes from my back door. The council guys were pollarding willows when the large cat passed them, just 30 metres away. It emerged from a thick tangle of brambles, seemingly disturbed by the sudden chainsaw. Two of the men made separate reports to Frank, and there was little room for doubt as the two corroborated each other. They had seen its eyes clearly as it looked at them. They sensed no fear and were awestruck. The oily-black panther then took off at rapid speed. 'When it ran, it moved like a wave, in massive effortless bounds,' said the foreman of the crew to Frank.

I chatted to the golf course groundsman the next day. The incident gave him a possible explanation for the mute swans which had been pre-dated on the course's lakes during that and the previous winter. With several swans being taken, he'd wondered how foxes could be so bold, and he'd asked for advice from experts from nearby Slimbridge, the Wildfowl and Wetlands Trust HQ. The bramble thicket where the cat emerged was perfect shelter for a resting cat, I thought. It was tucked away at the edge of the course, where the groundstaff deposited grass cuttings. It was a half-hidden wasteland, yet I'd been walking nearby for more than 15 years and it had never registered. Any passing panther would feel undisturbed here, and could snack away on the bounty of rabbits, let alone the swans around the corner. How had I missed this perfect felid bolt hole?

For the next few weeks I was cautious in the evening. I locked the cat flap to stop our two mogs going out at night. I checked that the shed door was firmly shut, and beamed the torch into the bramble thicket between our back track and the golf course, half expecting to see some giant watchful eyes. The reality of a possible panther, seeing to its needs in my own space, thinking that rabbits in the surrounding hedgerows might be its prey, was with me at last, nagging away. I laughed at my own plight. I felt I deserved to feel the tension I so often heard from others – now it was my turn. After a few weeks, the influence of the cat wore off and I became more relaxed. I was half-relieved, half-regretful. I have not yet sensed the cat again, but now every winter I note the arrival of the golf course swans, because a wild predator, a giant feline, might be doing the same thing.

THE PEOPLE'S VERDICT

As well as giving talks and helping run meetings on big cats across the country, I do several briefings on the topic throughout Gloucestershire each year, often with Frank Tunbridge. Civic Societies, Women's Institutes, Young Farmers' Clubs and similar bodies have all held meetings where people come to hear about the evidence, learn from others who've had sightings and ask questions. The hall or meeting room will often be packed; people from all walks of life come along, pleased to talk through what is often regarded as a fringe and difficult topic. In 2011, in Nailsworth near Stroud, one lady had phoned Frank three days before a scheduled talk. She lived half a mile from the venue, and had just seen a big black panther from her kitchen window, sniffing around the bird table scraps in her garden. She was horrified. She never wanted to see the animal again – what could Frank do about it? Frank encouraged her to come to the talk to learn a bit about the cats, and to hear views on big cats from other people in her area. We weren't sure she'd attended until a phone call to Frank a few days later. She said she'd enjoyed the event and was now more at ease. In fact, her husband was cleaning the windows and getting the camera ready, in case the cat came back.

Rick Minter (left) and Frank Tunbridge give regular talks on big cats, including at outdoor events.

At tea-break during the talks we sample people's views. We give them a list of statements about big cats, as reproduced below. We ask the participants to identify the two comments which most closely resemble their own views. We do the exercise in different ways, sometimes on a chart with sticky dots, sometimes with personal survey sheets. We often change the order of the statements, in case people have a tendency to tick the top ones more than the bottom. But whichever way we do it, the results are similar, and remarkably so. A distinct message comes across about the presence here of big cats: the majority of responses are pretty equally divided between 'Leave them alone', 'It's exciting' and 'Survey them'. Intolerant views, such as 'Cull them', are rare. This has been the common pattern in nine different talks over three years, which provides a sample of over 600. Yes, the people who attend the talks are self-selecting, but a wide range of backgrounds and ages, including farming families, are represented at most events. In my view, any bias in the sample is slight. The response numbers listed below, from a 2011 talk in Nailsworth in the Stroud Valleys, offer a standard example of the proportions we get across the different categories of feedback.

**Survey feedback at Big Cat talks in Gloucestershire
Representative example from Nailsworth, Gloucestershire,
January 2011**

Sample of 52 respondents with two votes each

Big Cats in the wild here? Your view…

Use them to promote tourism in the area	2
It's worrying	2
It's exciting	25
Cull them	0
Leave them alone	30
Put up Information Signs	11
Survey them	28
Not sure about it	5
Don't believe it	1
Other comments…	See examples below

People at the talks are also invited to write a comment to supplement their survey response. Few people do add anything, but reproduced below are a range of the kinds of comments received from talks in 2010–2011.

'I would like to see the big cats protected.'
'Trap them and DNA identify.'

'Do a scientific survey. Include witness reports from the public but encourage general public to leave them alone.'

'My daughter didn't believe I'd seen a big cat – she does now.'

'I'm from Canada. I spotted a large black cat in Dartmoor in winter 2006–2007. It was at the back of my hotel and activated the security lighting as I watched from the window. It rolled on the ground and I gauged scale as a panther-size cat.'

'I've often heard the [leopard-type] noises as demonstrated by Frank in my local area near Stroud.'

'Having lived in Africa I appreciate that big cats will keep away from humans. If they are reported locally I would take extra care with domestic pets.'

'At first, when I felt I'd seen a big cat I was very curious and excited. I have heard about these kinds of sightings before, yet nothing really out of the ordinary has happened to me, so it was definitely a feeling of 'It's exciting!' It wasn't until I'd had a look at the area where I saw the cat that it dawned on me I could be putting myself, my son-in-law and my dogs at terrible risk, so it quickly flipped to 'It's worrying!' I definitely would not cull them though. Survey them certainly. It's fascinating!'

The above quotes illustrate views from people who are largely positive about the cats and find them intriguing. But a small proportion find big cats problematic, as indicated in the following statements:

'It's worrying – I've got dogs.'

'These animals are not native to the UK and should be eliminated before their numbers get out of control.'

'I value the general safety and absence of dangerous wild animals in our countryside, so would like to see research, a count, and some control before there's an incident.'

The comments from the talks reveal the fascination people have with the cats, and the considered feedback they make. People can detect the mix of emotions at stake, and often express this in the final discussion session. It is rare to come across naked prejudice or a complete redneck reaction. Many times, for instance, I've seen landowners state 'Leave them alone', and families, including from farming backgrounds, express not just one but a range of views which show that they appreciate the jumble of feelings bound up with these animals. People recognise the genuine challenge of the cats, and can see there is no correct or easily deliverable measure. A good proportion of people say they would love to see one, and there are always eyewitnesses willing to describe their particular incident. At the end of a talk in Stroud, one man described his wonder at the big cats and concluded by expressing his inner concern: 'I just hope they keep behaving themselves.'

If I could sum up one main strand of opinion I pick up from participants at the talks, I would put it like this:

'The cats seem to be established here. Part of the fascination is that they are truly wild. They do not appear to be aggressive in normal circumstances. If they are doing no harm to us and to the environment, then leave them be. We deserve to know more about them, to understand rather than risk messing with this incredible surprise in nature.'

In case we might think these sentiments are peculiar to Gloucestershire and its hinterland, here is a statement from an eyewitness in Norfolk. This came from Paul, after his sighting of 'a large black cat with shiny short fur and a powerful lean body', near Palgrave in March 2010.

> I guess that seeing – or rather witnessing – something so unique was so incredible that I wanted to tell someone that I felt would treat it with a bit more than 'I don't believe you,' or 'Are you sure it wasn't a dog?' I felt very privileged to have seen the big cat and wanted others to know whom I felt would be excited/respectful to hear of my sighting. However, if I felt that they would simply want to hunt/kill the cat I would certainly not wish them to know.
>
> Finally, I guess the uniqueness of the cats and their environment needs to be surveyed so that we can understand them more: their habits, patterns and lifestyle. Are they a danger to humans? Do they kill prey to survive or simply because they can? How have they adapted to their surroundings? All questions that culling and killing wouldn't answer.

I take heart from the thrust of these messages and from people's calls to have the cats better understood and studied. This reaction from the grassroots, expressing a need to learn about these new animals, has helped clarify my own view and is why it forms a central proposition of this book.

THE PREDATOR'S STARE AND THE REALITY OF RISK

Might some of our assortment of big cats pose an inherent danger to us? What about the worry over 'an incident', expressed in the quote above from the Gloucestershire talks? It is a view I'm exposed to from within my own family, as my father feels it strongly. To him, large carnivores roaming free in a landscape spell trouble. To countenance their presence means putting ourselves in danger. As an artist, he recognises as much as anyone that exotic cats are awesome creatures which many people revere. But for him, the risk they pose is paramount – all other factors, the pros and the cons, are relegated. He knows the theory that large carnivores seldom bare their teeth at humans and tend to avoid our presence, and yet the unpredictability is there. An acquaintance of his was killed by a bear in North America. For my dad, the exception is not an abstract notion.

There is a dilemma in admitting a large predator has the potential to be dangerous. It can seem like scaremongering. Any attack or defensive reaction of a large cat on a human could be horrific in nature. But we need a sense of proportion. Dogs injure people, and it is not just children who are at risk. The NHS figures show that strikes and bites by dogs can happen to any person of any age. The total number of dog-related incidents (defined by the NHS as 'attack and collision') in 2007–2008 resulted in 4,699 people admitted to patient care in Britain. A good proportion of those may well have happened in people's own homes. But it is not just carnivores that can have effects: herbivores – weighty animals that can charge and move at rapid speed – have the potential to be dangerous, too. And it's not just bulls which can be problematic. Unexpectedly aggressive behaviour in cows can occur when they feel their calves are threatened and when they are spooked by dogs, especially if those dogs are not being responsibly walked by their minders. According to figures collected over recent years by the Health and Safety Executive, an average of one fatality per year to a member of the public is caused by cattle, including bulls. We need to get these rare problems from grazing livestock in perspective too, for they are abundant in their number and distribution. Deer can be dangerous to humans, especially males at rutting time, and walking in the hours of darkness can carry risks where people may carry rifles. I knew somebody who was shot through the lung in southeast England when out watching owls late one evening. He only survived after urgent surgery.

Chris Johnston, featured in Chapter 4, is both an animal behaviourist and a big cat researcher. He offers the following perspective on this matter: 'I have been attacked by two German Shepherds and several border collies in the countryside. I have seen two big cats in the countryside and they posed no threat to me and left me alone, and I have heard the warning sound of a leopard at close quarters when I was tracking one after a sighting reported to me. I think we need to find a balance.'

We should not dodge people's worries about the possible danger from big cats. Many people feel positive, 'in awe', even, and very few people show animosity towards the cats. But people are sometimes shocked and scared, and so much depends on the circumstance. We should avoid

mushy thinking and face up to the capability of large carnivores to pose the occasional slight risk, especially if the human reaction is an inappropriate one. But we also need the measured perspective that most people who come to the talks readily recognise.

In usual circumstances here in Britain, it seems that the cats are not under stress: their territories are not congested and their food is everywhere. They are not persecuted and they would not grow up sensing us as trouble. So despite the fact that they are hunter and carnivore, while we are soft-skinned, slow moving and with poor hearing, it appears that we are not in their sights. It would be dangerous to meet a large cat in a confined space, like a barn, shed, blocked-off tunnel or cave, where it might feel threatened and want to flee while we are in line with its escape route. It would also be dangerous to be near a large cat when it happens to be in stalking mode, poised and fixed on its natural prey. But in a situation where a cat is close by, staying confident seems to be the key advice, to ensure that a predator does not detect fear and a sense of submission. Facing a cat and backing off slowly, neither intimidating nor worrying it and certainly not turning from it, is another message. And doing anything which could aggravate a large cat is unwise.

One has to be cautious in looking at North American puma incidents on the web and in literature. Organisations which are pro-puma may play down the risks, while less tolerant groups can spin the dangers. The topic is also tricky because puma attacks are the exception, and each offending cat often acts unpredictably, defying the standard US briefing on what to do when faced with a puma close up.

The raw statistics of North America's puma attacks involving injuries and fatalities over recent decades are set out on page 192. Looking beyond these decades, three times as many people were attacked in the 1990s as in the entire previous century. One factor may be that expanding settlements are encroaching more into prime puma habitat, making occasional conflicts with the cats more likely. Another reason may simply be hunger among parts of the puma population, with some of the culprits found to be in poor condition, struggling to feed themselves. These may not be the only influences, but they seem to be part of the equation. As we've already discussed, lack of food supply does not apply to the cats in Britain. Superficially, though, we mirror this new American scenario of residential areas merging with the cats' living space. Big cats are sometimes seen on people's properties in Britain, treating them as part of their beat. There may be a difference in the UK, though – maybe more of our big cats have grown up from the start in the thick of human activity and know how to dodge it. I offer more on this point at the end of the chapter.

Puma/cougar attacks in US and Canada		
1970s	17 attacks	4 fatalities
1980s	20 attacks	2 fatalities
1990s	37 attacks	8 fatalities
2000–2005	28 attacks	3 fatalities
2006–2010	19 attacks	1 fatality

Source till 2005: (*Calgary Herald*; 01/04/01)

As further context for the above figures, according to *National Geographic* magazine, current puma numbers in the whole of North America are estimated to be approximately 50,000. And here is more perspective, this time from an Amazon website reviewer of a book on cougars: 'But being attacked by a cougar is much less likely than being struck by lightning or being stung to death by bees, wasps or hornets. I sure don't let lightning or bees keep me from enjoying the outdoors. I just use common sense.'

THE FLEEING AFRICAN LEOPARD

If we prefer to hold the view that unstressed leopards in the wild are ultra-wary of humans and will almost always keep away, then the work of Theodore N. Bailey is of interest. His book, *The African Leopard*, first published in 1993, is a scholarly and readable account of fieldwork with leopards. The book charts two years of close observation of leopards in Kruger National Park in South Africa. He made over 100 direct observations of leopards, learnt from over 2,500 radio-tracking locations, and undertook 112 live captures. Bailey travelled around his study area by vehicle and on foot. Here is a key part of his account of leopard behaviour he experienced:

> Leopards were seldom aggressive toward me. Male 3 once snarled for 10 minutes at a distance of 20 metres, so I retreated. I was uncertain, however, whether he was threatening me, another leopard, or a nearby hyena... Once, when I stepped from my vehicle, a radio-collared female rushed me from dense cover. But she stopped 15 metres away with her ears laid back, front teeth widespread and lips curled back, snarling. Then she slowly turned and calmly walked away. The only leopards that did not flee upon my approach were females with cubs. On 15 to 20 occasions when I approached three different females that had young, they remained motionless and would not leave the area. To prevent aggressive behaviour, I did not approach within ten metres of females with cubs.

Radio-collared leopards fled when I was as far as 80 metres from them. But on 20 occasions I stalked within 20 metres and on three occasions within ten metres of leopards before I observed them. Once I heard a leopard breathing before I could see it, and on another occasion I discovered a leopard sleeping at the base of a tree only three metres away. All close approaches occurred during the wet season when dense vegetation provided ideal stalking cover.

Bailey was studying leopards in Africa. We should be tentative, of course, in drawing conclusions about the circumstances of big cats in the wild in Britain.

UNDER PRESSURE IN ASIA – WHEN LEOPARDS LASH OUT

In some parts of India we can get a different perspective on leopards. There are instances of leopards having attacked people, especially children, and especially near the edges of some main settlements. But it is crucial to grasp the cause and effect here. Some people fear leopards when they see them, and a mob can quickly form to descend on the cat. Inevitably this aggravates the leopard, and the chances of one of the assailants being fish-hooked by the desperate animal are high. You can view exactly these sorts of cases in India on YouTube. In one distressing clip the mass stoning of a leopard is graphically filmed, and it soon succumbs. In another we learn how leopards have taken to lurking in the sugar cane, which allows easy access to villagers' dogs and goats. Small children then become at risk. This worrying state of affairs has partly arisen from encroachment on a wild animal's territory and the predator starts struggling for its natural food.

According to the New Delhi edition of *The Telegraph* of April 2011, leopards have attacked more than 560 people in the past ten years in Uttarakhand, while Maharashtra has reported about 240 such attacks, most taking place in villages and semi-urban areas, confirming the scenario above. New guidelines for leopard management were issued by the Indian Environment and Forests Ministry in 2011, as reported in the same newspaper. The guidelines recommend that leopards trapped after deliberate attacks on humans should never be released into the wild. The preferred option is euthanasia. But accidental attacks should be treated differently, resulting in trapped animals released within 10 km of the capture site. Forest officials in India have sometimes met obstructive crowds when trying to capture leopards. The guidelines call for crowd management through trained response teams. The advisers on the guidelines have emphasised that not all leopards seen in croplands should be assumed as dangerous.

The situation in India has clearly escalated, as villagers don't wish to take a chance with any leopard in view. It is a truly sad story, in which nature fights back if we show we do not understand it.

WHEN CATS GET CLOSE – WHAT CAN WE ASSUME?

In January 2011, two young women arrived home south of Gloucester in a taxi after being out clubbing. It was 1.30 a.m. Their house was at an isolated spot along a main road. As the taxi pulled up they were greeted by something – a large animal, a huge and thick-set black panther. As the security lights flicked on in the driveway, it circled the vehicle. Once it had gone, the startled women jumped out, but instantly the big cat returned and they rushed back to the vehicle. It eventually moved off and the women made their way to the house. For two weeks the family's dogs, large German Shepherds, refused to wander their normal routes in the adjacent paddock and stuck close to the house when they exercised. The police were asked for advice, and Frank was invited to brief the family. A burger seller, close by in a lay-by, had also seen the cat.

We do not know the intent of the animal, almost resembling a black jaguar in its muscular build, and why it singled out this particular vehicle to inspect. Maybe, as the women had returned from a nightclub, there was a waft of perfume, as cats can find these scents attractive? One particular brand is used as a lure for cats in preference to catnip. Life is back to normal in that particular household, but sightings in the general vicinity and along that road in particular are something we have come to expect.

In the past five years I can recall three instances of children racing home from play areas in different parts of Gloucestershire after a big cat arrived on the scene. Their parents sensed something was up, such was the anxious state of the kids on arrival. In spring 2010, another case made the local and national press, this time in Ruspidge, deep in the Forest of Dean. Mark Fletcher described the incident in *ECOS* magazine: 'Fifteen year old Kim Howells and her eight year old cousin Sophie Gwynne were followed by a massive black wild cat… Kim described the 'panther' as about the size of a Great Dane, with big eyes, paws and a long tail: 'We cut through the brambles and just started running.' The girls fled home. Their feet were all cut and Sophie was in tears. They feared they had had a lucky escape, though I don't believe the cat, if it was a big cat, was actually stalking them, or meant them any harm.'

Ruspidge gets a mention elsewhere in the book where the deer carcasses are shown. Fallow deer like that are what a panther is mainly fixed on. I recall the reaction to the reports of these girls' encounter at the time. On the newspaper website there was scepticism and scorn, as people accused the girls of wanting their fifteen minutes of fame. In contrast, though, there was real alarm too, from those who felt this was a defining moment, proof that big cats were around and posed a threat. And here, of course, is the quandary – a polarisation of views. We are dammed if we do respond in any way to such incidents, and dammed if we don't. Public bodies could be accused of alarmism and wasting money with any signs and educational briefings, while such measures might be seen as too soft, too tentative, by others. It is far easier, of course, to dither.

A FACE-OFF AT THE COTSWOLD EDGE

The stalking cat, eyeing up other wildlife, pumped full of adrenalin before the ambush, is the one, we all think, to avoid. If small children accidentally entered this sort of space, would the cat consider the human option? It seems this situation was recently tested, in April 2011, not far

An example of public information on pumas in the United States. Signs like this are used at locations such as reserves and trails which lie within the habitat of pumas. Photo: The Midpeninsula Regional Open Space District, California, USA

from me on the east side of Cheltenham. Luckily, the four children returned home safely from an event which will live long in the family's lore. My account of it below is taken directly from BBC Radio Gloucestershire's interview with family members after they first described the event to Frank Tunbridge.

During the Easter holidays, on 19 April, from their house on the edge of Cheltenham, four children took their dogs up the hill between Harp Hill and Cleeve Hill on the Cotswold edge. 13-year-old Grant described what happened after the children watched deer running away before them. They advanced to get a better look when the youngest girl, at the head of the group, said, according to Grant, 'Run, quickly!' She had spotted a panther in the vegetation. Grant added: 'I saw a panther square up to one of my friends' face, like only four yards away. Me and my friends started crying because we were really worried. We just ran.' Asked to describe the animal, Grant reported that it was, 'Really big. About four foot high, and his teeth quite big.' Grant's parents were interviewed too: 'I didn't know what to believe, but they've seen something, because they were really shook up,' said his mother. The five-year-old girl had fled directly through stinging nettles at the sight of the animal.

The father discussed the incident at length with Frank Tunbridge. They concluded the children had disturbed the big cat stalking the deer. The radio reporter asked Grant if he would return to the location. 'Only with adults,' he stated. Even on the return, during the second part of the interview, Grant was not keen to venture near the undergrowth from where the animal appeared. The reporter described the vegetation as 'thick brambles'. I phoned the family to agree to their mention in the book. It was a month after the incident and they had since met other dog walkers from the vicinity, using that part of the Cotswold slope. The parents were now even more inclined to believe the kids, for other people had mentioned seeing a local panther too. In the textbooks we can read of a warning charge from a leopard if you intrude into its space, but there is extra relief in this example, given the big cat's apparent stalking mode amongst the deer.

UK CAT INCIDENTS – THE ALLEGED BITES AND SCRATCHES

Across Britain there have been a few alleged attacks from big cats, restricted to superficial bites and scratches. Here is a brief summary of some of the incidents. Fuller accounts of these and others can be found on the web if you want to read more. Some of these reports have been controversial and were doubted by various observers - again, the differing opinions can be read online. All these examples were treated seriously by the local police.

2000: Trellech, Gwent

Several web sites – including BBC Wales – describe the Josh Hopkins case from 2000 in south east Wales. According to these reports, Josh, who was 11 at the time, described how a large black cat reared up at him as he disturbed it in long grass when searching for the family's domestic cat near his home in Trellech. The big cat reportedly took him unawares, biting him on the head and scratching him superficially on a cheek.

2002: Insch, Aberdeenshire

According to the *Press & Journal* newspaper, Doris Moore of Insch in Aberdeenshire suffered puncture wounds to her thigh after an animal rushed at her, disturbed from the nearby stable, as she walked to her car. A watching friend confirmed the incident, reporting the animal as black and feline in appearance. As a poet the incident moved her to write about the encounter. Reproduced in the local *Press & Journal*, her 'Shadow of the Cat' poem sets the scene with 'A chance encounter never meant to be, would chill the heart of you or me…' It goes on to convey the difficulty she had of convincing people of the attack.

2002: near Gravesend, Kent

Reported in *The Observer*, Mike Cole, an optician, thought an animal present in his garden was a fox until it apparently growled and lashed out, cutting open his hand. As described in the *The Observer*: 'He staggered back, bleeding, and watched in astonishment as a lynx the size of a Labrador bounded from his Kent lawn. Feline experts were unanimous that only a big cat could deliver the two gouges that still disfigure the optician's right hand.'

2008: Alness, Scotland

As explained on BBC News web pages and in the *Press & Journal*, Pat Macleod needed stitches in deep wounds on her leg and suffered cuts on her hands after being attacked by a large animal which dragged her. Quoted in the above media at the time, she said: 'A very large animal came bounding out of the shadows… It leapt at me, gripping my leg. I was knocked over by the propulsion of the beast and I thought "how do I get rid of this animal?" I pulled over the dustbin for protection and the animal came over the top, gripping my left leg and the top of my right arm. I would say from nose to the tip of its tail it was about 4ft long.' She described the animal as a grey cat with a dark dorsal mark along its back and a long tail. She was still bandaged from the wounds when she reported that the animal repeated the attack a few days later and ran off. Both the local police and Scottish Natural Heritage followed up the incident.

THE TABLOIDS – CALLING THE SHOTS?

In May 2011 the area around Loch Ness, of all places, continued to receive reports of one or more large black panthers. This is no surprise to seasoned observers who have known of big cat sightings in the area for many years. Amidst the concern expressed by some locals, there was a suggestion that the loose animal should be trapped. Police indicated that clearer evidence would be required to prompt any effort to humanely capture a large cat. 'Forget Nessie…Big cat is stalking locals' said the report in *The Sun*, under the unforgettable headline, 'The Loch Ness Mogster'.

I often feel the tabloids are smarter than we think. Yes, they do indulge in 'beast savages sheep' headlines, even when it might be lurchers on the loose, but they side with their readers too. They have backed their readers who report big cats, and they have mocked the authorities for not realising cats are here, under their nose. But the key question remains: would an unfortunate episode involving a big cat tip the tabloid press into a hostile reaction? What would this precipitate, and in what ways could it influence wider opinion and force the issue into the policy arena?

I will address part of this concern immediately. There is nothing practical and affordable that can be done on a wide scale if policy-makers ever wished to get tough with our feral big cats. The main options would all be clumsy and would generate great controversy. The measures would not have compliance from some landowners. Poisoned bait would be ill-targeted and endanger domestic and native animals, as we have mentioned in Chapter 8. A bounty on the cats would be reckless, making humans far more dangerous than the animals they were seeking. Trapping is also fraught with difficulty: the cages would need constant vigilance, with birds, squirrels, badgers and people's dogs invading them before any big cats got close. The method of following feline tracks with trained hounds, used for pumas in North America and resulting in a treed cat, would also mostly be useless. The cats can easily slip away, and we have plenty of roads and boundary fences to contend with in Britain. In addition, some cats, the ones unrelated to pumas, might not respond to this method and they could turn on the dogs and cause mayhem as happened in Siberia where this approach was tested just once. What would surely need to happen is that any specific big cat known to have caused genuine human strife, whether due to rogue behaviour or because it was provoked, would need to be tracked down, difficult as that would be. We know that police sometimes deploy heat-seeking helicopters, as discussed in the last chapter, and humane trapping overseen by experienced professionals is an option.

BOUNTY – REWARDING THE SMALL-MINDED?

Occasional rumours break out about people who offer rewards for bagging a local big cat. Gossip has it that someone in a southern county has offered £1,000 for their local beast. This has upset some locals, some of whom side with the cat, while others are quite content to leave it to prey on the excessive numbers of deer. It is perhaps irresponsible to encourage trigger-happy behaviour, and £1,000 is a paltry sum. The rewards for a clinching photo of the cat would be far higher.

My friend Peter Taylor once phoned a police officer, who was reported in the press to be out with a gun following up a big cat incident in south Wales. Peter spoke to the officer on his mobile who said he was there to 'show a presence' to local people. He'd taken aim at a large cat two years previously, but realised the folly of his action – an injured predator is pretty much guaranteed to be dangerous.

In 2007 Gail and Nigel Cooke managed to watch a black panther in the Nailsworth area of Gloucestershire for nearly 15 minutes. It seemed to be foraging at a field edge, aware of their presence but ignoring them. Gail has been on the look out for it ever since and now always carries a camera, but she is worried about other people carrying guns:

> Seeing the big cat at such a close range was a thrill. We had heard stories about them being around the area, but to see one was brilliant, and we do hope to have another sighting some day. We are not at all worried about big cats roaming the countryside around Nailsworth, they are not causing any harm. Our worry is that someone from the government might decide to hunt them down and kill them, which would be a great shame. Observe, photograph, and film but we hope they are left to roam free.

The fear of hunters, and of irresponsible gun-wielding people taking an interest in our big cats, is a main barrier to people reporting the animals. Sightings reports, information about locations and hard evidence all remain suppressed because of people's caution about the consequences of hunting. It remains one of the main influences on whether and how people decide to impart the information they have.

OFF THE LEAD AND MISSING

Have you seen many 'Dog missing' signs pasted on telegraph poles down the rural lanes near you, or 'Cat missing' ones, for that matter? I admit I'm on the lookout, but I notice plenty. I'm not saying all our lost dogs have become a panther's meal but some, at least, may have met their end this way. Leopards target dogs in Africa and India, and pumas do so in the US and Canada. In North America people have left dogs chained to their kennels at night but found them gone in the morning. I suspect that our smaller dogs, and dogs out at night, are more at risk. I know of two farmers who are sure they have lost dogs to big cats, having last seen them at a time when a cat was on their land. One of these farmers eventually found the dog's body, clearly eaten by a carnivore. He is forgiving of the culprit, despite being an expert marksman.

At a talk I did with Frank in February 2007, I met a woman who had travelled over an hour to be present. At the questions, she explained why she'd come along. She'd had a remarkable and shocking encounter ten years before, when walking her dog in a forest ride in Herefordshire: 'My dog froze. Then I realised why – although still on the lead that I was holding, a big panther at the edge of the wood was stalking him, close by. I couldn't believe it and was terrified. Eventually I think it recognised there was a human about too, and pulled out of the attack. It bolted away along the ride at dramatic speed. It was ten years ago but the moment still haunts me now.' Being at the talk and getting feedback from us after-wards seemed a help to her. I think – and hope – that she left with a sense of closure on this troubling experience. Like so much else about the big cats' lives, the extent to which they eye up our dogs is unknown. Do they do so in a calculated way, seeing them as easy pickings, or are any kills opportunistic, timed for when a dog runs innocently by, or sniffs out and hassles a big cat of which it has no fear and pays the price? If we ever get a tide of opinion in some quarters against the cats, maybe it will be the plight of our pets which will spark it off.

WHISPER AND THE PANTHER

Other instances of dog walkers being followed by big cats have reached Frank and me, but I stress that these are rare. The latest one, summarised below, sounds dramatic as I quote from the lady involved. Bear in mind, though, that nothing happened, and she believes that responsible educa-tion is important so that people do not provoke any cat that comes close by.

On 26 May 2011 a retired woman from Painswick was walking her Lakeland terrier in the local Cotswold woods. Her experience compelled her to speak to the *Stroud Life* newspaper the following day, which re-sulted in the headline: 'I won't go back to woods after big cat stalked me'. The situation she described mirrored three others reported to Frank and myself over the previous three years, in which dog walkers noticed big cats tailing them. I felt it important to speak to her direct to learn what had happened first-hand, and she was pleased to get my call. Her first remark was one of relief, glad to speak to someone who might believe her. Then, before she recounted the event, she insisted: 'I don't want any harm to come to the animal. It's got as much right to be in those woods as I have to walk in them.'

She'd known of the area's big cats from a report from her daughter two years before, in a sighting east of Stroud, backed up with photos of tracks in the snow. The one she'd met in the woods was a bigger animal. She referred to it as a 'he'. She was ten minutes into the walk, a familiar stroll near a golf course. Whisper the terrier was beginning to get edgy, tightening up. She noticed that all had gone quiet: no background noise, no birds, just her own and Whisper's rustling of the leaves. At this stage Whisper was rigid, totally stiff and having to be dragged. She sensed another dog around. Sure enough, she heard a different shuffle in the deep layer of leaves – a larger dog-sized animal, she thought. She looked around and saw a tail of an animal keeping to cover, but it was no ordinary tail: 'black, long and silky, with like a pipe at the end'. It was definitely time to go, she felt. Then she heard a sound from the direction of the animal, 'like engine trouble from an aeroplane,' she said. As she strode back, tugging the dead weight of Whisper, she kept glancing back. The animal was gaining ground, making up half the distance, first 40 metres away, now 20. Each time she fully turned and looked, 'it bellied down'. 'I saw the rump, and a tail go down – it was like satin in the light. Definitely black, a beautiful black, like satin,' she said.

By now, fear was setting in. 'I was looking at Whisper thinking, "We're in trouble." I kept walking, and talking out loud, partly in case anyone was around, but also to mask my fear, so the cat wouldn't pick it up. I spoke up in a loud voice, "If anyone is there, would you please come here, because I really would be glad to see somebody right now."' By now she noticed the animal keeping to a ridge above her, amidst holly trees. 'I was accelerating, not knowing my old legs could move like it. I thought it might jump from the ridge as we entered the last stretch, an open area. I was literally dragging the dog – his eyes had turned white. Still, every time I looked round, the cat bellied down, just showing its hind. I prayed. Then, getting in sight of the road, a coach was at the junction. The driver was really revving it before moving off. I thought, "Now's the time to edge along even faster with the distraction of the noise." I walked briskly sideways, focused on the ridge all the time. I made it back, and Whisper wet himself as I lifted him through the stile. Walking home along the road I spent 20 minutes gathering my composure and catching my breath. I have a heart condition, and had to up the dose of my pills over the weekend, such was the effect.'

She spoke to the newspaper to report her concern. Half-term week was coming, and she thought children should be accompanied in the wood. She herself was now only going again with Whisper in the company of other people. She wonders what has made this cat bolder, although she realises the dog was a key factor. She believes responsible education and awareness of the cats is needed in the future.

It sounds a troubling incident that none of us would like. It may be difficult to draw lessons from it, but here are some tentative observations, or rather questions:

When anxious, we may talk with a fearful tone in our voices which dogs are able to sense, however much we try and cover this. Would a leopard-type cat or a puma-type big cat also sense a person's unease?

If the panther was going to charge the lady and take the dog, it had time to do so, but it did not. Did it assess the situation on whether an attack on the dog was viable or was it just curious?

Finally, the chances of encountering a large cat are remote, and it is even more unusual to experience one up close in a situation like this. But if we do, any action that risks aggravating a nearby cat, or making it feel threatened, whatever its mood, could be risky.

STAYING A PREDATOR, NOT A SCAVENGER

If and when predators turn into habitual scavengers, they risk becoming a problem and a possible danger to us and to themselves. Here in Gloucestershire, drivers have sometimes reported a big cat sniffing at bin bags on a verge, while in Leicestershire, researcher Nigel Spencer has had several witness reports of big cats seen at the back of fast food premises, perhaps attracted by the kitchen smells. Thankfully, the scavenging sometimes reported by big cats here seems occasional and opportunist, not routine and systematic.

DECIDING THE RULES – FOR THE WILD AND THE TAME

There is no right or wrong way to perceive a predator, although we must recognise that the natural world, and any ecosystem, needs predators of different kinds to function fully. People do not tend to have half-hearted opinions on large carnivores. Some people's dislike of wolves, for instance, is visceral, despite the negligible accounts of them attacking humans across their natural ranges. But, as we've noted above, there is little animosity towards the big cats that have turned up here in Britain, despite the fact that some people, in the abstract at least, can have a loathing of 'snarly' predators.

I once dropped into a Tooth & Claw photography exhibition on tour in Gloucester, displaying the impressive range of prints by Peter Cairns and Mark Hamblin. The pictures ranged across iconic European beasts, like wolves and brown bear, and included our own Scottish wildcat. Birds included sea eagles, golden eagles and peregrines, all of which grace the elegant book of that name, produced by Whittles in 2007. Like the book, the exhibition illustrated these predators in their natural homes in the wild, and the photographs were poignant, subtle, vivid, and spectacular. The photographs showed the various predators in different roles: looking lavish, seeming invincible, interacting with humans and being the villain – taking livestock or snaffling prized pigeons, for example. The intention was to show an honest spectrum of predator actions, and of our relationships with them. Comments in the visitors' book revealed the mix of reaction: 'Stimulating – makes you think' and 'Magnificent creatures!' were amongst the mostly positive jottings. But aggressive remarks were there too: 'Disgraceful' and 'I am disgusted!' were ones which stood out as a reminder that some people can feel offended by the action of predators doing what they do in the wild. Feeling stroppy, my daughter scribbled 'Moody' against these carping comments. She marvels at the charismatic predators, the hunters of nature's food chain. Yet Bambi-lookalike deer, all deer, and even rabbits are precious to her too. Like many of us who are much older, her outlook is partly realistic but also, perhaps, overly sentimental. A predator's actions can crash through our sympathies. It confronts us with inconvenient truths.

Another factor which influences each one of us is the unread rules by which we live, both in relation to other animals and to the great outdoors itself. In the wild places of any nation we should expect more risks from the terrain, the remoteness, extreme weather and from some of the uncompromising plants and animals which occupy the severe conditions. So we should be prepared to take risks, mentally and physically, in places where they can be expected. The difficulty comes when nature brings risk close to our own homes and to the situations and places where we expect to relax rather than be on edge. It is the proximity to big cats when they turn up on the edge of towns, in a community woodland or even in our gardens which may test our resolve. They are not just seeking refuge in the wilder parts of our landscape.

SIDING WITH THE ANIMAL

It is consistent among big cat reports to find a good proportion of people showing admiration for the animal and sometimes expressing concern for what they see as its plight, perhaps viewing it as a lone creature struggling to cope in a foreign land. Dr Samantha Hurn, an anthropologist at the University of Wales, Lampeter, picked up this sentiment in an area she sampled. She found that some farmers and rural residents near Lampeter who claimed to have seen a local panther or found livestock kills suspected to be the work of a big cat, regarded it as one of their own. They saw it as a symbol of marginalisation, reflecting their own geographical isolation. According to her findings, another factor which generated sympathy for the cat was the presumption that it had been cast out following the Dangerous Wild Animals Act. Locals felt a common hardship and related to it as a fellow victim of English legislation.

THE WILL TO COMPLY

Humans and animals have to operate in their own contexts and by their own codes. But there may be different rules that should apply in different situations. In some places, big cats may have to conform to our rules, especially around residential areas and where people need to make their living from the land. But in other places, more wild and secret ones, we may deem it to be appropriate and even an asset to be aware of the big predator asserting its role, so long as it does not impinge on people's livelihoods. Many people and landowners work by such a code with foxes. A neighbouring farmer, while discussing his colourful collection of fowl and chickens with me, once said: 'If I don't lock up these birds correctly at night, then that's my lookout, but if the fox takes anything during the day, that's his lookout.' Compliance amongst all parts of the animal kingdom has to be worked out. We are not exempt from this deal – humans have a role, and maybe we are acting it out. Is that what we are doing in our 'Leave them alone' reaction to the cats, and the police's realisation that taking aim is an unwise move? We are working out our relationship with the big cats – there may be need for give and take but, so far, I'd suggest that the big cats, with all their cunning and resourcefulness, mainly know and keep to their place.

The compliance was perfectly illustrated in the 1960s, when attention was on the Surrey puma. Writing in *The Surrey Puma* booklet, author Roman Gollicz describes how the big cat of the time was felt to be living its stealthy existence amidst the south east's farmland, concentrating its territory at a farm called Bushylease:

'But why Bushylease Farm? The Blanks family held all wildlife in the highest regard: they were not interested in chasing and capturing the puma after the few initial attempts had failed. They left it alone and it left them alone. Apart from a few attacks on farm livestock, which Nick Blanks maintains was accepted as a natural loss, after 1964 the puma learnt to keep away from Bushylease Farm livestock, appearing to understand that it would not then be molested. Indeed, after the period of fevered newspaper involvement, the Blanks family did not even publicise the puma's subsequent appearances. As Edward Blanks stated and Nick Blanks confirms, they just 'put up with it' until it disappeared altogether in about 1970. As a territorial animal, which clearly had settled at Bushlease Farm, always returning there after its periodic roaming, it is reasonable to suppose that the flesh-and-blood puma died at about that time, aged 10 to 12 years.'

The account of Bushylease Farm is one that seems familiar, nearly 50 years on. I regularly meet farmers and landowners who have learnt to accept that a big cat may return to their land. They could get exercised over it, but decide not to, given that livestock losses are occasional and low, at levels and rates people can live with, and there may be what the farmer regards as benefits from the cat. A relationship has been struck. The cat is keeping to mutually acceptable rules.

SELF-DETERMINATION?

We might not have guessed that people would show such tolerance – sympathy, even – for the mystery cats. It continually contradicts what we expect. In my day job as a facilitator and analyser of people's attitudes on the environment and nature, I am meant to assume that people with rural land and businesses will be anti-predator, and I am supposed to think that people will be worried, too scared of fierce creatures to want to live alongside them. And some surveys done in the abstract would back this up, suggesting people's perception even of a middle-sized carnivore like the humble lynx is wary, and that they would need convincing of the merits of officially bringing back this lost native mammal. The reality, though, is somewhat different. Now with a range of large cats fused into the landscape, people are not being forever snarled at on walking trails or ambushed in the woods, and farmers are not suffering more than the

Rick Minter hosts the Big Cats discussion stall
at the 2011 Stroud Festival of Nature.

occasional loss of an individual lamb or ewe. So far, at least, the big cats are 'behaving themselves' and there is no rural revolt. People in the know are thinking through the issues for themselves, and realising that something interesting is afoot, as nature takes another twist. And, as Frank Tunbridge himself says: 'In the future we should learn to live with big cats within the UK without due fear, as they do not pose a threat to the human population unless we alter the balance by our own rash motives and actions.'

A RESOLUTION OR A PROCESS?

I was recently posed a question by a farmer, somebody who might have been tempted to tick the 'Cull them' box above. After losing three prize sheep, she was struggling to see any upside of having big cats around, but could see the complexities. 'Do you see a resolution?' she asked. I think the answer is yes, if we treat this as a process, and if we recognise that when management becomes required, it should be thoughtful not hasty, and that we still need to learn, as Paul from Norfolk suggests in the quotes above. And whilst we learn, there are some steps we could take to support those who need it. Here are just a few ideas:

Survey high-density sighting areas: our learning will mainly stem from tracking, filming and studying a sample of cats in the areas where they roam, and by having a rapport with the people who are encountering them.

Awareness-raising through school posters: schools in areas of regular cat sightings could be invited to do big cat awareness posters, knowing the challenge of getting the right tone, not off-putting and not whipping up a frenzy. The posters need not actually be deployed. The process of children, teachers and parents thinking what to communicate on a poster, and learning the basics of the cats' behaviour, would offer benefits in itself and might bring creative ideas.

Landowner support and networking: I enjoy my discussions with farmers, landowners and others who feel they need to come to terms with the occasional big cat visit. They mostly have similar queries and they learn and adapt fast. They might do well to share ideas and to network. What experience have some got with llamas as stock guardians, probably used in relation to dogs and foxes? Which, if any, types of fencing or responsible deterrents work? And in what ways do landowners view the transient cats as an asset? Perhaps these and other issues could be networked over the web on a forum tailored for the purpose.

Guidance for countryside management staff: the staff of councils, charities, utilities and public agencies who manage places of amenity and wildlife importance are naïve about the possibility of big cats. Some training could give them an induction. With several reports of big cats

tailing people in my area, some professionals should perhaps be told what this means in terms of a cat's behaviour, and what briefing and advice to offer visitors using woodlands, trails and reserves.

I hope these ideas are amongst the measured options available. They seem to me to be actions which are realistic and affordable to help us acclimatize. If they are seen as a culture shock they'll probably never happen, but I detect their time is coming.

As I finish my case for the covenant of understanding, I leave the last words of this section to someone who has studied the animals longer than most. Writing from North Devon, naturalist Trevor Beer offers this advice:

> The big cats are with us due to people causing escapes and releases. They include black leopard and puma. If you see one, leave well alone, do not attempt to corner them nor bait them with food. Treat them with respect. They deserve that and if left to their own devices will do us no harm. The mortality rate of young is high, thus if there are no further releases the situation will remain low-key, leaving a feral situation which should not be a problem. Certainly no organisation should waste time hunting down and persecuting these fine animals.

Views on big cats, as sampled in 2011 at the Big Cats discussion stall over a day in Stroud, Gloucestershire.

EVERY POSSIBLE HUMAN

Below are summaries of the various views people may have on big cats. They reflect the opinions of those groups most likely to encounter them occasionally or to have an interest in the topic. The lists start with a general range of views that anyone may have, whatever their background and affiliations. Specific types of groups are then set out, followed by the possible viewpoints prevailing amongst them. You might recognise yourself somewhere. The lists are simply meant to indicate how opinions and experiences may vary, often within the same camp. An individual's view can also change depending on information and experience. Perhaps we are best off sharing our ideas, whatever our starting points.

General span of views on UK big cats across all stakeholder groups

- Unaware
- Uninterested
- Disbelieving
- Agnostic – no view
- Open-minded – wanting more evidence?
- Sceptical – polite
- Sceptical – hostile
- In denial
- Believe and 'So what? Just a few big cats'
- Believe and worried – public safety, livestock, pets
- Believe and neutral – 'If the cats behave, then fine…'
- Believe and enthusiastic – new experience, wild nature, wild predator
- Believe and protectionist – the cats have rights, majestic animals

Key groups with possible connections to UK big cats

The list below shows professions, occupations and types of activities which may sometimes have links to aspects of UK big cats.

Bushcrafters
Cryptozoologists
Dog walkers
Farmers and landowners
Fishermen
Horse riders
Lampers
Outdoor recreation
Poachers
Police
Ramblers and walkers

Taxidermists
Vets
Managers of countryside sites and amenity areas
Wildlife practitioners and natural history specialists
Zoo and wildlife park staff

Main stakeholders and their possible views on UK big cats

Landowners and farmers

Positive: natural vermin control. The cats go unnoticed. Something new and interesting
Neutral: if the cats 'behave', or if benefits outweigh problems, then fine
Negative: potential impacts on stock. Worry over presence of a large predator

Foresters

Positive: adds to deer management, intrigue at new and hidden predator
Neutral: if the cats 'behave', or if benefits outweigh problems, then fine
Negative: worry over presence of a large predator

Game sector (gamekeepers, deer managers, stalkers)

Positive: natural vermin control, intrigue at new and hidden predator, future game?
Neutral: if the cats 'behave' or if benefits outweigh problems, then fine
Negative: interference from large predator

If you wish to follow up points raised in this book or discuss any of the topics, a blog site has been created for this purpose:
www.bigcat101.wordpress.com

A CALLING FROM THE
WILDWOOD

The big cats visit me in my dreams – I'd be amazed if they didn't. They play with my emotions. I sometimes sense a dark panther. It seems a mutant, composite cat, merging with the blackness of the night. The eyes are piercing and neon. It is a menacing, stylised image, signifying power and otherness. It seems apt to call this one 'beast'. Then I meet pumas, mother and juveniles, settled around a deer kill in a local wood. They are aware of my presence but dismiss me as they gorge their prey. The contrast with the restful landscape disturbs me. The predator's raw power has visited this wood and I should keep to my own space for now.

But it is the lynx that I feel most strongly, through the ethereal world it enters. I am at the edge of a forest. It is a dark European wood of vast scale, except it is in Britain. There are conifers at the fringe but they give way to a regenerating native wood. I tread watchfully… then it happens. I glimpse an animal thought not to be here, missing for countless generations in our native fauna, yet here it is, utterly in command. It flits amongst trees, but I miss a convincing view. I start questioning myself. Am I creating this bewitching cat? But it comes again. It teases me, darting through shade, edging closer, but vanishing. The scene could be Narnia, as Mr Tumnus the Faun comes into focus.

Eventually the lynx is present, in clear view. It seems disconcertingly close. I am both scared and overcome, captivated by its sleek perfection. But then it ends, and I feel cheated, as a compelling dream fades away. I wonder what, if anything, the lynx is communicating? I guess it is signalling transformation, our forests being restored to native woodland that will enrich our lands. Perhaps the shy and secret predator is simply confirming that it is here – it has a foothold. It is beyond our desire to order and to boss Mother Nature. It is doing as it needs in our woods, now truly wild woods of Britain.

But another dream was better – stunning, even. The lynx spoke. The voice was Germanic and stilted, it was copying and repeating people's phrases it had heard in the forest. Here was a tape of the human history of the wood, a record of how people eked out an existence and lived alongside the natural rhythm of the land, back through centuries. Lest

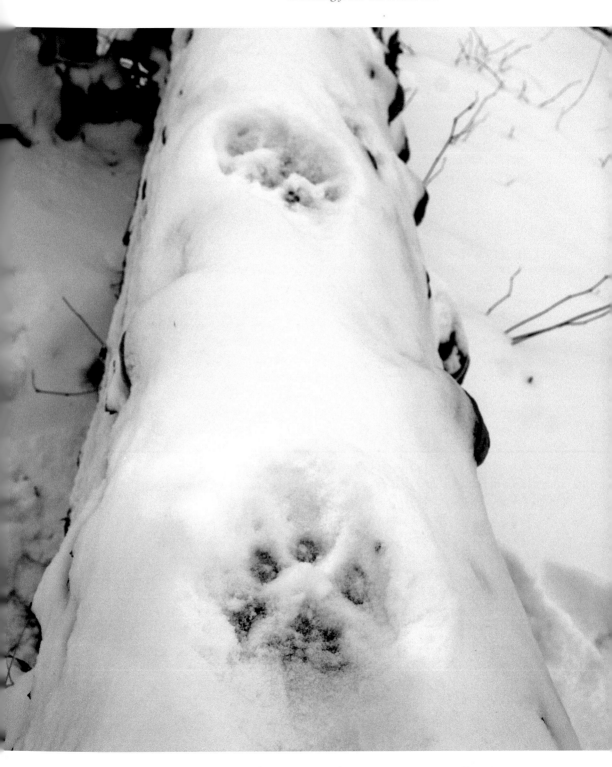

Lynx footprints in northern Dinaric Mountains, Slovenia.
Photo: Miha Krofel

we forget, we are bound with nature, we are not something separate. The lynx was proving its heritage, alongside and as a part of our own.

This may feel like a rather profound note on which to end, but these dreams were genuine. I have not embellished them, just guessed at their meaning. I hope they offer relevant points on which to dwell. Could the arrival of big cats, coupled with our complicity, be telling us something? Perhaps our recognition of the cats is as much about the rediscovery of our wild side, the power of our senses when they brush with something elemental. This is happening to many people as an inner response to our materialistic trappings. It doesn't need a big cat experience to spark it. All manner of wildlife encounters or experiences of outdoor adventure can help tune people to a wilder and more fulfilled self. Maybe, though, encounters with a large carnivore, one of our big cats, can take it to a deeper level. I sense that some people have tasted this already. They have had the adrenaline rush and the magic lives on.

Chris Packham once made a TV documentary, 'Big Cats in a Little Country', for part of a series called *The X Creatures*. It was a half-decent programme for the time, 1998, before some of the more convincing sightings had taken place. He seemed undecided about their existence then, but he concluded by emphasising a message of respect: 'Remember – any big cats that are around didn't ask to be put here.' That seemed fitting, regardless of one's understanding and one's attitude towards any feral big cats. But now, over ten years on, and very much in the era of discovery, the cats already have their protection society. I feel it at every turn of studying them and meeting people who know of them. As we have seen, the cats are admired much more then they are feared. People do not want to betray them.

Time, then, for just one more example. I call it the Panther and the Stag, and no, it is not the name of a pub, although maybe it should be. It comes from a gentleman who approached me during a break at one of my evening talks in a Gloucestershire village hall. He was a clean-cut figure from the professional middle classes. He was well-spoken and wearing a tie, seeming to have come straight from work. He apologised for having to leave early, but wanted to relay something as he departed. His comments were spoken in the tone of a club member: 'I've seen one...' he began, as so many people do. He explained that he was a keen birdwatcher and had arrived at a bird reserve in the Forest of Dean early one Saturday morning. He enjoyed the rewards of being amongst the first visitors, but on this winter morning nature conjured up a special memory. As he strode out to one of the hides he heard a large animal crashing across the forest floor. 'I looked up and it was a stag,' (most likely a roe buck or a fallow buck). He said it briefly slowed as it noticed him in passing, its breath rising vapour-like in the cold air. But the animal quickly pounded on its way through the wood, for it was not alone. Seconds later, a silent animal followed the same path. A large black panther was on its tail, fixed on its prey…

As we've seen and discussed, many people's reports of big cats seem special and a proportion, like this one, involve deer in flight. But somehow, this event, at a site famed for its pied flycatchers, did seem the ultimate. It wasn't that the informant was building it up – he was telling it as it was. In the scheme of things, it was just another in the steady stream of reports. On that evening of the talk, it was a way of introducing himself and marking his connection with the topic. But I think it was also much more – I detected it was a neat way of signalling to me: 'I'm with you. I know of the rich sensation this subject brings. Thank you for being a fall guy.'

Our relationship with the big cats will be personal. Each one of us will have a different take. The vibes may be strong or weak, maybe enchanting for some, less so – or even hostile – for others. Sometimes, of necessity, the response will be pragmatic, as simple as shutting the outbuildings or keeping the dogs in at night. Other than on rare occasions, we will meet the cats in our minds or dreams, if at all. They will stay secret – the puma treads with soft moccasins, the leopard is known as the invisible one. But it is no bad thing to share and discuss our views, to ask questions and to admit our wonder or our fears. These are conversations worth having. Adapting to big predators when they have long been absent from our realm takes us to a fresh association with nature and for some, perhaps for many people, towards a new awakening. Whether, and how, to realise this is up to us.

Illustration by Robert Hines. Originally produced courtesy of the North American Wildlife Foundation.

A Eurasian lynx stays wary in its habitat enclosure in the
Dinaric Mountains of Slovenia. Photo: Miha Krofel